Computational Modeling: Principles and Practices

Computational Modeling: Principles and Practices

Edited by
Tom Halt

www.willfordpress.com

Published by Willford Press,
118-35 Queens Blvd., Suite 400,
Forest Hills, NY 11375, USA

ISBN: 978-1-68285-411-2

Cataloging-in-Publication Data

Computational modeling : principles and practices / edited by Tom Halt.
    p. cm.
Includes bibliographical references and index.
ISBN 978-1-68285-411-2
1. Computer simulation. I. Halt, Tom.
QA76.9.C65 C66 2018
003.3--dc23

For information on all Willford Press publications
visit our website at www.willfordpress.com

Contents

Preface

Computational modeling uses computers to understand and study the behavior of complex systems. This process encompasses subjects such as mathematics, physics and computer science. Computational models are mostly used in weather forecasting models, flight simulator models, molecular protein folding models, neural network models, etc. This book contains some path-breaking studies in the field of computational modeling. It elucidates the concepts and innovative models around prospective developments with respect to computational modeling. This book explores all the important aspects of computational modeling in the present day scenario. It aims to serve as a resource guide for students and experts alike and contribute to the growth of the discipline.

This book is a comprehensive compilation of works of different researchers from varied parts of the world. It includes valuable experiences of the researchers with the sole objective of providing the readers (learners) with a proper knowledge of the concerned field. This book will be beneficial in evoking inspiration and enhancing the knowledge of the interested readers.

In the end, I would like to extend my heartiest thanks to the authors who worked with great determination on their chapters. I also appreciate the publisher's support in the course of the book. I would also like to deeply acknowledge my family who stood by me as a source of inspiration during the project.

Editor

The multi-axial material fatigue under the combined loading with mean stress in three dimensions

F. Fojtík[a,*], J. Fuxa[a]

[a]Faculty of Mechanical Engineering, VŠB – Technical University of Ostrava, 17 listopadu 15, 708 33 Ostrava-Poruba, Czech Republic

Abstract

This contribution describes the application of Fuxa's conjugated strength criterion on the experimental results under combined loading of specimens made from common construction steel 11523.0, melt T31052. The specimens were stepwise loaded by the torque amplitude, combination of torque amplitude and tension pre-stress, further by the amplitude of the torque in combination with inner overpressure and axial tension force. The last set of specimens was loaded by the torque amplitude in combination with inner and external overpressure and with axial tension force. To obtain the data required as the input values for the conjugated criterion the stress/strain analysis of the specimens by the finite element method in software ANSYS was performed. The experiments were performed on modified testing machine equipped by overpressure chamber.

Keywords: high-cycle fatigue, experiment in multi-axial fatigue, mean stress effect, combined loading

1. Introduction

To verify the multi-axial Fuxa's conjugated strength criterion and to determine the proper constants the new test jig was developed which generalizes the possibilities of reconstructed testing machine SHENCK type PWXN [1, 2]. In this case the testing device was newly equipped by a multifunctional pressure chamber. This chamber makes possible to load the specimen by the inner/external overpressure in addition or independently in combination with torque amplitude. The constant tension/pressure pre-stress can be added into this system. The proper stress state combinations with the influence of mean stress can be realized in this way. Four types of experiments were performed which will be described in the following. The first two experiments serve to find the data required for the conjugated stress criterion. The third and fourth loading type overtakes this criterion setting and applies it on the experimental results.

2. Alternating torsion – experiment

The specimens were manufactured from the steel 11523.0, melt T31052. Their parameters are mentioned in Fig. 1. Those specimens were subsequently loaded by nominal amplitude of the torque with test frequency of 25 Hz. The amplitude of torque was gradually decreased until the limit 10^7 cycles was reached. The results experiment are placed in tab. 1. In the fig. 2 can be seen measured values, Fuxa's approximation curves (1) [5]. Point of crack initiation under static torsion was measured by reconstructed testing machine INOVA [3].

---

*Corresponding author. e-mail: frantisek.fojtik@vsb.cz.

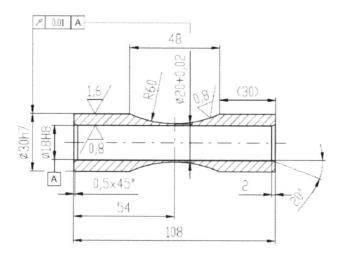

Fig. 1. Specimen

Table 1. Experimental results for alternating torsion

Specimen Nr.	Stress amplitude τ_a [MPa]	Number of cycles	Notes
1	214,4	30 800	
2	196,3	67 500	
3	178,2	683 620	
4	176,3	2 703 000	
5	172,2	10 810 000	No crack generated
6	516,6	0,25	τ_f

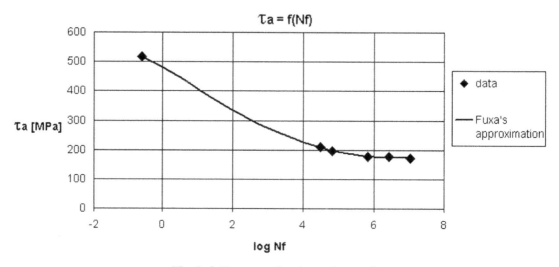

Fig. 2. S-N – curve for alternating torsion

Fuxa's approximation:

$$\tau_{aF} = (\tau_f + \tau_C)/2 + [(\tau_f - \tau_C)/2] \cdot \cos\{\pi \cdot [\log(4 \cdot N_f)/\log(4 \cdot N_C)]^{a_1}\}, \qquad (1)$$

for N_f in interval $[1/4; N_C]$ and τ_{aF} in interval $[\tau_f; \tau_C]$.

τ_f (516,6 MPa) is a value of real shear strength, τ_C (172,9 MPa) is the stress at the fatigue limit, N_C (6 400 000) is number of cycles at the fatigue limit, a_1 is constant, τ_{aF} is the limit stress amplitude under alternating torsion and N_f is the limit number of cycles until crack initiation. The mentioned values were obtained by nonlinear regression methods.

3. Alternating torsion – tension prestress – experiment

For this way of testing the same specimen as in previous case were used fig. 1. The specimens were loaded in every series by the constant tension pre stress and consequently by nominal amplitude of the torque until the crack initiation. This amplitude was gradually decreased until the value when was the specimen able to endure 10^7 of cycles. The testing frequency was also 25 Hz.

The experimental results are shown in the tab. 2 and figured in fig. 3. The results are here approximated by Fuxa's approximation (2, 3, 4, 5) which takes the influence of the mean stress into the account. Particular approximations are based on measured number of cycles which is mentioned in fig. 3.

Table 2. Experimental results for alternating torsion and tension prestress

Specimen Nr.	Tension Stress σ_t [MPa]	Stress amplitude τ_a [MPa]	Number of Cycles	CH_F [%]	Notes
1	266,1	154	401 000	3,82	
2	266,1	145,5	637 600	1,42	
3	266,1	136,6	10 487 000	2,42	No crack generated
4	191,6	178,5	110 300	1,69	
5	191,6	162,3	310 500	3,06	
6	191,6	146,5	11 300 000	2,34	No crack generated

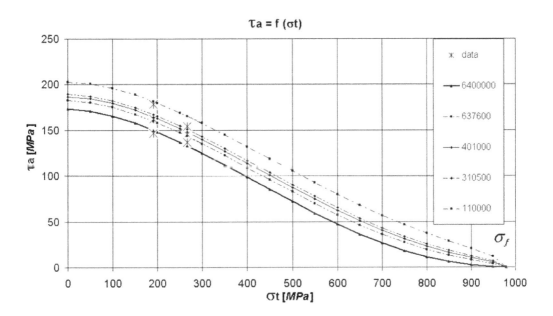

Fig. 3. Fuxa's approximation for combined torsion – tension loading

Fuxa's approximation with influence of mean stress:

$$\tau_{aF2} = \left(\tau_f^* + \tau_C^*\right)/2 + \left[\left(\tau_f^* - \tau_C^*\right)/2\right] \cdot \cos\left\{\pi \cdot \left[\log\left(4 \cdot N_f\right)/\log\left(4 \cdot N_C\right)\right]^{a_1}\right\}, \quad (2)$$

$$\tau_f^* = 1/\sqrt{3} \cdot \left(\left(\sqrt{3} \cdot \tau_f\right)^2 - 2 \cdot \sqrt{3} \cdot \tau_f \cdot B_O \cdot \sigma_t/3 + \sigma_t^2 \cdot B_O^2/9 - \sigma_t^2\right)^{1/2}, \quad (3)$$

where (4) is the static strength condition for $N_f = 1/4$ and constant B_O is equal to:

$$B_O = 3 \cdot \left(\sqrt{3} \cdot \tau_f/\sigma_f - 1\right), \quad (4)$$

$$\tau_C^* = \tau_C/2 \cdot \left\{1 + \cos\left[\pi \cdot \left(\sigma_t/\sigma_f\right)^B\right]\right\} \text{ is the strength condition for } N_f = N_C. \quad (5)$$

σ_f (979,2 MPa) is the real tension strength value, τ_f is a value of real shear strength, τ_C is the stress at the fatigue limit, N_C is number of cycles at the fatigue limit, a_1 and B are constants, τ_{aF2} is the limit amplitude of shear stress, σ_t is the constant tension stress and N_f marks the limit number of cycles until crack initiation. The absolute mean relative error value of used approximation is mentioned in tab. 2 and can be determined according to following formula:

$$CH_F = ABS\left(\tau_{ai} - \tau_{aFi}\right)/\tau_{ai} \cdot 100\ \%, \quad (6)$$

τ_{ai} are the measured stress amplitude values and τ_{aFi} are the values calculated according to the Fuxa's approximation (2).

4. Alternating torsion – inner overpressure and tension prestress – experiment

For this way of testing the same specimen as in previous case were used fig. 1. Every series of specimens was loaded by different constant overpressure. The torque amplitudes were chosen for every series. Specimens were loaded by that amplitude until the crack initiation. This amplitude was gradually decreased until the value when was the specimen able to endure 10^7 of cycles. The testing frequency was also 25 Hz. The results of those experiments are mentioned in tab. 3.

Table 3. Experimental results for alternating torsion and a inner overpressure

Nr.	Overpressure [MPa]	Tension mean Stress $\sigma_t = \sigma_a + \sigma_{t1}$ [MPa]	Stress amplitude τ_a [MPa]	Number of cycles	CH_F [%]	Notes
1	10	151,8	176,2	256 500	0,38	
2	10	151,8	162,3	1 475 600	0,68	
3	10	151,8	155,3	10 080 000	1,41	No crack generated
4	15	219	166,7	441 500	5,39	
5	15	219	160,1	1 234 000	6,92	
6	15	219	146,7	11 058 000	1,74	No crack generated
7	20	303,7	149,6	175 000	0,02	
8	20	303,7	134,6	2 374 000	6,72	
9	20	303,7	124,4	10 750 000	0,33	No crack generated

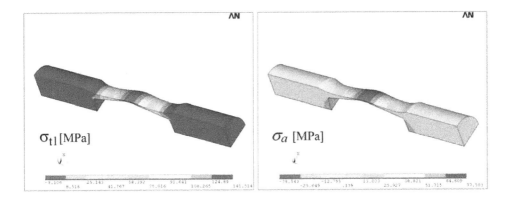

Fig. 4. Circumferential and axial stresses for inner overpressure 15 MPa

On the base of stress state evaluation of the specimen the significant circumferential σ_{t1} and axial σ_a stress can be observed on the surface. Hence this stress state had to be determined by finite element method in software ANSYS [6].

The static analysis was performed, where $1/4$ of specimen. The material parameter was obtained on the base of tensile test. The boundary conditions are chosen so that the resting $3/4$ of specimen is compensated by symmetry and further one point of specimen face is fixed in three directions (x, y, z). Opposite end of the specimen is free. On the relevant length the inner overpressure was applied thereby the axial force is put into the specimen. Results for given overpressure are in tab. 3. The calculated circumferential and axial stress (MPa) for the pressure of 15 MPa figured in fig. 4.

Results obtained from performed experiments and computation are on fig. 5. Those results are approximated Fuxa's approximation (2, 3, 4, 5) which takes into account the influence of mean stress. It is necessary to adjust equation (3) according to the strength criterion formulation [4] for obtained stress state.

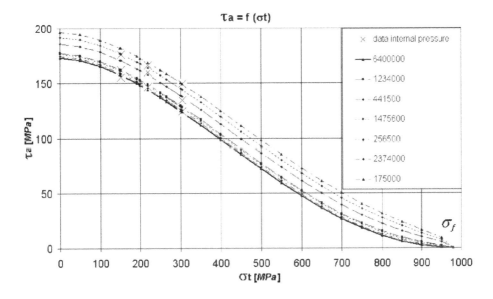

Fig. 5. Fuxa's approximation for combined torsion – inner overpressure loading

Particular approximations result from measured number of cycles written in tab. 3. The constant determined in previous experiment are used in this case. The curves at the fatigue limit are in the case of both described problems equivalent. The absolute value of mean relative error CH_F (6) is mentioned in tab. 3 as well.

5. Alternating torsion – inner and external overpressure and tension prestress – experiment

For this way of loading was the testing machine SHENCK type PWXN [1] equipped by a new type of specimen fixation which makes possible to use the overpressure chamber. This chamber is connected with multiplier and with hydraulic aggregate which serves for gaining of inner and external overpressure in the range 0–70 MPa. For this way of testing the same specimen as in previous case were used.

The tests were performed so that the first series of specimens was loaded simultaneously by inner and external overpressure of 40 MPa. For this inner/external overpressure the torque amplitude was chosen by which the specimen was loaded until the crack initiation. This amplitude was subsequently reduced until the value when the specimen was able to endure 10^7 of cycles. Those experimental results are in tab. 4.

Table 4. The experimental results for alternating torsion with the influence of mean stress from inner/external overpressure and tension loading

Nr.	Pressure [MPa]	Tension force [N]	Tension mean Stress $\sigma_t = \sigma_a + \sigma_{t1} + \sigma_R$ [MPa]	Stress amplitude τ_a [MPa]	Number of cycles	CH_F [%]	Notes
1	40	0	172,4	178	197 860	0,79	
2	40	0	172,7	169,1	1 261 800	6,38	
3	40	0	172,3	157,2	11 160 000	2,21	No crack generated
4	40	7 000	35,7	184	97 500	10,78	
5	40	7 000	35,7	174,8	1 022 500	1,69	
6	40	7 000	35,7	167,2	10 470 000	2,85	No crack generated

The second series of specimens was loaded by inner and external overpressure of 40 MPa simultaneously by axial tension force. The torque amplitude by which the specimen was loaded until the crack initiation was determined for this loading case as first. In case of following specimens this amplitude was subsequently reduced until the value when the specimen was able to endure 10^7 of cycles. Due to such complicated loading the mean stress in three dimensions was established in the specimen.

From the stress state analysis follows that in case of specimen loaded in described way the significant circumferential σ_{t1}, axial σ_a and radial σ_R stress appear. Those stresses can not be analytically determined in the simple way due the complicated shape of the specimen and faces where the inner and external overpressure is applied. Base on this fact the described stress state was determined by the finite element method in software ANSYS.

The static analysis was performed in both cases. The model was pen as $1/4$ of the specimen which was meshed by the SOLID186 element. The material parameters were obtained from the tension test. The boundary conditions were chosen so that the remaining $3/4$ of the specimen is substituted by the symmetry and further the displacement is constrained in three directions (x, y, z) on one face. The other end of the specimen is free. The inner and external overpressure was applied on the appropriate faces of the specimen. Those faces are based on the dimensions and sealing of the specimen. The simulation results for both series and given loading type are in tab. 4. The results of circumferential, axial and radial stresses (MPa) obtained from performed analysis by FEM for inner and outer overpressure of 40 MPa are in fig. 6.

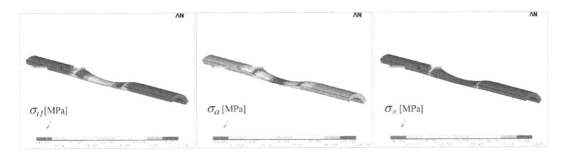

Fig. 6. Circumferential, axial and radial stresses for inner and external overpressure 40 MPa in specimen – Nr. 2. in tab. 4

The both experimental and simulation results are in fig. 7. Those results are approximated by described Fuxa's approximation (3, 4, 5, 6) which takes the influence of the three-dimensional mean stress into the account. It is necessary to adjust equation (4) into the shape which takes the influence of three-dimensional mean stress into the account for obtained stress state.

The particular approximations are based on the measured cycles number from tab. 4. The approximation on the fatigue limit is same as in the case of previous experiments. The same constants of used approximation are used here as well. In fig. 7 the good agreement between the obtained experimental results and proposed approximation can be seen.

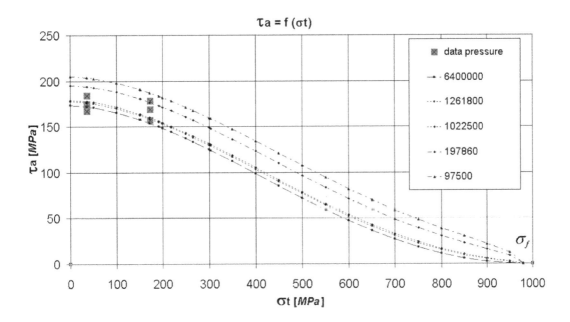

Fig. 7. The Fuxa's approximation for combined loading by torsion – inner, external overpressure and axial force

6. Conclusion

The four types of experiments on the specimens made from the steel 11523.0, melt T31052 are subsequently mentioned in this contribution.

First experiment – alternating torsion. Obtained results are approximated Fuxa's approximation. The Fuxa's approximation embodies a good agreement with experiment – see fig. 2.

Second experiment – combined loading by alternating amplitude of torque and by constant axial tension force. Also here the Fuxa's approximation embodies the good agreement with experiment – see fig. 3. The constants of strength criterion were tuned on this experiment.

The third experiment – combined loading by the amplitude of the torque with the influence of mean stress which is created by the inner overpressure and axial tension force here. The relevant hoop and axial stresses are obtained by the static stress/strain analysis by FEM. The experimental results are approximated by Fuxa's approximation whose constants result from previous experiment. The good agreement can be seen here and hence it is possible to state the appropriate constant tuning for further possible combined loading – see fig. 5. The maximum absolute mean relative error value of used approximation is here 6,92 %. Described approximation is a part of conjugated stress criterion, see [4] for more details.

The fourth experiment – combined loading by the amplitude of the torque with the influence of mean stress which is created by the inner and external overpressure and axial tension force here. The relevant circumferential, axial and radial stresses are obtained by the static stress/strain analysis by FEM in software ANSYS. The experimental results are approximated by the Fuxa's approximation of the Conjugated strength criterion. The good agreement with the experimental results in the area the fatigue limit can be seen here.

Acknowledgements

The paper was created under support of GACR, project no: 101/08/P141.

References

[1] Fojtík, F., The Experimental Machine for the Multiaxis Fatigue Testing of Material, Dissertation Thesis, FS VŠB-TU Ostrava, 2007.
[2] Fojtík, F., The Fatigue Testing Machine and Experiment, In: Applied Mechanics 2008, Wisla, Polsko, 2008.
[3] Fuxa, J., Fojtík, F., Kubala, R., Torque machine fit for high cycle fatigue of material testing, In: Experimental Stress Analysis 2007, Hotel Výhledy, 2007.
[4] Fuxa, J., Kubala, R., Fojtík, F., Idea of Conjugated Strength, In: Experimental Stress Analysis 2006, Červený Kláštor, Slovensko, 2006, pp. 125–130.
[5] Fuxa, J., Kubala, R., Fojtík, F., Poruba, Z., Reconstruction of the Torque Test Machine and Its Utilization for Strength Criterion Searching In: Experimental Stress Analysis 2005, Skalský dvůr, 2005.
[6] Fojtík, F., Fuxa, J., Examination of the Fatigue Life under Combined Loading of Specimens, Applied and Computational Mechanics, Volume 2, Number 1, 2008, pp. 37–44, ISSN 1802-680X.

2

Determination of the transient vibrations of a rigid rotor attenuated by a semiactive magnetorheological damping device by means of computational modelling

J. Zapoměl[a,*], P. Ferfecki[a], J. Kozánek[a]

[a]*Department of Dynamics and Vibrations, Institute of Thermomechanics, Department of Mechanics, Dolejškova 1402/5, 182 00 Praha 8, Czech Republic*

Abstract

Unbalance is the principal source of increase of time varying forces transmitted between the rotor and its stationary part. Their magnitudes can be considerably reduced if the rotor is flexibly suspended and if the damping devices are added to the support elements. Their damping effect must be high for low rotor velocities and small for velocities approximately higher than the critical one to minimize the transmitted forces and the vibrations amplitude. This implies to achieve maximum efficiency of the damping elements, their damping effect has to be adaptable to the current operating conditions. Such technological solution is offered by application of a squeeze film magnetorheological damper. Its hybrid variant consisting of two damping units (one controllable) in a serial arrangement is investigated in this paper. The damping takes place in two concentric lubricating films formed by normal and magnetorheological oils. The damper is equipped with an electric coil generating magnetic flux passing through the layer of the magnetorheological fluid. As resistance against its flow depends on magnetic induction, changing magnitude of the applied current enables to control the damping force. In the computational model, the rotor is considered to be absolutely rigid, unbalanced and the damping elements are represented by force couplings. The goal of the analysis is to study influence of the investigated magnetorheological damper on behaviour of a rigid rotor during different transient regimes. A special attention is focused on passing the rotor through the critical speed and on planning the dependence of the applied current on speed of the rotor rotation to achieve the optimum compromise between minimizing the transmitted forces and maximum attenuation of the rotor vibrations.

Keywords: rigid rotors, controllable damping, hybrid magnetorheological dampers, transient response

1. Introduction

Unbalance is the main source of time varying forces transmitted between the rotor and its frame. They cause fatigue loading of mechanical parts, which can arrive at occurrence of cracks and consequently at fractures. A frequently used technological solution for reducing these undesirable effects consists in application of a rotor flexible suspension.

Basic information on the influence of damping devices added to the constraint elements on rotor vibrations is provided by a simplified dynamical analysis assuming absolutely rigid rotor and linear properties of its flexible suspension (Fig. 1).

The dependences of amplitude of the force transmitted between the rotor and its casing on angular speed of the rotor rotation and on the coefficient of linear damping b_D of its suspension are drawn in Fig. 2. Fig. 3 shows the corresponding frequency responses.

*Corresponding author. e-mail: jaroslav.zapomel@vsb.cz.

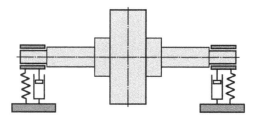

Fig. 1. Scheme of the simplified rotor system

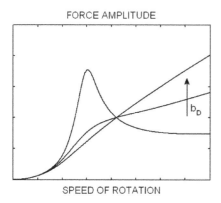

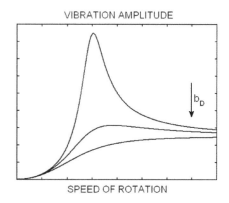

Fig. 2. Transmitted force – speed of rotation rela-   Fig. 3. Rotor frequency responses
tionship

It is evident from the analysis of Figs. 2 and 3 that the increasing damping reduces both the transmitted force and the vibration amplitude in the case of lower rotor angular velocities (approximately lower than the critical speed). On the contrary, the rising damping leads to significant increase of the transmitted force but has only small influence (or even negligible) on the attenuation of the rotor vibrations for higher speeds (approximately higher than the critical velocity). This implies to achieve efficient performance of the damping devices in the rotor supports in a wide range of running speeds the damping effect of which must be adaptable to the current operating conditions.

The squeeze film dampers lubricated by Newtonian oils are frequently used in practical rotor dynamic applications. One of the first reported works dealing with their control was published by Burrows et al. [1]. The authors examined the effect of the controlled oil-supply pressure on the change of the system damping coefficients and showed that the proposed approach reduced both the rotor vibrations and the forces transmitted to the machine frame. A different design of a controllable squeeze film damper was developed by Mu et al. [6]. Between the inner and outer rings of the damper there is a gap of a conical form filled with normal oil. The position of the outer ring in the axial direction is adjustable, which enables to change both the radial clearance and the land length of the damper and thus to control the damping force by the ring shifting.

A new concept of controlling the damping effects is represented by magnetorheological devices. As resistance against the flow of magnetorheological liquids depends on magnetic induction, the damping force can be controlled by changing the magnitude of electric current generating magnetic flux passing through the lubricating film. Wang et al. [7] studied the vibration characteristics and the control method of a flexible rotor equipped with a magnetorheological squeeze film damper by means of experiments. Forte et al. [4] presented results of the theoretical and experimental investigations of a long magnetorheological damping device. Wang et al. [8] developed a mathematical model of a long squeeze film magnetorheological damper based on the modified Reynolds equation. The results of experiments performed with a squeeze film magnetorheological damping element on a small test rotor rig were reported by Carmignani et al. [2, 3]. Zapoměl et al. [10] worked out a mathematical model of a short squeeze film magnetorheological damper, which can be applied for analysis of both the steady state and transient rotor vibrations.

A new hybrid variant of a magnetorheological damper intended for minimizing the force transmission between the rotor and its casing during unsteady operating regimes is investigated in this article. A squirrel spring of the damper supporting the rotor forms a flexible suspension. The rotor is considered as absolutely rigid. The damper is of a squeeze film kind and the dissipation of mechanical energy takes place in two concentric fluid layers of normal and magnetorheological oils arranged in a serial way. The damping effect produced by squeezing the layer of the magnetorheological oil is controlled by the change of magnetic flux generated in electric coils. The computational simulations showed that a suitable current control in dependence on speed of the rotor rotation enabled to achieve the optimum compromise between the reduction of the force transmitted through the constraint elements to the stationary part and the attenuation of the rotor vibrations during its acceleration and passing the critical velocity.

Proposal of a new design solution of the damping element, development of its mathematical model together with learning more on its effect on a rigid rotor behaviour represent the principal contributions of this article.

2. The hybrid squeeze film magnetorheological damping element with serial arrangement of the oil layers

The carried out simplified analysis shows that to achieve maximum efficiency of the damping elements placed between the rotor and its casing their damping effect must be as large as possible for lower velocities and minimum for angular speeds approximately higher than the critical one. This has arrived at the idea of investigating a concept of a hybrid damping element consisting of two independent damping units, from which one is controllable, in a serial arrangement. In this case, the resulting damping coefficient is always lower than the lower one from both individual damping units. This makes it possible to reach lower damping in the range of high rotor velocities than those produced by a compact device containing only one lubricating layer.

The principal parts of the proposed damping element (Fig. 4) are three rings, from which two are moveable. The clearances between the rings are filled with lubricating oils. The inner ring is coupled with the rotor journal by a rolling element bearing and with the damper's body by a squirrel spring. The outer ring is stationary and fixed to the damper housing. The lubricating films are concentric formed by normal (inner) and magnetorheological (outer) oils and are mutually separated by a thin ring flexibly coupled with the damper's housing. From the physical point of view, the lubricating films are arranged in a serial way. Because of the lateral vibrations of the rotor, the oil films between the rings are being squeezed, which produces the damping effect. A substantial part of the studied damper is an electric coil generating magnetic flux passing through the layer of the magnetorheological liquid. As resistance against its flow depends on magnetic induction, the change of the applied electric current can be used to control the damping force.

The developed mathematical model of the studied damping element is based on utilization of the classical theory of lubrication with some modifications. The magnetorheological oil is

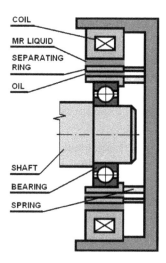

Fig. 4. Scheme of the damping device

represented by Bingham material with the yielding shear stress depending on magnetic induction. If no magnetic field is applied, it behaves as Newtonian liquid, as well as the normal oil. Further, it is assumed that the geometric and design parameters enable to consider the damping device as short (the length to diameter ratio of the rings is small, no or soft sealings are applied at the damper's ends).

Based on a simple geometric analysis, the relations for thicknesses of the thin films of normal and magnetorheological oils read (Krämer [5])

$$h_{NO} = c_{NO} - e_{NO}\cos(\varphi - \gamma_{NO}), \tag{1}$$

$$h_{MR} = c_{MR} - e_{MR}\cos(\varphi - \gamma_{MR}). \tag{2}$$

h_{NO}, h_{MR} are the thicknesses of the classical and magnetorheological oil films, c_{NO}, c_{MR} are the widths of the gaps between the rings filled with normal and magnetorheological oils, e_{NO}, e_{MR} denote the rotor journal and the separating ring eccentricities, φ is the circumferential coordinate and γ_{NO}, γ_{MR} denote the position angles of the lines of centres of the rotor journal and the separating ring respectively (Fig. 5).

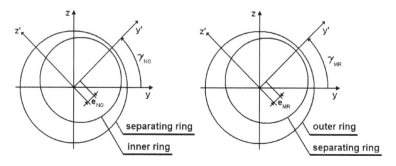

Fig. 5. The damper's coordinate systems

The Reynolds equations governing the pressure distribution in the layers of normal and magnetorheological oils adapted for short squeeze film dampers take the form (Krämer [5], Zapoměl et al. [10]),

$$\frac{\partial^2 p_{NO}}{\partial Z^2} = \frac{12\eta}{h_{NO}^3} \dot{h}_{NO}, \tag{3}$$

$$h_{MR}^3 p_{MR}'^3 + 3\left(h_{MR}^2 \tau_y - 4\eta_B \dot{h}_{MR} Z\right) p_{MR}'^2 - 4\tau_y^3 = 0 \quad \text{for } p_{MR}' < 0, \tag{4}$$

$$h_{MR}^3 p_{MR}'^3 - 3\left(h_{MR}^2 \tau_y + 4\eta_B \dot{h}_{MR} Z\right) p_{MR}'^2 + 4\tau_y^3 = 0 \quad \text{for } p_{MR}' > 0. \tag{5}$$

p_{NO}, p_{MR} denote the pressures in the layers of normal and magnetorheological oils respectively, η, η_B are the dynamical and Bingham viscosities of the normal and magnetorheological oils, τ_y represents the yield shear stress, Z is the axial coordinate and $(\dot{})$, $(')$ denote the first derivative with respect to time and coordinate Z. The Reynolds equations (4) and (5) are valid for $Z > 0$.

The governing equations (3)–(5) are solved for the boundary conditions expressing that the pressure at the damper's ends is equal to the pressure in the ambient space. Relationships (4) and (5) represent the polynomial algebraic equations of the third order for the pressure gradient. The sought root must fulfil the conditions: p_{MR}' is real (not complex), is negative for equation (4) or positive for equation (5) and it satisfies the relation

$$|p_{MR}'| > \frac{2\tau_y}{h_{MR}}. \tag{6}$$

After determining the pressure gradient from equations (4) or (5), the pressure distribution in the axial direction is calculated by the integration

$$p_{MR} = \int p_{MR}' \, dZ. \tag{7}$$

To solve equation (3) and integral (7), the constants of integration are determined for the boundary conditions which express the pressure at the damper's ends is equal to the pressure in the ambient space.

For the damper's simplest design arrangement, the outer and separating rings can be considered as a divided core of an electromagnet having the gap filled with the magnetorheological oil. Then dependence of yielding shear stress on magnetic induction can be approximately expressed

$$\tau_y = k_d \left(\frac{I}{h_{MR}}\right)^{n_y}, \tag{8}$$

where n_y is the magnetorheological liquid material constant, k_d is the design parameter depending on the number of the coil turns and material properties of the magnetorheological liquid and I is the applied electric current. More detailed information on determination of the yielding shear stress in the layer of the magnetorheological film can be found in [9, 10].

In the areas where the thickness of the lubricating films increases with time ($\dot{h}_{NO} > 0$, $\dot{h}_{MR} > 0$), a cavitation is assumed. In these regions, the pressure of the medium remains constant and equal to the pressure in the ambient space. In noncavitated areas, the pressure is governed by solutions of the Reynolds equation (3) and integral (7).

Consequently, components of the damping forces are calculated by integrating the pressure distributions around the circumference and along the length of the damping element taking into account the cavitation in the oil films. Then it holds

$$F_{MRy} = -2R_{MR} \int_0^{2\pi} \int_0^{\frac{L}{2}} p_{DMR} \cos\varphi \, dZ \, d\varphi, \tag{9}$$

$$F_{MRz} = -2R_{MR} \int_0^{2\pi} \int_0^{\frac{L}{2}} p_{DMR} \sin\varphi \, dZ \, d\varphi, \tag{10}$$

$$F_{NOy} = -2R_{NO} \int_0^{2\pi} \int_0^{\frac{L}{2}} p_{DNO} \cos\varphi \, dZ \, d\varphi, \tag{11}$$

$$F_{NOz} = -2R_{NO} \int_0^{2\pi} \int_0^{\frac{L}{2}} p_{DNO} \sin\varphi \, dZ \, d\varphi. \tag{12}$$

F_{NOy}, F_{NOz}, F_{MRy}, F_{MRz} are the y and z components of the hydraulic forces produced by the pressure in the films of normal and magnetorheological oils respectively, R_{NO}, R_{MR} are the mean radii of the layers of normal and magnetorheological oils, L is the axial length of the damping element and p_{DNO}, p_{DMR} denote the pressure distributions in the layers of normal and magnetorheological oils (taking into account different pressures in cavitated and noncavitated regions).

3. The investigated rotor system

The investigated rotor consists of a shaft and of one disc and it is coupled with the frame by the studied constraint elements at both its ends (Fig. 6). The rotor operates at variable angular speed and it is loaded by its weight and excited by the disc unbalance. The squirrel springs of the damping elements are prestressed to eliminate their deflection caused by the rotor weight. The whole system is symmetric relative to the disc middle plane.

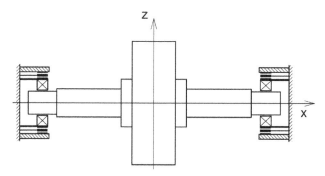

Fig. 6. Scheme of the investigated system

The technological parameters of the rotor system are: mass of the rotor 450 kg, stiffness of one squirrel spring 5 MN/m, the length of each constraint element 60 mm, widths of the clearances filled by the normal and magnetorheological oils 0.2 mm, 1.0 mm, middle radii of the layers of the normal and magnetorheological oils 55 mm, 75 mm, dynamical and Bingham viscosities of the normal and magnetorheological oils 0.004 Pa · s, 0.3 Pa · s, eccentricity of the rotor centre of gravity 0.1 mm, exponential material constant of the magnetorheological oil 2 and the value of the design parameter 0.001 N/A^2.

In the computational model, the rotor is considered as absolutely rigid and the constraint devices are represented by springs and force couplings. The task was to find an effective rule for controlling the damping force to achieve the optimum compromise between the reduction of the force transmitted to the rotor frame and minimization of the rotor vibration during its acceleration from angular velocity of 150 rad/s to 350 rad/s during the time period of 2 s (Fig. 7).

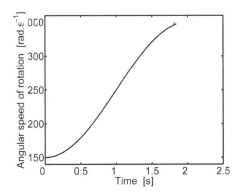

Fig. 7. Time history of required angular speed of the rotor rotation

The lateral vibration of the rotor system is governed by a set of four nonlinear differential equations

$$m_R \ddot{y}_R + b_P \dot{y}_R + 2k_R y_R = m_R e_T \left(\dot{\vartheta}^2 \cos\vartheta + \ddot{\vartheta} \sin\vartheta \right) + 2F_{NOy}, \tag{13}$$

$$m_R \ddot{z}_R + b_P \dot{z}_R + 2k_R z_R = m_R e_T \left(\dot{\vartheta}^2 \sin\vartheta - \ddot{\vartheta} \cos\vartheta \right) - m_R g + 2F_{PSR} + 2F_{NOz}, \tag{14}$$

$$m_{SR} \ddot{y}_{SR} + k_{SR} y_{SR} = -F_{NOy} + F_{MRy}, \tag{15}$$

$$m_{SR} \ddot{z}_{SR} + k_{SR} z_{SR} = -F_{NOz} + F_{MRz} - m_{SR} g + F_{PSSR}. \tag{16}$$

m_R is the rotor mass, b_P is the coefficient of the rotor external damping, k_R is the stiffness of the squirrel spring supporting the rotor, m_{SR}, k_{SR} are the mass of the ring separating the lubricating layers and the stiffness of its support respectively, e_T is the eccentricity of the rotor unbalance, θ is the angle of the rotor rotation about its axis, t is the time, y_R, z_R, y_{SR}, z_{SR} are the displacements of the rotor centre (centre of the rotor journal) and of the centre of the ring separating the lubricating layers in the horizontal and vertical directions, g is the gravity acceleration, F_{PSR}, F_{PSSR} are the forces prestressing the dampers' springs and (¨) denotes the second derivative with respect to time.

4. Results of the computational simulations

The time histories of the force transmitted between the rotor and its casing for two constant magnitudes of the applied current (0 A, 1.27 A) are depicted in Figs. 8 and 9. The corresponding time courses of displacements of the rotor and of the separating ring centres in the horizontal direction are drawn in Figs. 10–13. The results show that the applied current reduces the transmitted force and amplitude of the rotor vibration for lower velocities (approximately lower than the critical speed) but for higher angular speeds it leads to their increase. The vibration amplitude of the separating ring is attenuated in the whole extent of the rotor operating velocities (Fig. 13).

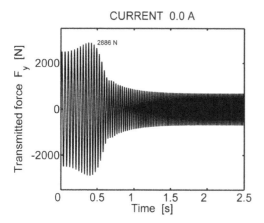

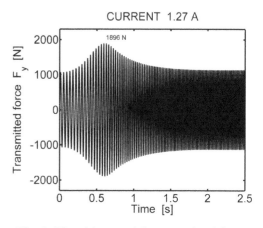

Fig. 8. Time history of the transmitted force   Fig. 9. Time history of the transmitted force

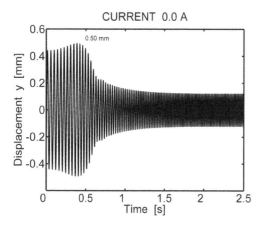

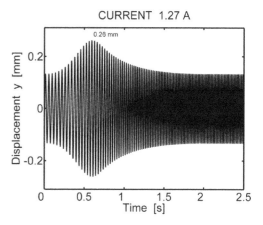

Fig. 10. Time history of the rotor displacement   Fig. 11. Time history of the rotor displacement

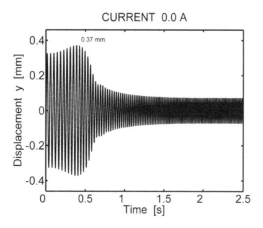

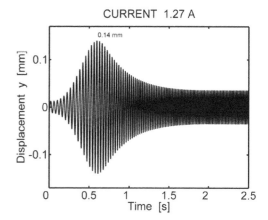

Fig. 12. Separating ring displacement   Fig. 13. Separating ring displacement

The rotor mass and the supporting squirrel springs stiffness determine the system undamped resonance frequency to 149 rad/s. Comparison of Figs. 8 with 9, 10 with 11 and 12 with 13 gives the evidence that increase of the hydraulic (damping) force shifts the system resonance frequency to a higher value, by employing diagram in Fig. 7, approximately to 169 rad/s if no current is applied and to 193 rad/s if the current is switched on.

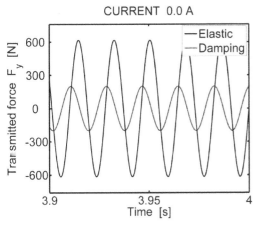

Fig. 14. Transmitted force components

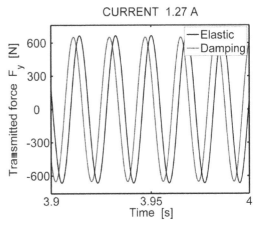

Fig. 15. Transmitted force components

The force between the rotor and its casing is transmitted through the squirrel spring (the elastic force) and the lubricating layers (the damping force) of the damping element. The time histories of components of both these forces referred to the rotor steady state vibration after finishing its acceleration are drawn for two magnitudes of the applied current in Fig. 14 and 15. It is evident that the applied current influences their magnitudes but has almost no effect on their mutual phase shift which is caused by their different physical substance (elastic and damping forces).

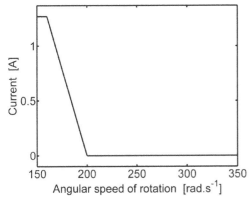

Fig. 16. Current angular speed of rotation history – variant 1

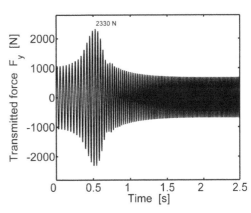

Fig. 17. Force time history – variant 1

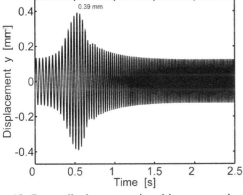

Fig. 18. Rotor displacement time history – variant 1

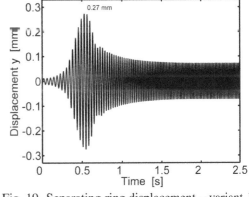

Fig. 19. Separating ring displacement – variant 1

Analysis of Figs. 8–11 shows that the maximum suppression of the transmitted force and of the rotor vibration requires to apply high current in the area of the rotor low velocities but to switch it off after crossing the critical speed.

Therefore, to achieve the optimum system response, several strategies differing in the moment of beginning, course and duration of switching off the current have been studied. The corresponding time histories of the transmitted force and the rotor oscillations, both in the horizontal direction, are drawn for three variants of dependence of the current on the rotor rotational speed in Figs. 16–27. It is evident that variant 3 gives the best results as it enables maximum reduction of the transmitted force and minimum elevation of the rotor vibration amplitude. Early starting this manipulation (variant 1) arrives at large increase of the transmitted force accompanied by large increase of vibration of the rotor and of the separating ring. Similarly, shifting the beginning of this manipulation to higher angular velocities and extending time of its duration (variant 2) does not lead to the rotor satisfactory behaviour.

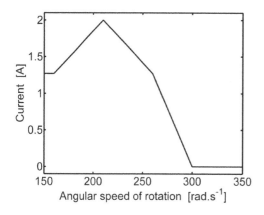

Fig. 20. Current angular speed of rotation history – variant 2

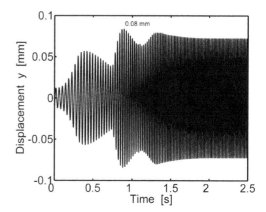

Fig. 21. Force time history – variant 2

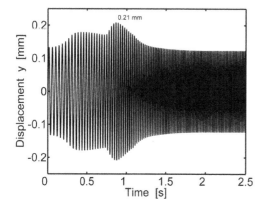

Fig. 22. Rotor displacement time history – variant 2

Fig. 23. Separating ring displacement – variant 2

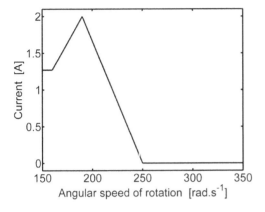

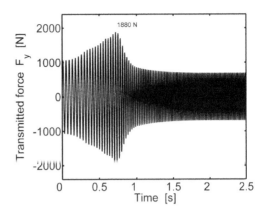

Fig. 24. Current angular speed of rotation history –
variant 3

Fig. 25. Force time history – variant 3

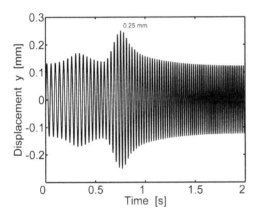

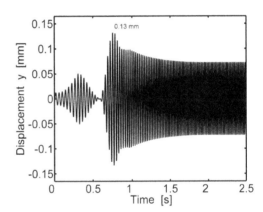

Fig. 26. Rotor displacement time history – variant 3

Fig. 27. Separating ring displacement – variant 3

5. Conclusions

A flexible suspension of rigid rotors is an often used technological solution that enables reduction of the forces transmitted between the rotor and its casing. The carried out computational simulations confirmed that the dampers added to the rotor supports had significant influence on both the magnitude of the transmitted force and the amplitude of the system vibrations.

The advantage of the studied damping device is that it enables to change the damping effect by controlling electric current and thus to adapt its performance to the current running conditions. The damper works on a semiactive principle and thus it does not require a complicated and expensive control system for its operation.

The theory confirmed by results of computational simulations shows that the damping effect of the damping devices added to the rotor supports should be high for velocities approximately lower than the resonance frequency and minimum for higher angular speeds. The studied design represents a hybrid variant of a magnetorheological damping element consisting of two lubricating layers in a serial arrangement. It enables to achieve larger reduction of the damping force in the range of higher rotor angular velocities than a compact damping device that has only one lubricating film. The results of performed computational simulations give the evidence that the change of the current (the current switching off) must not be sudden but that it has to be distributed over a certain speed interval so that the optimum performance of the damping element could be achieved. The efficiency of this manipulation depends on the moment of its starting and on the time of its duration.

Acknowledgements

The work reported in this article has been done with the institutional support RVO:61388998.

References

[1] Burrows, C. R., Sahinkaya, M. N., Turkay, O. S., An Adaptive Squeeze-Film Bearing, ASME Journal of Tribology 106(1)(1984) 145–151.

[2] Carmignani, C., Forte, P., Badalassi, P., Zini, G., Classical control of a magnetorheological squeeze-film damper, Proceedings of the Stability and Control Processes 2005, Saint-Petersburg, Russia, 2005, pp. 1 237–1 246.

[3] Carmignani, C., Forte, P., Rustighi, E., Design of a novel magneto-rheological squeeze-film damper, Smart Materials and Structures 15(1)(2006) 164–170.

[4] Forte, P., Paterno, M., Rustighi, E., A magnetorheological fluid damper for rotor applications, International Journal of Rotating Machinery 10(3)(2004) 175–182.

[5] Krämer, E., Dynamics of Rotors and Foundations, Springer-Verlag, Berlin, 1993.

[6] Mu, C., Darling, J., Burrows, C. R., An appraisal of a proposed active squeeze film damper, ASME Journal of Tribology 113(4)(1991) 750–754.

[7] Wang, J., Meng, G., Hahn, E.-J., Experimental Study on Vibration Properties and Control of Squeeze Mode MR Fluid Damper-Flexible Rotor System, Proceedings of the 2003 ASME Design Engineering Technical Conference & Computers and Information in Engineering Conference, Chicago, USA, 2003, pp. 955–959.

[8] Wang, G.-J., Feng, N., Meng, G., Hahn, E.-J., Vibration Control of a Rotor by Squeeze Film Damper with Magnetorheological Fluid, Journal of Intelligent Material Systems and Structures 17(4)(2006) 353–357.

[9] Zapoměl, J., Ferfecki, P., A numerical procedure for investigation of efficiency of short magnetorheological dampers used for attenuation of lateral vibration of rotors passing the critical speeds, Proceedings of the 8th IFToMM International Conference on Rotordynamics, Seoul, Korea, 2010, CD 1–8.

[10] Zapoměl, J., Ferfecki, P., Forte, P., A computational investigation of the transient response of an unbalanced rigid rotor flexibly supported and damped by short magnetorheological squeeze film dampers, Smart Materials and Structures 21(10)(2012) art. no. 105011.

3

Application of selected multi-axial fatigue criteria on the results of non-proportional fatigue experiments

F. Fojtík[a,*], J. Fuxa[a], Z. Poruba[a]

[a]*Faculty of Mechanical Engineering, VSB – Technical University of Ostrava, 17 listopadu 15, 708 33 Ostrava-Poruba, Czech Republic*

Abstract

The contribution describes the experimental results obtained from the combined loading of the specimens in the field of high-cycle fatigue. Those specimens were manufactured from common construction steel 11523.1, melt T31052.

The following experiments were performed: The first set of the specimen was loaded by the alternating bending amplitude. The second set was loaded by the amplitude of the bending in combination with constant inner overpressure. The results were evaluated by the conjugated strength criterion and another generally used multiaxial fatigue criteria. The stress-strain analysis of the specimens by FEM was performed to determine parameters (constants) of particular strength criteria.

Keywords: combined loading, experiment, high-cycle fatigue, multiaxial analysis

1. Introduction

Although the material failure phenomenon in the conditions of multiaxial fatigue is investigated for many years by world-known research institutes, the reliable mathematical description making possible to describe this boundary state was not introduced yet. Hence, it is still necessary to perform expensive prototype verification. The evidence of this fact is number of laboratories especially in aircraft and automotive industry. We bring another build-stone into the mosaic of this interesting technical field in this contribution.

Number of fatigue experiments using both the reconstructed and new proposed devices [1], were performed at the Department of Mechanics of Material, VSB-TU Ostrava. The aim was to verify the ability of the conjugated strength criterion [2] proposed at our department and to use it for coupling of static and fatigue multiaxial strength criterion.

Our contribution describes certain findings obtained from four different types of mechanical material loading. The experiments were performed on hollow specimens manufactured from the steel 11523.1. The experimental data obtained at the fatigue limit were judged primarily, i.e. for specimens which were not damaged after 10^7 cycles. The below presented methodology is made for this lifetime. The experimental data obtained for given combinations of loading even for the fields of lifetime strength are mentioned in this contribution as well. Those experiments were performed with the testing frequency of 25 Hz. The obtained data were used to determine the constants of conjugated strength criterion whose application can be suitable even for prediction of boundary cycle number in the field of lifetime strength [3].

---

*Corresponding author. e-mail: frantisek.fojtik@vsb.cz.

2. Experimental material

The experiments were performed on the hollow specimens (fig. 1) manufactured from low carbon steel CSN 411523.1 melting T31052. Those specimens were polished on the outer diameter. The chemical content and basic mechanical properties of this material are summarized in table 1 and table 2.

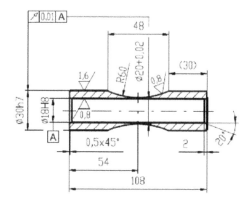

Fig. 1. Testing specimen

Table 1. Chemical properties of the specimen material

C	Mn	Si	P	S	Cu
%	%	%	%	%	%
0.18	1.38	0.4	0.018	0.006	0.05

Table 2. Mechanical properties of specimen material

Ultimate tensile strength [MPa]	Tensile yield stress [MPa]	Elongation at fracture [%]	Reduction of area at fracture [%]
560	400	31.1	74.0

The following material parameters were experimentally found out for the setting of below mentioned fatigue criteria.
tensile modulus: $E = 2.06 \cdot 10^5$ MPa,
Poisson's ratio: $\mu = 0.3$.

Other material parameters determined via experiment for given material and melting which are necessary for setting of given fatigue criteria.
fatigue limit in fully reversed torsion: $t_{-1} = 160$ MPa,
fatigue limit in fully reversed plane bending: $f_{-1} = 311$ MPa,
fatigue limit in repeated bending: $f_0 = 380$ MPa,
tensile true fracture strength: $\sigma_f = 979.2$ MPa,
torsion true fracture strength: $\tau_f = 516.6$ MPa.

3. Used multiaxial fatigue methods

The following generally used fatigue strength criteria were used for the analysis of performed experiments. The results obtained in experimental way for given loading combination on the fatigue limit will be judged by those criteria.

3.1. Crossland method

Crossland published his results in the 50th of previous century. His criterion uses the square root from tho second invariant of stress tensor. This invariant is determined from the stress amplitude. Another term added to the equation is the hydrostatic stress calculated from maximal stress values [4]

$$a_C \cdot \left(\sqrt{J_2}\right)_a + b_C \cdot \sigma_{H,\max} \le f_{-1}, \tag{1}$$

where coefficients a_C and b_C are defined as:

$$a_C = \frac{f_{-1}}{t_{-1}},$$
$$b_C = \left(3 - \frac{f_{-1}}{t_{-1}}\right), \tag{2}$$

other parameters in the equation are:
J_2 second invariant of stress tensor deviator, f_{-1} fatigue limit in fully reversed axial loading (in tension, in bending or in rotating bending), $\sigma_{H,\max}$ maximum value of hydrostatic stress during load history, t_{-1} fatigue limit in fully reversed torsion.

3.2. Sines method

Sines published his results in the same period as Crossland. The formulation of both criteria as similar, they differ in the determination of hydrostatic stress. Sines calculate this stress from mean stress values [5]

$$a_S \cdot \left(\sqrt{J_2}\right)_a + b_S \cdot \sigma_{H,m} \le f_{-1}, \tag{3}$$

where coefficients a_S and b_S are defined as:

$$a_S = \frac{f_{-1}}{t_{-1}},$$
$$b_S = 6 \cdot \frac{f_{-1}}{f_0} - \sqrt{3} \cdot \frac{f_{-1}}{t_{-1}}, \tag{4}$$

where f_0 is fatigue limit in repeated bending, $\sigma_{H,m}$ mean value of hydrostatic stress during load history, other parameters in the equation are defined as in the case of Crossland Method.

3.3. Dang Van method

This criterion belongs to the mesoscopic criteria. The mesoscopic criteria have their common point in an assumption that not the apparent macroscopic quantities, but their mesoscopic counterpart related to the least homogenous agglomerates of grains should be checked for fatigue evaluation. Dang Van initiated the solution and presented a way of transforming the mesoscopic quantities towards macroscopic stresses [9]. Dang Van criterion can be written for the lifetime at the fatigue limit in following way:

$$a_{DV} \cdot C_a + b_{DV} \cdot \sigma_{H,\max} \le f_{-1}, \tag{5}$$

where

$$a_{DV} = \frac{f_{-1}}{t_{-1}},$$

$$b_{DV} = 3 - \frac{3}{2} \cdot \frac{f_{-1}}{t_{-1}},$$

where C_a is shear stress amplitude on an examined plane, $\sigma_{H,\max}$ maximum value of hydrostatic stress during load history.

3.4. McDiarmid method (McD)

This criterion is widely used. On the base of number of experiments McDiarmid proposed the following form of the criterion:

$$\frac{f_{-1}}{t_{AB}} \cdot C_a + \frac{f_{-1}}{2 \cdot S_u} \cdot N_{\max} \leq f_{-1}, \tag{6}$$

where C_a is shear stress amplitude on an examined plane, f_{-1} is fatigue limit in fully reversed axial loading, $N_{\max}$ is maximum normal stress on the plane examined, S_u is tensile strength, t_{AB} is fatigue limit in fully reversed torsion with crack in A or B system. The crack parallel with the surface is typical for the type A. The crack leading inside down from the surface is typical for type B [6]. The following equivalence was used for the solution: $t_{AB} = t_{-1}$.

3.5. Papadopoulos method (Papad)

The Papadopoulos method is based on the Dang Van Criterion. However this method integrates the input variables in all planes. The method can be found in following form [7]:

$$\sqrt{a_p \cdot (T_a^2)} + b_p \cdot \sigma_{H,\max} \leq f_{-1}, \tag{7}$$

where

$$a_p = 5 \cdot \kappa^2, \qquad b_p = 3 - \sqrt{3} \cdot \kappa, \qquad \kappa = \frac{f_{-1}}{t_{-1}},$$

where T_a is resolved shear stress (a projection of shear stress into a given direction), K is ratio of fatigue limits.

3.6. Papuga PCr method

Papuga proposed the criterion on the base of long-term studies of multiaxial fatigue criteria in following form (7) [8]. According to his research embodies this criterion the most accurate results for wide range of materials

$$\sqrt{a_C \cdot C_a^2 + b_C \cdot \left(N_a + \frac{t_{-1}}{f_0} \cdot N_m \right)} \leq f_{-1}. \tag{8}$$

It is valid for following ratio of fatigue limits:

$$\kappa < \sqrt{\frac{4}{3}} \cong 1.155, \text{ is:}$$

$$a_C = \frac{\kappa^2}{2} + \frac{\sqrt{\kappa^4 - \kappa^2}}{2}, \qquad b_C = f_{-1}$$

$$\kappa \geq \sqrt{\frac{4}{3}} \cong 1.155, \text{ is:}$$

$$a_C = \left(\frac{4 \cdot \kappa^2}{4 + \kappa^2}\right), \qquad b_C = \frac{8 \cdot f_{-1} \cdot \kappa^2 \cdot (4 - \kappa^2)}{(4 + \kappa^2)^2}.$$

3.7. Matake method

The Matake criterion is the critical plane criterion of the following form [7, 9]

$$a_M \cdot C_a + b_M \cdot N_{\max} \leq f_{-1}, \tag{9}$$

where

$$a_M = \frac{f_{-1}}{t_{-1}},$$

$$b_M = 2 - \frac{f_{-1}}{t_{-1}}.$$

Here C_a is shear stress amplitude on the plane experiencing maximum shear stress range, $N_{\max}$ maximum normal stress on the same plane.

3.8. Conjugated strength criterion

This criterion was proposed by Fuxa [2]. For the crack initiation in N-th cycle it can be written in following form:

$$\frac{f_{-1} \cdot (A_N - B_N \cdot \sigma_R)}{S_\sigma} \leq f_{-1}, \tag{10}$$

where S_σ marks the stress intensity and is defined as:

$$S_\sigma = \frac{1}{\sqrt{2}} \cdot \left[(\sigma_1 - \sigma_2)^2 + (\sigma_2 - \sigma_3)^2 + (\sigma_3 - \sigma_1)^2\right]^{\frac{1}{2}}, \tag{11}$$

σ_R is the reference stress value producing the identical value as the octaedric normal stress and can be written as:

$$\sigma_R = (\sigma_1 + \sigma_2 + \sigma_3)/3, \tag{12}$$

where σ_1, σ_2, σ_3 are the principal stresses. The value A_N can be considered as dependent on the cycle number N and is written as:

$$A_N = (A_O + A_C)/2 + (A_O - A_C)/2 \cdot \cos\left\{\pi \cdot \left[\log(4 \cdot N)/\log(4 \cdot N_C)\right]^a\right\}. \tag{13}$$

A_O is the constant of the static reference strength criterion and can be determined based on the torsion test:

$$A_O = 3^{1/2} \cdot \tau_f. \tag{14}$$

A_C the stress intensity at the fatigue limit in torsion, N_C number of cycles at the fatigue limit, a material constant, B_N is the constant equal to:

$$B_N = 3 \cdot \left(\sqrt{3} \cdot \tau_f / \sigma_f - 1 \right), \tag{15}$$

where σ_f is the value of true fracture strength in tension and τ_f is the value of true fracture strength in torsion.

3.9. Fatigue index error

All mentioned criteria according to the results from (1, 3, 5, 6, 7, 8, 9, 10) judge if the component is able to transfer the infinity of loading cycles. Evaluate of those criteria the fatigue index error ΔFI is used. It shows the rate of deviation from the ideal equilibrium of the left and right hand sides of mentioned criterion relations [9]

$$\Delta FI = \frac{LHS(load) - f_{-1}}{f_{-1}} \cdot 100 \%, \tag{16}$$

where LHS is the left hand side of the equation. The relation $LHS(load) \leq f_{-1}$ has to be fulfilled. If LHS is greater, the component may fail.

4. First experiment — alternating bending

The first set of specimens was loaded by the nominal amplitude of the bending. In the case of first specimen the proper amplitude was set and the number of cycles until failure was registered. In case of other specimens, the amplitude was stepwise reduced until the fatigue limit — 10^7 cycles — was reached. The experiments were performed at the frequency 25 Hz. The experimental results are summarized in table 3 where σ_a is the stress amplitude in bending and σ_p is the constant inner overpressure. The resulting stress was obtained via stress/strain analysis using FEM in the software ANSYS. The limit stress intensity leading to the crack initiation in N_f cycles is depicted in fig. 2. It is calculated from obtained stress values.

Table 3. Experimental results for alternating bending

Nr.	σ_a [MPa]	σ_p [MPa]	N_f [−]	Notes
1	376.9	0	89 700	
2	352.4	0	196 635	
3	336.8	0	214 430	
4	324.8	0	1 262 300	
5	319.0	0	5 037 000	
6	311.0	0	11 631 000	No crack generated

5. Second experiment — alternating bending and inner overpressure

The second set of specimens was loaded in every series by the nominal amplitude of the bending moment and constant inner overpressure until the crack initiation. The loading of the specimen is described in fig. 3. This amplitude was gradually decreased until the value when was the

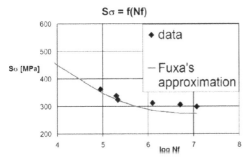

Fig. 2. S-N curve for alternating bending

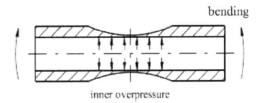

Fig. 3. The loading of the specimen

specimen able to endure 10^7 of cycles. The experiments were performed at the frequency 25 Hz again. The experimental results are summarized in table 4.

The dominant components of the stress tensor for both stress states are in table 4. The other components of the stress tensor are significantly smaller and were neglected in the analysis.

It was determined in the critical spot of the specimen using the FEM analysis in software ANSYS.

Table 4. Experimental results for alternating bending and inner overpressure

Nr.	σ_a [MPa]	σ_p [MPa]	N_f [–]	Notes
1	339.1	203.8	81 900	
2	314.8	205.5	172 200	
3	301.7	207.3	299 000	
4	296.0	203.8	813 000	
5	286.7	202.0	10 200 000	No crack generated
6	293.7	312.9	266 800	
7	281.8	312.9	894 400	
8	274.4	312.9	11 050 000	No crack generated

6. Experimental results analysis

The obtained experimental results from all described experiments were used for the analysis of above mentioned fatigue stress criteria. Only those experimental results were analyzed where the failure was not reached until 10^7 cycles. The software Pragtic was used for the analysis. This software is free accessible at http://www.pragtic.com [9]. It contains all mentioned criteria with the exception of Conjugated stress criterion which was proposed at the authors' laboratory. The program in Microsoft Office Excel was created for the analysis of this criterion. The results of this study are depicted in table 5.

Table 5. Experimental results analysis

Nr.	σ_a [MPa]	σ_p [MPa]	ΔFI (%)							
			Sines	Crossland	Dang Van	McD	Papad	Papuga PCr	Matake	Fuxa
1	311.0	0.0	12.2	0.0	0.0	11.1	0.0	0.0	0.0	2.8
2	286.7	202.0	36.8	−15.8	−6.0	11.3	−15.8	−6.8	−6.0	18.7
3	274.4	312.9	50.7	−24.1	−8.9	11.9	−24.1	−10.2	−8.9	4.4

7. Conclusion

The common used multi-axial strength criteria (see above) and the conjugated strength criterion [2] proposed by the authors of this contribution with the aim of coupling the static and fatigue multi-axial criterion, have been described in this contribution.

The three sets of experiments have been performed on the hollow, thin-walled specimen made of steel 11523.1. The different stress states were generated in the specimens during the loading: alternating bending, alternating bending with constant inner overpressure with two levels. The results of the experiments have been applied to verify the mentioned strength criteria.

According to the values of the fatigue index error ΔFI stated in table 5 the best results are achieved by using Dang Van and Matake criteria. The good results have been reached using Papuga PCr method as well. The next has been the Conjugated strength criterion (Fuxa) and other criteria.

Acknowledgements

The paper was created under support of GACR, project no: 101/08/P141.

References

[1] Fuxa, J., Fojtík, F., Kubala, R., Torque machine fit for high cycle fatigue of material testing, Experimental Stress Analysis, Hotel Výhledy, 2007.

[2] Fuxa, J., Kubala, R., Fojtík, F., Idea of Conjugated Strength Criterion, Acta Mechanica Slovaca, Vol. 1, 2006, p. 125–130.

[3] Fojtik, F., Fuxa, J., The multiaxial material fatigue under the combined loading with mean stress in three dimension, Applied and Computational Mechanics, Vol. 3, 2009, p. 267–274.

[4] Crossland, B., Effect of large hydrostatic pressure on the torsional fatigue strength of an alloy steel, In: Proc. Int. Conf. on Fatigue of Metals, Institution of Mechanical Engineers, London, 1956, p. 138–149.

[5] Sines, G., Behavior of metals under complex static and alternating stresses, In: Metal Fatigue. Red. G. Sines a J. L. Waisman, New York, McGraw Hill 1959, p. 145–469.

[6] McDiarmid, D. L., A general criterion for high cycle multiaxial fatigue failure, Fatigue Fract. Engng. Mater. Struct., 14, 1991, No. 4, p. 429–453.

[7] Papadopoulos, I. V., Davoli, P., Gorla, C., Filippini, M., Bernasconi, A., A comparative study of multiaxial high-cycle fatigue criteria for metals, Int. J. Fatigue 19, 1997, No. 3, p. 219–235.

[8] Papuga, J., Růžička, M., Two new multiaxial criteria for high cycle fatigue computation, Int. J. Fatigue 30, 2008, No. 1, p. 58–66.

[9] Papuga, J., Španiel, M., PragTic Fatigue Freeware and FatLim Databáze, MECCA, Vol. 5 (2007), No. 3.

4

Self-contained gas turbine unite with turbine expander drive of the compressor for the gas distribution station

A. Zaryankin[a], S. Arianov[b], S. Storoguk[c], A. Rogalev[a,*]

[a]Department of Steam and Gas turbines, Moscow Power Engineering Institute (Technical University),
Krasnokazarmennaya 14, 111250 Moscow, Russia

[b]JSC "ENTEK", Krasnokazarmennaya 17-G/3, 111116 Moscow, Russia

[c]JSC "RAO Energy System of East", Timura Frunze 11/15, 119021 Moscow, Russia

Abstract

This paper deals with the gas turbine installation with turbine expander drive of the compressor. It is shown that the offered installation has greater power capacity in comparison with the existent power turbo expanders and this unit can work in the regardless of steam turbine mode.

Keywords: turbine expander drive of the compressor, gas turbine

1. Introduction

In connection with uninterrupted growth of the energy consumption and limited sources of hydrocarbon fuel, the currency of waste energy utilization grows. Among the waste energy utilization problems, the important problem is excessive gas pressure utilization on the gas-distribution stations and in the first place on the gas-distribution station of the thermal power plant, where the natural gas flow is very big.

At present this problem is solving by application of the turbine expanders used the potential energy of natural gas and directly connected with electric generator.

However the opinion about the reasonability of the usage of such units on the thermal power plants is argued.

It should be taken into consideration that the gas directed to the consumer with lower pressure then in the gas-main pipeline must have near the same temperature, which was at the inlet of the turbo expander. Therefore the gas must be heated behind or after the turbo expander and the quantity of the heat input must be equivalent to the additional generated power.

From this point of view the turbo expander unit is the transformer of the thermal energy into electric one. However if this installation is included in thermal scheme of the thermal power plant and for the gas heating the steam bled form the steam turbine is used the steam turbine power capacity decrease induced by the steam extraction appears less than the power capacity generated by the turbo expander.

This research deals with the methodology of the additional power capacity estimation which generated by the turbo expander and with the dependence of power capacity from the gas expansion ratio. These results are compared with results which can be reaches in case of the

*Corresponding author. e-mail: R-Andrey2007@yandex.ru.

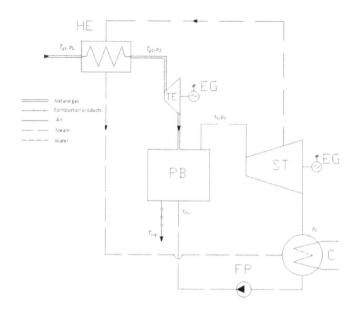

Fig. 1. Thermal diagram of the turbo expander installation: HE – heat exchanger for gas heating; TE – turbo expander; EG – electric generator; PB – power boiler; ST – steam turbine; C – condenser; FP – feed pump

application of gas turbine unit with the turbo expander drive of the compressor on the thermal power plant.

Naturally such gas turbine units which aren't connected with the objects which consume the gas behind turbo expander can operate at the various gas expansion ratios with the high electric efficiency level.

2. The estimation of the efficiency of the turbo expanders application in the thermal power plants thermal schemes

At present the simplest scheme of the natural gas potential energy utilization is used on the thermal power plants. This scheme is presented in Fig. 1.

In this scheme the high-pressure gas goes to the power boiler through the turbo expander directly connected with electric generator. In the expand process the gas pressure and temperature decrease. So far as the gas entered to the boiler must have definite temperature and pressure the heat exchanger is installed in front of turbo expander where the gas is heated by the bled steam of turbo installation. The steam condensate generated in the heat exchanger goes back to the cycle and enter to the boiler.

The steam extraction from the steam turbo installation cycle leads to decreasing of the steam turbine power. The effectiveness of the turbo expander application will be determined by the difference value between the turbo expander power capacity and decrease of steam turbine power capacity.

The useful electric power of the turbo expander is determined by the following expression:

$$N_{te} = B \cdot c_{p\_ch4} \cdot T_{g2} \cdot (1 - \delta^{-m_{ch4}}) \cdot \eta_{te} \cdot \eta_m \cdot \eta_{eg}, \qquad (1)$$

where B – the natural gas flow through turbo expander; c_{pm} – the average gas heat capacity in the expansion process; T_{g2} – the gas temperature in front of turbo expander; δ – the gas expansion ration in the turbo expander; η_{te} – the turbo expander internal efficiency factor; η_m – mechanical efficiency of the turbo expander; η_{eg} – efficiency of the electric generator; m_{ch4} – is defined by the adiabatic index of the natural gas by the expression:

$$m_{ch4} = \frac{k-1}{k}.$$

It is supposed that the required natural gas temperature in front the boiler equals to the natural gas temperature in front of the heat exchanger $t_{g2} = t_{g1}$. Then the gas temperature in front of turbo expander defines by the following expression:

$$T_{g2} = \frac{T_{g1}}{1 - (1 - \delta^{-m_{ch4}}) \cdot \eta_{te}}. \tag{2}$$

The substitution of the expression (2) in to (1) takes us the expression for the turbo expander power capacity:

$$N_{te} = B \cdot c_{p\_ch4} \cdot T_{g1} \cdot F(\delta) \cdot \eta_m \cdot \eta_{eg}, \tag{3}$$

where $F(\delta)$ is the gas expansion ratio function in the turboexpander:

$$F(\delta) = \frac{(1 - \delta^{-m_{ch4}})}{1 - (1 - \delta^{-m_{ch4}})}. \tag{4}$$

Let's find the steam turbine power capacity decrease resulted from the steam extraction for the gas heating. Let thinking that the steam turbine internal efficiency doesn't change because of little steam extraction. In this case the steam turbine power capacity decrease may be estimated by the following expression:

$$\Delta N_{st} = G_{extr} \cdot (h_{extr} - h_c), \tag{5}$$

where G_{extr} – the flow of extracted steam, h_{extr} – the extracted steam enthalpy, h_c – the steam enthalpy at the end of expansion process.

After the proper transformations the expression (5) may be presented it the following view:

$$\Delta N_{st} = c_{p\_ch4} \cdot B \cdot T_{g1} \cdot \eta_{te} \cdot F(\delta) \cdot Y(p_n, t_n, \eta_{oi}, \delta), \tag{6}$$

where $Y(p_n, t_n, \eta_{oi}, \delta) = \frac{h_{extr} - h_c}{h_{extr} - h_s}$.

In the issue the additional power capacity which may be obtained in case of application of the turbo expander scheme presented on the figure 1 is estimated by the following expression:

$$N_1 = N_{te} - \Delta N_{st} = B \cdot c_{p\_ch4} \cdot T_{g1} \cdot F(\delta) \cdot \eta_{te} \cdot \eta_m \cdot \eta_{eg} \cdot \left(1 - \frac{Y(p_n, t_n, \eta_{oi}, \delta)}{\eta_{eg} \cdot \eta_m}\right).$$

For $m_{ch4} = 0.218$ and $\eta_{te} = 84\,\%$, the function $F(\delta)$ will be as it is presented in Fig. 2 (curve 1).

It is required to know the expansion process in the steam turbine for the function

$$1 - \frac{Y(p_n, t_n, \eta_{oi}, \delta)}{\eta_{eg} \cdot \eta_m}$$

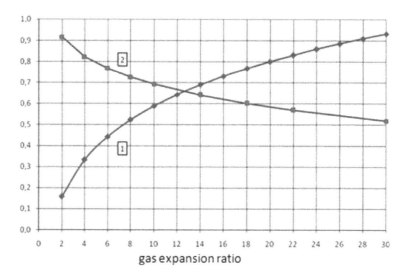

Fig. 2. $F(\delta)$ and $1 - \frac{Y(p_n,t_n,\eta_{oi},\delta)}{\eta_{eg}\cdot\eta_m}$ as a function of the gas expansion ratio in the turbo expander δ

estimation. For example, let us consider this process for the steam turbine K-300-240 of LMZ. Let's take the subcooling δt in the heat exchanger equals to 7 K and the natural gas heat capacity c_{p_ch4} equals to 2.39 kJ/kg.

Then the function $1 - \frac{Y(p_n,t_n,\eta_{oi},\delta)}{\eta_{eg}\cdot\eta_m}$ will take on a form as it is presented in Fig. 2 (curve 1).

Deficient for the calculation values are the following: the mechanical and electric efficiency – $\eta_{eg} = 99\ \%$, $\eta_m = 99\ \%$, the gas temperature in the gas-main pipeline $T_{g1} = T_{g3} = 288.15$ K.

The results of calculations of additional power capacity N_1 which generated at the expense of turbo expander application for the selected steam turbine are presented in Fig. 3 and in Table 1.

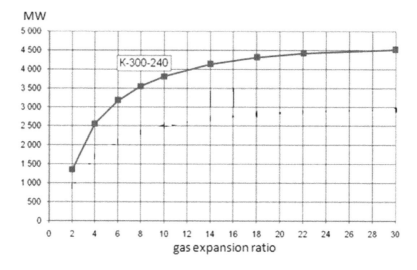

Fig. 3. The addition power capacity of the power generating unit induced by the turbo expander application as a function of the gas expansion ratio δ

Table 1. The results of calculations

No.		parameter	value
1	G_2	Gas flow, kg/s	16.45
2	δ	Gas expansion ratio (from gas-main pipeline to the boiler)	8
3	t_{g1}	The gas temperature in the gas-main pipeline, °C	15
4	t_{g2}	The gas temperature in front of turbo expander, °C	141.9
5	p_{extr}	The pressure in the steam extraction manifold, MPa	0.53
6	t_s	Saturation temperature at the steam extraction pressure, °C	154
7	G_{extr}	Steam flow for the gas heater, kg/s	2.074
8	N_{te}	Turbo expander power capacity, kW	4 893.5
9	ΔN	The steam turbine power capacity decrease because of the steam extraction for the gas heating, kW	1 391.6
10	N_{usf}	The useful power capacity of the unit, kW	3 501.8
11	η_{te}	The turbo expander efficiency, N_{te}/Q	0.98
12	η_{usf}	The efficiency of addition power generation for the whole power generation unit, N_{usf}/Q	0.7

The results of the calculations have shown we can obtain the additional power capacity from 1 400 to 4 500 kW subject to the gas expansion ratio in the turbo expander for the steam turbine K-300-240. So far as the gas expansion ration in the turbo expander is determined by the gas pressure in the gas-main pipeline and by the gas pressure in front of the boiler burners then for the conventional power boilers the value of the gas expansion ratio δ changes in the short range from 6 to 8. Then in according to the curve in Fig. 3 the additional power capacity changes from 3 200 kW to 3 500 kW.

The power capacity of the turbo expander unit subject to the gas expansion ratio lies in the range from 1 500 kW to 8 800 kW. The steam turbine power decrease does not exceed 4 000 kW.

The data in Table 1 show that for the gas expansion ratio in the turbo expander δ equal to 8 in case of the application of the turbo expander in the gas system of the power generation unit K-300-240 LMZ the power capacity of the turbo expander N_{te} is equal to 4 893kW and additional power capacity N_{usf} reaches 3 500 kW.

3. Recovery gas turbine unit with turbo expander drive of the compressor for gas-distribution stations

The executed estimations of the turbo expanders application in the power plants thermal schemes are shown that we can obtain the power capacity increase of power generation unit

K-300-240 by 1 %. This increment may be considerably increase if we will use self-contained gas turbine installation with the turbo expander drive of the compressor on the gas-distribution stations. The scheme of such installation is considered in the works [3, 4] and presented in Fig. 4.

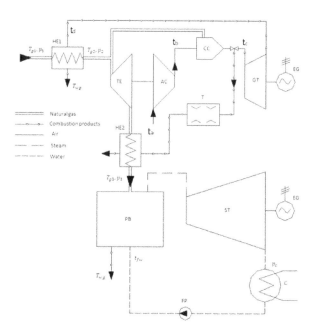

Fig. 4. Thermal scheme of the gas turbine unit with turbo expander drive of the compressor in the power boiler gas feed system: HE – heat exchanger for the gas heating; HE2 – heat exchanger for the gas heating the varying duty; TE – turbo expander; AC – air compressor; GT – gas turbine; EG – electric generator; PB – power boiler; ST – steam turbine; C – condenser; FP – feed pump, T– throttle

In this scheme the high pressure gas goes through the heat exchanger HE1 where it is temperature grows up to $100\,°C$. Such temperature level ensures required temperature in front of the power boiler. Behind the heat exchanger part of the gas flow goes to the gas turbine combustion chamber and the other part enter to the turbo expander. After the expansion in the turbo expander gas enter to the power boiler as in the conventional scheme. The turbo expander drives the air compressor which supplies the combustion chamber with compressed air. The fuel combustion is realized in the combustion chamber. The combustion products expands in the gas turbine which generate the useful electric power and the waste gases of the gas turbine is utilized in the heat exchanger HE1 where the natural gas is heated up to required temperature.

The whole turbo expander power capacity is used for the compressor rotation:

$$N_c = N_{te}.$$

Using this condition and taking the air compression ratio value, we can estimate the air flow through the compressor by the following expression:

$$G_{air} = \frac{N_c}{c_{p\_air} \cdot T_a \cdot \frac{(\varepsilon^{m_{air}} - 1)}{\eta_c}}, \tag{7}$$

where ε – air compression ratio, c_{p_air} – average air heat capacity in the compression process, T_a – air temperature in front of the compressor, η_c – compressor internal efficiency.

The air temperature behind the compressor is estimated by the following expression:

$$T_b = T_a \cdot \left(1 + \frac{(\varepsilon^{m_{air}} - 1)}{\eta_c}\right).$$

The combustion products temperature must be so that the this products may heat the natural gas in the heat exchange HE1 up to the required temperature.

Let us estimate the required combustion product temperature in front of the heat exchanger from the heat balance equation:

$$T_d = T_{wg} + \frac{B \cdot c_{p\_ch4} \cdot (T_{g2} - T_{g1})}{c_{pg} \cdot G_{air}}.$$

The gas temperature in front of the gas turbine is determined in the following way:

$$T_c = \frac{T_d}{1 - (1 - (\lambda \cdot \varepsilon)^{-m_g}) \cdot \eta_{gt}},$$

where λ – hydrodynamic loss coefficient in the gas turbine and in the heat exchanger; η_{gt} – internal efficiency of the gas turbine.

In the issue the useful power of the gas turbine may be estimated by the following expression:

$$N_2 = c_{pg} \cdot c_{p\_ch4} \cdot T_{g1} \cdot B \cdot F(\delta) \cdot X(\varepsilon) \cdot \eta_{te} \cdot \eta_{gt} \cdot \eta_c \cdot \eta_m \cdot \eta_m \cdot \eta_{eg}. \qquad (8)$$

$X(\varepsilon)$ – the function of the air compression ratio in the compressor:

$$X(\varepsilon) = \frac{1}{c_{p\_air} \cdot \eta_m} \cdot \left[\frac{c_{pg} \cdot T_{wg} \cdot \eta_m \cdot \eta_c}{c_{p\_air} \cdot T_a \cdot (\varepsilon^{m_{air}} - 1)} + 1\right] \cdot \left[\frac{1 - (\lambda \cdot \varepsilon)^{-m_g}}{1 - (1 - (\lambda \cdot \varepsilon)^{-m_g}) \cdot \eta_{gt}}\right].$$

Let us calculate the absolute efficiency η_{GTU} of the concerned installation, which defines as a ration of the useful power N_2 to the combustion chamber heat power Q_{CC}:

$$\eta_{GTU} = \frac{N_2}{Q_{CC}}.$$

In its' turn Q_{CC}:

$$Q_{CC} = \frac{c_{pg} \cdot G_{air} \cdot (T_c - T_b)}{\eta_{cc}}.$$

Then

$$\eta_{GTU} = \frac{c_{pg} \cdot c_{p\_ch4} \cdot T_{g1} \cdot B \cdot F(\delta) \cdot X(\varepsilon) \cdot \eta_{te} \cdot \eta_{gt} \cdot \eta_c \cdot \eta_m \cdot \eta_m \cdot \eta_{eg} \cdot \eta_{cc}}{c_{pg} \cdot c_{p\_ch4} \cdot T_{g1} \cdot B \cdot F(\delta) \cdot Z(\varepsilon) \cdot \eta_{te} \cdot \eta_m \cdot \eta} = \qquad (9)$$

$$= \frac{X(\varepsilon)}{Z(\varepsilon)} \cdot \eta_{gt} \cdot \eta_m \cdot \eta_{eg} \cdot \eta_{cc},$$

where

$$Z(\varepsilon) = \frac{1}{T_a \cdot c_{p\_air} \cdot (\varepsilon^{m_{air}} - 1)} \cdot \left[\frac{T_{wg} + T_a \cdot \frac{c_{p\_air}}{c_{pg}} \cdot \frac{(\varepsilon^{m_{air}} - 1)}{\eta_m \cdot \eta_c}}{1 - (1 - (\lambda \cdot \varepsilon)^{-m_g}) \cdot \eta_{gt}} - T_a \cdot \left(1 + \frac{\varepsilon^{m_{air}} - 1}{\eta_c}\right)\right].$$

The derived expression (9) shows that the gas turbine installation with outer turbo expander drive of the compressor efficiency at the fixed waste gases temperature and specified hydrodynamic loss coefficient λ depends on the air compression ratio in the compressor only. This dependency is shown in Fig. 5 and all characteristic quantities for the concerned self-contained gas turbine installation with turbo expander drive of the compressor operating jointly with turbo installation K-300-240 LMZ are presented in Table 2.

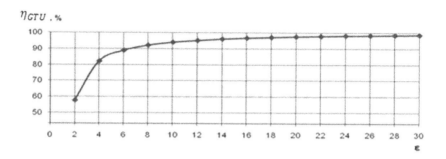

Fig. 5. The gas turbine unit with turbo expander driver of the compressor as a function of the air compression ratio

The thermal scheme calculations of the conventional turbo expander unit connected directly with electric generator and the calculations of the alternative self-contained gas turbine unit with the turbo expander drive of the compressor shows that the passage to more difficult installation utilized the compressed gas power allows us to considerably increase the generating power at the same natural gas flow. So the application of such installation on the thermal power plant gas-distribution station supplying the steam boiler of the power-generating unit K-300-240 the useful power capacity increases from 3.5 MW up to 6.8 MW.

The efficiency of the addition power generation in case of the conventional turbo expander unit is 70 % as the usage of the extracted steam for the gas heating leads to power decrease of the main power-generation unit but in case of the gas turbine installation with turbo expander drive of the compressor application the addition power generation efficiency reaches 98 %. The efficiency is high because the both units utilize the energy of the compressed natural gas at the equivalent temperatures in front of and behind the turbo expander ensuring in such way the transformation of the thermal energy delivered to the heat exchanger into electric one.

If the air compression ratio ε is more than 4, the efficiency of such installation considerably exceed the modern power-generating units of the thermal power plants. Thereafter the specific fuel consumption on the concerned self-contained gas turbine installations with turbo expander drive of the compressor appears considerably lower than the specific fuel consumption on the power-generating units.

4. Conclusions

1. The application of the self-contained gas turbine unit with turbo expander drive of the compressor on the gas-distribution stations allows to increase the additional power generated on the base of compressed natural gas energy in 1.6–2 times in comparison with the conventional turbo expanders.

Table 2. Parameters of self-contained gas turbine installation

No.		parameter	value
1	δ	Gas expansion ratio	8
2	t_{g1}	Gas temperature in the gas-main pipeline, °C	15
3	t_{g2}	Gas temperature in front of the turbo expander, °C	141.9
4	N_{te}	Power capacity of the turbo expander and air compressor, kW	4 893.5
5	ε	Air compression ratio in the air compressor	14
6	t_b	Air temperature in front of the combustion chamber, °C	401.5
7	G_{air}	Air flow at the compressor inlet, kg/s	12.73
8	t_c	The combustion product temperature in front of the gas turbine, °C	874.4
9	t_d	The combustion product temperature behind the gas turbine, °C	402.6
10	T_{wg}	Waste gases temperature behind the heat exchanger, °C	60
11	B	Air flow entered to the combustion chamber, kg/s	0.155
12	N_{gc}	Power consumption for the gas compression in front of the combustion chamber, kW	55.7
13	N_{gt}	Gas turbine power capacity, kW	6 730.4
14	Q_{CC}	Heat power of the combustion chamber, kW	6 871.3
15	η_{te}	Turbo expander efficiency, N_{gt}/Q_{CC}	98

2. So far as the gas temperature in front of and behind the turbo expander must be about the same that for this conditions ensuring all installations which utilize the energy of compressed natural gas must operate with heat supply equivalent to the turbo expander power. From this point of view all considered installations almost completely transforms the delivered heat energy into electric one with very high efficiency.

References

[1] Ohotin, V. S., Thermodynamic analysis of the turbo expanders in the thermal scheme of the steam turbine installations with gas heating by extracted steam, MPEI bulletin (4)2004 34–40.

[2] Truhniy, A. D., Thermodynamic foundation of utilization turbo expanders units application, MPEI bulletin (5)1999 11–15.

[3] Zarjankin, A. E., Simonov, B. P., Jesionek, K. J., The use of turbocompressor blocks in the utilizing systems of gas turbines at natural gas transfer station units. VDI Berichte, 1995, Nr. 1 208, St. 153–159.

[4] Simonov, B. P., Zarjankin, A. E., Autonomous twin-shaft disposal plant for gas-filling stations, Proceedings of the Conferinta Internationala TURBO '98, Bucharest, Editura Printech, 1998.

5

Finite element modelling of vocal tract changes after voice therapy

T. Vampola[a,*], A. M. Laukkanen[b], J. Horáček[c], J. G. Švec[d]

[a]*Department of Mechanics, Biomechanics and Mechatronics, Faculty of Mechanical Engineering, Czech Technical University in Prague, Karlovo nám. 13, 121 35 Prague 2, Czech Republic*

[b]*Department of Speech Communication and Voice Research, University of Tampere, FIN 33014 Tampere, Finland*

[c]*Institute of Thermomechanics, Academy of Sciences of the Czech Republic, Dolejškova 5, 182 00 Praha 8, Czech Republic*

[d]*Department of Experimental Physics, Faculty of Sciences Palacký University Olomouc, 17. listopadu 12, 771 46 Olomouc, Czech Republic*

Abstract

Two 3D finite element (FE) models were constructed, based on CT measurements of a subject phonating on [a:] before and after phonation into a tube. Acoustic analysis was performed by exciting the models with acoustic flow velocity at the vocal folds. The generated acoustic pressure of the response was computed in front of the mouth and inside the vocal tract for both FE models. Average amplitudes of the pressure oscillations inside the vocal tract and in front of the mouth were compared to display the cost-efficiency of sound energy transfer at different formant frequencies. The formants F1–F3 correspond to classical vibration modes also solvable by 1D vocal tract model. However, for higher formants, there occur more complicated transversal modes which require 3D modelling. A special attention is given to the higher frequency range (above 3.5 Hz) where transversal modes exist between piriform sinuses and valleculae. Comparison of the pressure oscillation inside and outside the vocal tract showed that formants differ in their efficiency, F4 (at about 3.5 kHz, i.e. at the speaker's or singer's formant region) being the most effective. The higher formants created a clear formant cluster around 4 kHz after the vocal exercise with the tube. Since the human ear is most sensitive to frequencies between 2 and 4 kHz concentration of sound energy in this frequency region (F4–F5) is effective for communication. The results suggest that exercising using phonation into tubes help in improving the vocal economy.

Keywords: biomechanics of human voice, voice production modelling, vocal exercising, voice training

1. Introduction

Earlier observations have shown that sound pressure level (SPL) tends to increase after vocal exercising on semi-occlusions like voiced fricatives and phonation into a tube [1]. Applying computer simulation with a self-oscillating vocal fold model and an interactive vocal tract model, Titze [4] concluded that a semi-occlusion at the lips strengthens the interaction between the voice source and the vocal tract by raising the mean supraglottal and intraglottal pressures. Impedance matching by a sufficient vocal fold adduction and narrowing of the epilaryngeal tube may improve the efficiency and economy of voice production. Based on modelling results it was hypothesized [5] that an artificial extension of the vocal tract leads to a more efficient and economic phonation, especially if narrowing of the epilaryngeal region occurs at the same time. This in turn is also prone to lead to formant clustering around 3–3.4 kHz [6].

---

*Corresponding author. e-mail: tomas.vampola@fs.cvut.cz.

These and other studies suggest that the phonation into a tube leads to beneficial effects in voice production. What has not been clear, however, is what changes remain in the vocal tract after the tube has been removed. To address these questions, the Computerized Tomography (CT) methods was recently used to visualize the shape of the vocal tract of a female subject before, during and after phonation into a tube [8]. The CT results showed clear changes of the vocal tract after phonation into a tube. These changes include widening the frontal part of the oral cavity and of the lower pharynx (just above the epiglottis), and narrowing in the region between the lower part of the tongue body and the back wall of the pharynx. Acoustic recordings showed slightly lowered formant frequencies F1, F2, F4 and F5 and slightly raised formant F3. The overall sound pressure level (SPL) of voice increased by 3 dB.

The present study investigates the effects of the vocal tract changes on the sound energy transfer through the vocal tract. Three-dimensional (3D) finite-element (FE) models of the vocal tract created from the CT measurements were used to investigate the changes in the transfer function of the vocal tract and in the acoustic pressure radiated out of the mouth. The investigations aimed at determining the acoustic consequences of the changes of the supra-glottal spaces before and after phonation into the tube.

2. CT data and acoustic data acquisition

The CT data were obtained using the Light Speed VCT GE – 64 (General Electric) device. A female subject volunteered to be the experimental subject. She had an extensive experience in voice training and in using the 'resonance tubes'. She signed a consent form allowing the CT examination to be performed. For the measurement details, see [8]. The midsagittal and corresponding coronal slices obtained from the CT measurements are shown in Fig. 1 for phonation the vowel [a:] before and after phonation into the resonance tube (made of glass, length 28 cm, inner diameter 7 mm). The airways of the vocal tract are clearly distinguishable from the surrounding tissues here.

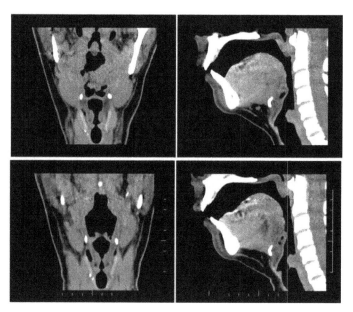

Fig. 1. Coronal (on the left) and midsagittal (on the right) images of the vocal tract for the vowel [a:] obtained from the CT scannings performed before (upper panel) and after (lower panel) phonating into the tube

When performing the examination, the subject was given a sign through the CT intercom system to start phonating. First, the subject produced the vowel [a:] for c. 4 seconds, then took a breath and produced the vowel [a:] again for c. 4 seconds. The first phonation was used as a sign of the subject's readiness. The CT scanning occurred immediately after the subject started the second phonation (see Fig. 2).

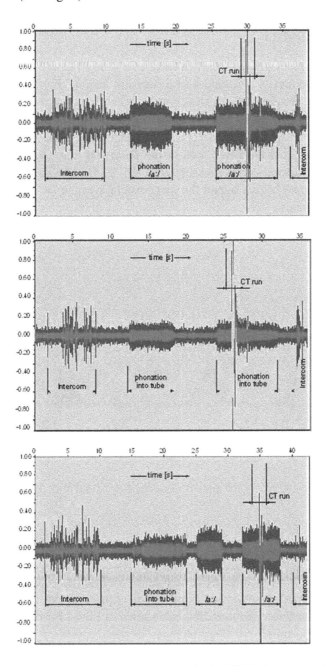

Fig. 2. Audio signal samples measured during phonation in the CT device: phonation /a:/ before phonation into the tube (upper panel), phonation into the tube (middle panel), phonation /a:/ after the tube (bottom panel)

A relatively high background noise level in the room with the CT apparatus is also visible in the figure. This procedure was repeated twice before phonation into the tube, twice during phonation into the tube and twice after phonation into the tube. For the after-tube examination, the subject performed the phonation into the tube first and then immediately continued by phonating without the tube.

3. Analysis of acoustic data

The analysis of the formant frequencies was done using the LPC analysis that yielded formant values, fundamental frequency (F0) and sound pressure level (SPL). The histograms from the LPC-obtained formant frequencies for the acoustic recordings before and after the phonation into the tube are shown in Fig. 3. The figure reveals that the largest changes occurred in the 3rd formant, which increased by c. 150 Hz after the tube-phonation. The sound pressure level (SPL) was c. 2.4 dB higher after than before the phonation into the tube. The fundamental frequency F0$\cong$171 Hz decreased on average by c. 9.5 % after the phonation into the tube, the third formant increased by c. 7.5 % and the first formant by c. 3 %. The changes in the other formants were rather small.

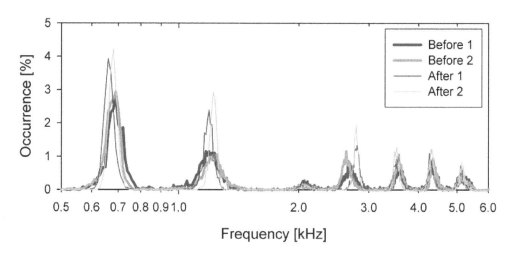

Fig. 3. LPC formant histogram for the audio recordings before and after the phonation into the tube

4. Volume and finite element models

The recorded CT images were first segmented and processed into 3D volume models of the vocal tract. The developed volume models of the vocal tract for the vowel /a:/ positioned into the backbones of the skeleton and mandible are shown in Fig. 4 for two cases, i.e. before and after phonation into the tube. No large changes in the position of the larynx related to the vertebrae before and after phonation into the tube can be visible, but a wider mouth opening after phonation into the tube can be recognized here.

The volume models of the vocal tract for phonation before and after tube-phonation are compared in Fig. 5, where the epilaryngeal airways, the piriform sinuses and the valleculae are clearly visible. The shape of the vocal tract appears to be visually similar before and after tube-phonation with one major difference: before the tube-phonation the velar passage port to the

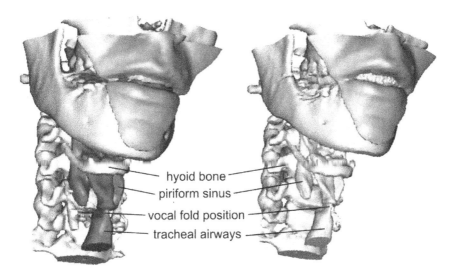

Fig. 4. Volume models of the vocal tract positioned in the mouth and neck bones during phonation of vowel /a:/ before (on the left) and after (on the right) phonation into the tube

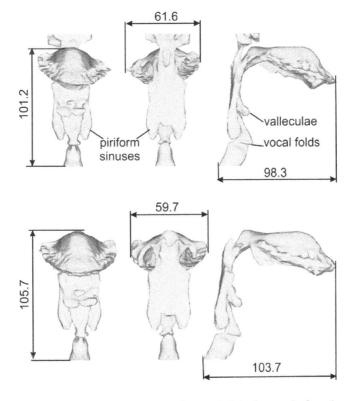

Fig. 5. Volume models of the vocal tract for phonation on [a:] before and after phonation into the tube

nasopharynx was open, whereas after the tube-phonation it was closed. There are no remarkable changes of the airways in the glottal region near the vocal folds.

The total volume of the acoustic vocal tract spaces was considerably larger after the tube-phonation; it increased by 38.5 %. The total length of the vocal tract after the tube-phonation was increased by 4.2 %. The volume of the valleculae and piriform sinuses increased on average by c. 64 % and 7 %, respectively. The volume of the epilaryngeal tube did not show much difference after the phonation into the tube.

After meshing the volume models, two 3D finite element (FE) models of the vocal tract were constructed for phonation on [a:] before and after tube-phonation. The models were created within the framework of the code ANSYS. Since the CT scans did not provide complete information on the nasal tract, in the case of velopharyngeal opening (recall Fig. 5), the connection of the supraglottal and nasal spaces had to be disregarded and the passage was artificially closed. The FE models consisted of about 125 000 and 175 000 acoustic finite elements for phonation before and after the tube, respectively.

In order to simulate the radiation of the sound out of the mouth, the head was modelled approximately as a sphere with a diameter of about 15 cm and the surrounding air was modelled as a set of finite elements filling in the space between the head and an outer sphere at the distance of c. 10 cm from the head (Fig. 6). The outer sphere was modelled with infinite, non-reflecting elements FLUID130. The following material parameters of the acoustic tetrahedral finite elements FLUID30 were considered: speed of sound 350 m/s, air density 1.2 kg/m3 and the dimensionless sound absorption coefficient 0.0005 at the walls of the acoustic spaces. The acoustic space between the spheres was modelled by about 515 000 finite elements with an average element size of c. 5 mm.

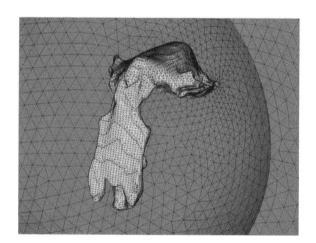

Fig. 6. FE model of the vocal tract for phonation on the vowel [a:], which includes also the surrounding infinite acoustic space allowing simulation of the sound propagation out of the mouth

5. Acoustic modal analysis of the FE models of the vocal tract

Acoustic modal analysis was performed on the FE models while considering, for simplicity, the following boundary conditions: zero acoustic pressure ($p = 0$) at the lips, closed vocal tract at the level of the vocal folds and no acoustic damping ($\mu = 0$) on the walls of the acoustic spaces (see Fig. 7). Nine formant frequencies were observed within the frequency range from zero up to c. 5 200 Hz. The first three eigenmodes for the frequencies F1–F3 are typical fundamental modes. The acoustic characteristics of these eigenmodes are similar like in a simple tube when the propagation of the longitudinal waves in the vocal tract is dominant and when the acoustics of the vocal tract can be described by a simple 1D acoustic theory (see, e.g. [7]). The higher eigenmodes for the formant frequencies F4–F9, however, are associated with cross-sectional

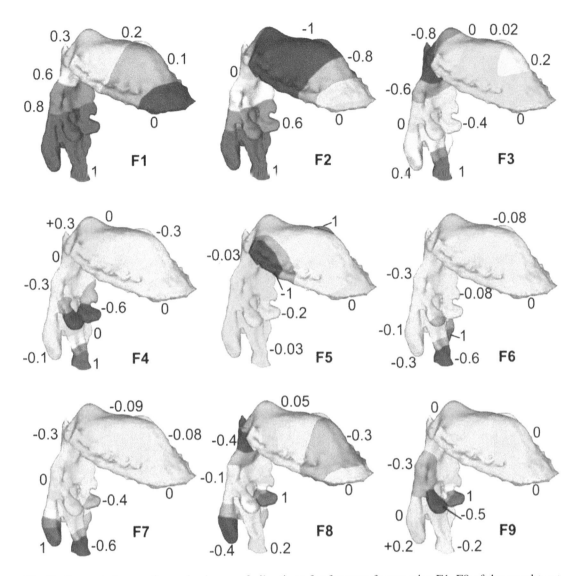

Fig. 7. Computed acoustic mode shapes of vibrations for formant frequencies F1–F9 of the vocal tract model of vowel [a:] after phonation into the tube

waves (see, e.g., the mode shape for the frequency F5) or notably 3D internal resonances in the laryngeal-pharyngeal part where the piriform sinuses, valleculae, laryngeal ventricles and the space between the false vocal folds just above the vocal folds play an important role (see the mode shape for the frequencies F4 and F6–F9, where the dominant antinodes for the pressure are situated in the above mentioned places). The acoustic mode shapes of vibrations did not essentially between the models for the vowel [a:] before and after the tube phonation.

6. Transient analysis of the FE models of the vocal tract

The supraglottal spaces of the FE models were excited at the level of the vocal folds by a very short impulse of acoustic flow velocity covering a broad band frequency range from zero up to about 5 kHz (see Fig. 8). The transient analysis was performed with the time step $\Delta t = 0.5 \cdot 10^{-4}$ s and the total simulated time was $T = 0.1$ s, resulting in the frequency

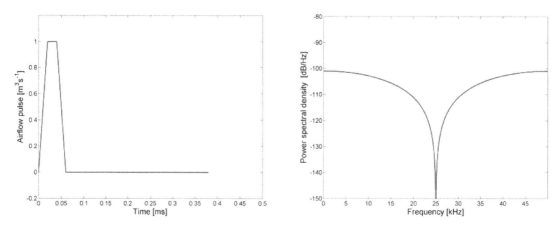

Fig. 8. The airflow velocity pulse used for the excitation of the FE models shown in the time and frequency domain

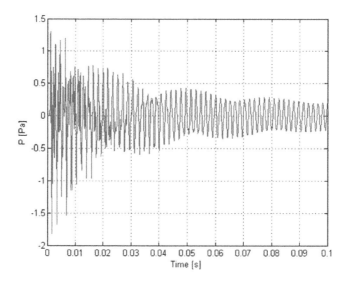

Fig. 9. Transient response in time domain of the acoustic pressure computed at the distance of 10 cm in front of the mouth excited by a short airflow velocity pulse at the vocal folds

resolution 10 Hz in the spectra. The acoustic pressure and the spectrograms of the response computed at the distance of 10 cm in front of the mouth are presented in Figs. 9 and 10. The transient time response of the pressure (see Fig. 9) shows a more sinusoidal waveform with increasing time, which is due to higher radiation losses for higher frequencies.

The numerically simulated spectrograms for the vowel [a:] before and after tube phonation are compared in Fig. 10. Formant F3 increased after phonation into the tube while the formants F1, F2, F4 decreased. Formation of a stronger cluster of formants (corresponding to the speaker's formant, see [2, 3]) is clearly visible around 4 kHz for phonation after the tube.

The power spectral densities computed at the distance of 10 cm in front of the mouth for the cases of before- and after-tube phonations are compared in Fig. 11. The computed resonance frequencies R1, R2 and R4 decreased down after phonation into the tube (about 1 % for R1, 5.1 % for R2 and 2.9 % for R4) and only the R3 increased by c. 5.1 %. While the frequencies of

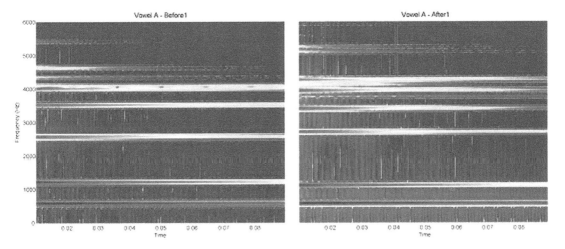

Fig. 10. Numerically simulated spectrograms of the excited sound in front of the mouth for the vocal tract models before (left) and after the tube-phonation (right)

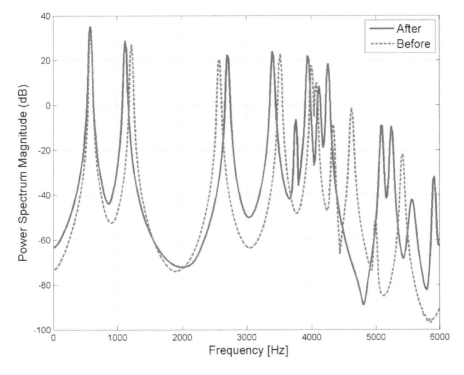

Fig. 11. Power spectral densities of the acoustic pressure computed in the distance of 10 cm in front of the mouth excited by a short airflow velocity pulse at the vocal folds

these resonances do not match perfectly the LPC-derived formant frequencies from the recorded acoustic signals, the general tendency of the resonance changes resembles the earlier observed tendency of the formant F3 to increase while the formants F1, F2 and F4 decrease.

Apart from the changes of the resonance frequencies, important differences can be seen in the spectral amplitudes of the resonance peaks. The peaks for the first four resonances (R1–R4) reach values, which are c. 3–4 dB higher for the case of the phonation after the tube. Even larger differences can be seen for the higher formants in the frequency region of 4–5 kHz, where some of the resonant peak levels are up to c. 20 dB higher after than before the tube phonation. However, in this frequency region is difficult to determine corresponding resonances before and after the tube, because of a complete restructuring of the spectra.

7. Modelling of vocal tract transfer efficiency

For comparison of the efficiency of the acoustic pressure transfer through the vocal tract from the vocal folds to the distance 10 cm in front of the mouth we introduced the quantity EF (transfer efficiency) that characterizes the effectiveness of the sound pressure transfer from the vocal tract to the surroundings:

$$EF(f) = SPL_{out}(f) - SPL_{in}(f), \tag{1}$$

where SPL_{out} [dB] is the sound pressure level of the acoustic pressure *in front of the mouth* given as

$$SPL_{out}(f) = 20 * \log(|^{out}p(f)|/20 * 10^{-6}), \qquad {}^{out}p(f) = \mathrm{Re}^{out}p(f) + \mathrm{i\,Im}^{out}p(f), \tag{2}$$

and $^{out}p(f)$ is the acoustic pressure in pascals in front of the mouth at the frequency f, SPL_{in} [dB] is the sound pressure level of the average acoustic pressure *inside the vocal tract* given as

$$SPL_{in}(f) = 20 * \log\left(\tfrac{1}{N}\sum_{j=1,N} |^{in}p_j(f)|/20 * 10^{-6}\right),$$
$$^{in}p_j(f) = \mathrm{Re}^{in}p_j(f) + \mathrm{i\,Im}^{in}p_j(f), \tag{3}$$

where $^{in}p_j(f)$ is the acoustic pressure in the j-node inside the FE model and N is the number of nodes inside the FE model of the vocal tract.

The acoustic pressures $^{out}p(f)$ in front of the mouth and $^{in}p_j(f)$ inside the vocal tract were computed by harmonic analysis with the frequency step $\Delta = 1$ Hz in selected narrow frequency regions around the detected formants (recall Fig. 11). The computed transfer efficiency (EF) of sound energy transfer at different formant frequencies is shown in Fig. 12. The maximum efficiency is possible to detect after the tube phonation in the frequency region 3.5–4 kHz, i.e. in the region of the so-called speaker's formant.

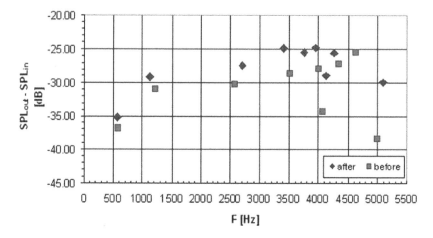

Fig. 12. Computed transfer efficiency of sound energy transfer at the formant frequencies for numerically simulated phonation before and after the tube-phonation

8. Conclusion

The lower formants F1–F3 represent classical vibration modes, which can be obtained also with 1D vocal tract models. At higher formants, however, more complicated transversal 3D modes of vibration are prominent, which require a 3D modelling approach. Comparison of the relative amplitudes of the pressure oscillations inside the vocal tract with the acoustic pressure in front of the mouth showed that formants differ in their efficiency; the formants (F4–F6) between 3.5–4.5 kHz, i.e. at the speaker's or singer's formant region were found to be the most effective. The human hearing threshold is also relatively low between 2 and 4 kHz. Consequently, sound energy concentration around 3.5 kHz (F4) region is useful to assure maximum audibility of the produced sound and can thus play a role in communication both from the point of view of production and perception.

The c. 3 dB-increase in SPL after the phonation into a tube observed here qualitatively corresponds to previous experimental findings. A tendency for SPL increase has been observed in earlier studies, e.g. measurements by Laukkanen [1]. An important finding of this study is that the c. 3 dB increase in SPL was possible to obtain through the vocal tract modelling, even without considering the interaction between the vocal tract and the vocal fold vibration.

The results suggest that exercising using a resonance tube can help in optimizing the vocal tract configuration for improved energy transfer from the vocal tract and thus improved vocal economy.

Acknowledgements

The research was supported by the grants GACR No. 101/08/1155 *Computer and physical modelling of vibroacoustic properties of human vocal tract for optimization of voice quality*, and No. 106139 *Biomechanical study on the traumatizing mechanisms in vocal fold vibration* awarded by the Academy of Finland and by the COST Action 2103 *Advanced Voice Function Assessment*. The authors are also very grateful to Doc. MUDr. Petr Krupa from the Hospital U Svaté Anny in Brno for providing the CT data of a human vocal tract during phonation.

References

[1] Laukkanen, A. M., On speaking voice exercises. A study on the acoustic and physiological effects of speaking voice exercises applying manipulation of the acoustic-aerodynamical state of the supraglottic space and artificially modified auditory feedback, Ph.D. thesis, Acta Universitatis Tamperensis ser A, Vol. 445, University of Tampere, 1995.

[2] Leino, T., Long-term average spectrum study on speaking voice quality in male actors, Proceedings of the Stockholm Music Acoustics Conference 1993, Stockholm, The Royal Swedish Academy of Music, 1994, pp. 206–210.

[3] Nawka, T., Anders, L. C., Cebulla, M., Zurakowski, D., The Speaker's formant in male voices, Journal of Voice 11(4) (1997) 422–428.

[4] Titze, I. R., Voice training and therapy with a semi-occluded vocal tract: Rationale and scientific underpinnings, Journal of Speech Language and Hearing Research 49 (2006) 448–459.

[5] Titze, I. R., Laukkanen, A. M., Can vocal economy in phonation be increased with an artificially lengthened vocal tract? A computer modeling study, Logopedics Phoniatrics Vocology 32 (2007) 147–156.

[6] Titze, I. R., Story, B. H., Acoustic interactions of the voice source with the lower vocal tract, Journal of the Acoustical Society of America 101(4) (1997) 2 234–2 243.

[7] Vampola, T., Horáček, J., Švec, J. G., FE modeling of human vocal tract acoustic. Part I: Production of Czech vowels, Acta Acoustica United with Acta Acustica 94 (2008) 433–447.

[8] Vampola, T., Laukkanen, A. M., Horáček, J., Švec, J. G., Vocal tract changes caused by phonation into a tube: A case study using computer tomography and finite element modeling, Journal of the Acoustical Society of America (2010), DOI: 10.1121/1.3506347. (in print)

6

A computational investigation of vibration attenuation of a rigid rotor turning at a variable speed by means of short magnetorheological dampers

J. Zapoměl[a,*], P. Forfooki[a]

[a]*Institute of Thermomechanics, branch Ostrava, Czech Academy of Science, 17. listopadu 15, 708 33 Ostrava, Czech Republic*

Abstract

Rotors of all rotating machines are always slightly imbalanced. When they rotate, the imbalance induces their lateral vibration and forces that are transmitted via the bearings into the foundations. These phenomena are significant if the rotor accelerates or decelerates and especially if it passes over the critical speeds. The vibration can be reduced if the rotor supports are equipped with damping elements. To achieve optimum performance of the damper, the damping effect must be controllable. At present time, semiactive magnetorheological squeeze film dampers are a subject of intensive research. They work on a principle of squeezing a thin film of magnetorheological liquid. If magnetic field is applied, the magnetorheological liquid starts to flow only if the shear stress between two neighbourhood layers exceeds a limit value which depends on intensity of the magnetic field. Its change enables to control the damping force. In the mathematical models, the magnetorheological liquid is usually considered as Bingham one. Application of the computer modelling method for analysis of rotors supported by rolling element bearings and magnetorheological squeeze film dampers and turning at variable angular speed requires to set up the equations of motion of the rotor and to develop a procedure for calculation of the damping force. Derivation of the equations of motion starts from the first and second impulse theorems. The pressure distribution in the thin lubricating film can be described by a Reynolds equation modified for the case of Bingham liquid. In cavitated areas, it is assumed that pressure of the medium remains constant. The hydraulic force acting on the rotor journal is then obtained by integration of the pressure distribution around the circumference and along the length of the damper. Applicability of the developed procedures was tested by means of computer simulations and influence of the control of the damping force on vibration of the rotor was analyzed.

Keywords: accelerating rotors, magnetorheological dampers, critical revolutions, vibration damping

1. Introduction

Because of manufacturing and assembling inaccuracies, rotors of all rotating machines are always slightly imbalanced. When they rotate, the imbalance produces their lateral vibration and the forces that are transmitted via the bearings into the stationary part and into the foundations. This results into reduction of the service life of all machine components, into the noise increase and in propagation of vibration and mechanical waves into the ambient space. These effects are significant especially if the rotors pass the critical speeds during their starting or running out.

The vibration amplitude and magnitude of the forces transmitted via the bearings are considerably influenced by a flexible suspension and by damping elements placed between the rotor and the stationary part. The damping effect depends on modal properties of the rotating machine and on the operation conditions. To achieve the optimum compromise between amplitude

---

*Corresponding author. e-mail: jaroslav.zapomel@vsb.cz.

of the vibration and the forces transmitted through the bearings, it is desirable to use dampers that enable to control magnitude of the damping effect and thus to adapt their performance to the current operating conditions.

At present time, a considerable attention is paid to investigation of controllable semiactive magnetorheological squeeze film dampers because their application has a number of advantages. Their design is simple, they do not require a complicated and expensive feedback control system, they work on the principle of dissipation of mechanical energy and therefore they do not destabilize vibration of the rotor. In addition, their mounting and maintenance is not much demanding.

Even if the problem of passing the rotors over the critical revolutions is very important from the technological point of view, almost all publications and computer procedures from the field of rotor dynamics are related only to the case when the rotor turns at a constant angular speed. In [1, 2, 3, 4], there are given the equations of motion of a flexibly supported disc performing a spherical movement. The system has only two degrees of freedom and its vibration is described by two equations. The equations of motion of a symmetric rotating disc having four degrees of freedom have been derived in [5]. Using assumption of small displacements and rotations, the authors simplified the Euler dynamic equations. But the resulting relationships are referred again only to the disc rotating at constant angular speed. In addition, unfortunately, some authors analyzing the rotors turning at variable speed use incomplete or even wrong equations of motion [6, 7].

At present time, the magnetorheological dampers are a subject of intensive experimental and theoretical research in the field of rotor dynamics. In [8], Wang and Meng studied experimentally the vibration properties and the control method of a flexible rotor supported by a magnetorheological squeeze film damper. In [9], Forte et al. presented results of the theoretical and experimental investigation of a long magnetorheological damper. In [10], Wang et al. developed a mathematical model of a long squeeze film magnetorheological damper based on modification of a Reynolds equation in which the authors included influence of the change of the width of the gap around the damper circumference on the yield shear stress of the magnetorheological liquid.

The principal intention of this article is to derive the equation of motion of a statically unbalanced rigid rotor turning at variable angular speed which is supported by rolling-element bearings and short magnetorheological squeeze film dampers and to test the influence of control of the yielding shear stress of the magnetorheological lubricant on the damping effect during passing the rotor over the critical revolutions.

2. Determination of the damping force of a short magnetorheological squeeze film damper

The magnetorheological squeeze film dampers (fig. 1) are semiactive damping devices. The damping effect is reached by squeezing a thin film of magnetorheological liquid whose resistance against the flow is controlled by intensity of the magnetic field. Magnetorheological fluids are colloidal suspensions consisting of carrying liquid (usually oil), tiny ferromagnetic particles dispersed in it and of a stabilizing agent that prevents coupling the particles due to action of the van der Waals surface forces. If the magnetorheological liquid is not effected by magnetic field, the ferromagnetic particles are dispersed in a random way and the liquid behaves as newtonian one. But when the magnetic field is applied, the particles start to form small chains and the flow occurs only if the shear stress between two neighbouring layers exceeds a limit value

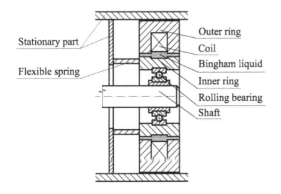

Fig. 1. Scheme of a MR damper

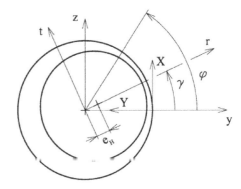

Fig. 2. The damper coordinate system

(yield shear stress). Its magnitude depends on intensity of the magnetic flux and this enables to control the damping effect.

It is assumed in the mathematical model, that (i) the inner and outer rings of the damper are absolutely rigid and smooth, (ii) the width of the damper gap is very small relative to the radii of both rings, (iii) ratio of the length of the damper to the diameter of its outer and inner rings is small, therefore it can be considered as short, (iv) the lubricant is Bingham liquid, (v) the yield shear stress depends on magnitude of the magnetic induction, (vi) the flow in the oil film is laminar and isothermal, (vii) pressure of the lubricant in the radial direction is constant, (viii) the lubricant is considered to be massless and (ix) influence of the curvature of the oil film is negligible.

Distribution of the pressure gradient in the lubricating film is described by a Reynolds equation modified for the case of Bingham liquid. Its derivation for a short damper has been performed in [11]

$$h^3 p'^3 + 3\left(h^2 \tau_y - 4\eta \dot{h} Z\right) p'^2 - 4\tau_y^3 = 0 \quad \text{for} \quad \dot{h} > 0, \tag{1}$$

$$h^3 p'^3 - 3\left(h^2 \tau_y + 4\eta \dot{h} Z\right) p'^2 + 4\tau_y^3 = 0 \quad \text{for} \quad \dot{h} < 0. \tag{2}$$

Z is the axial coordinate, p' is the pressure gradient in the axial direction, τ_y, η are the yield shear stress and viscosity of the Bingham liquid and h is thickness of the lubricating film. Dot ($\cdot$) denotes the first derivative with respect to time.

Determination of the pressure gradient as a function of the axial coordinate Z leads to solving cubic algebraic equations (1) or (2). Solution of each of them gives three roots. The searched one must be real (not complex).

The yield shear stress τ_y is proportional to the square of the magnetic induction B [8, 12]

$$\tau_y = k_\tau B^2. \tag{3}$$

Parameter k_τ is a material constant which depends on concentration of the ferromagnetic particles and on other liquid properties. Its magnitude is either given by the manufacturer or it must be determined experimentally for the concrete magnetorheological fluid.

For the simplest design of the dampers, it holds with sufficient accuracy

$$B = \mu^2 N_C \left(\frac{I}{2h}\right)^2. \tag{4}$$

I is the electric current, μ is permeability of the magnetorheological liquid and N_C is number of the coil turns. In more complicated cases the current – magnetic induction relationship must be determined e.g. by application of a finite element method.

Thickness of the lubricating film depends on position of the inner damper ring relative to the outer one

$$h = c - e_H \cos(\varphi - \gamma). \tag{5}$$

c is the width of the gap between the inner and outer rings of the damper, e_H is the journal eccentricity, φ is the circumferential coordinate and γ is the position angle of the line of centres (fig. 2).

The pressure is obtained by integration of the pressure gradient

$$p = \int p' \, dZ \tag{6}$$

with the boundary condition

$$p = p_A \quad \text{for} \quad Z = \pm \frac{L}{2}. \tag{7}$$

p_A is the pressure in the surrounding space (atmospheric pressure) and L is the length of the damper.

If the pressure drops to a critical value, a cavitation takes place. It is assumed that pressure of the medium in cavitated areas remains constant. Then it holds with sufficient accuracy

$$p_d = p \qquad \text{for} \quad p \geq p_{CAV}, \tag{8}$$
$$p_d = p_{CAV} \quad \text{for} \quad p < p_{CAV}. \tag{9}$$

p_d is the pressure distribution in the layer of lubricant and p_{CAV} is the pressure in cavitated regions.

Components of the damping force are obtained by integration of the pressure distribution around the circumference and along the length of the damper

$$F_{dy} = -R \int_0^{2\pi} \int_{-\frac{L}{2}}^{\frac{L}{2}} p_d \cos \varphi \, dZ \, d\varphi, \qquad F_{dz} = -R \int_0^{2\pi} \int_{-\frac{L}{2}}^{\frac{L}{2}} p_d \sin \varphi \, dZ \, d\varphi. \tag{10}$$

F_{dy}, F_{dz} are y and z components of the damping force, R is the inner ring radius.

3. Derivation of the equations of motion of a rigid statically unbalanced rotor

It is assumed that the investigated rotor is absolutely rigid and is supported by rolling element bearings mounted with cage springs which are coupled with the casing. Damping of the system is realized by magnetorheological squeeze film dampers placed between the cage springs and the stationary part. The rotor rotates at variable angular speed and is loaded by its weight. In addition, it is excited by its imbalance. The stationary displacement of the rotor caused by its weight is eliminated by prestressing the cage springs. The squeeze film dampers are implemented into the mathematical model by means of nonlinear force couplings. As their length to diameter ratio is assumed to be small, they are considered as short in the analysis.

To describe position of the rotor, three coordinate systems are used (fig. 3). The first one $(Oxyz)$ is fixed. Its axis x is coincident with the centre line of the rotor in undeformed state and connects centers of the bearings. Axes x', y', z' of the second coordinate system are parallel

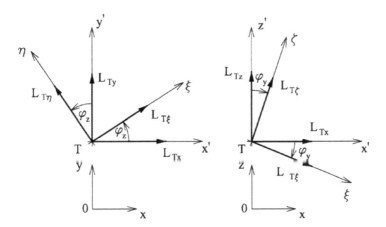

Fig. 3. Coordinate systems and components of the rotor moment of momentum L_{Tx}, L_{Ty}, L_{Tz}, $L_{T\xi}$, $L_{T\eta}$, $L_{T\zeta}$ denote components of the moment of momentum of the rotor

with corresponding axes x, y and z and its origin lies in the centre of gravity T of the rotor which is because of imbalance slightly shifted from the rotor axis. The third coordinate system has its origin in the centre of gravity T and its axes are denoted ξ, η, ζ. It slides together with the frame of reference $Tx'y'z'$ and slightly rotates about axes y' and z' so that its plane $\eta\zeta$ remains perpendicular to the axis of the rotor.

Making use of fig. 3, the equations of motion of the rotor are derived from the first and second impulse theorems

$$\frac{d}{dt}(m\dot{y}_T) = F_{Cy}, \qquad \frac{d}{dt}(m\dot{z}_T) = F_{Cz}, \tag{11}$$

$$\frac{d}{dt}(J_D\dot{\varphi}_y + \omega J_A\varphi_z) = M_{Cy}, \qquad \frac{d}{dt}(J_D\dot{\varphi}_z - \omega J_A\varphi_y) = M_{Cz}. \tag{12}$$

m, J_D, J_A are the mass and moments of inertia (diametral and axial) of the rotor, y_T, z_T are the horizontal (y) and vertical (z) displacements of the rotor centre of gravity, φ_y, φ_z are small rotations of the rotor about axes y, z, ω is angular speed of the rotor rotation, F_{Cy}, F_{Cz} are the sum of components of all forces acting on the rotor (applied, damping, elastic produced by deformation of the cage springs, rotor weight) in the horizontal and vertical directions, M_{Cy}, M_{Cz} are the sum of components of all moments acting on the rotor relative to its centre of gravity (which is because of small deformations the same as to the rotor centre) in the y and z directions, t is time.

After performing the differentiations and taking into account the relations between displacements of the rotor centre (displaced point O) and its centre of gravity T

$$y_T = y + e_T \cos\varphi_T, \tag{13}$$
$$z_T = z + e_T \sin\varphi_T, \tag{14}$$

the equations of motion obtain the form

$$m\ddot{y} = F_{Cy} + m \cdot e_T\varepsilon\sin\varphi_T + m \cdot e_T\omega^2\cos\varphi_T, \tag{15}$$
$$m\ddot{z} = F_{Cz} - m \cdot e_T\varepsilon\cos\varphi_T + m \cdot e_T\omega^2\sin\varphi_T, \tag{16}$$

$$J_D \ddot{\varphi}_y + \omega J_A \dot{\varphi}_z + \varepsilon J_A \varphi_z = M_{Cy}, \qquad (17)$$
$$J_D \ddot{\varphi}_z - \omega J_A \dot{\varphi}_y - \varepsilon J_A \varphi_y = M_{Cz}. \qquad (18)$$

y, z are the horizontal and vertical displacements of the rotor centre, e_T, φ_T are eccentricity and position angle of the rotor centre of gravity and ε is angular acceleration of the rotor rotation. Dots ($\cdot\cdot$) denote the second derivative with respect to time.

4. Methodology of determination of the current – magnetic induction relationship

The magnetorheological damper presented in [9] was used to demonstrate the methodology of determination of the current – magnetic induction relationship.

The schema of the investigated damper is drawn in fig. 4. The damper consists of one outer and one inner ring, two electric coils and their casings, a flexible spring and of a ball bearing which is mounted with a sleeve made of aluminium alloy and coupled with the shaft. The gap between the rings is filled with magnetorheological liquid whose properties are controlled by intensity of the magnetic field produced by the coils supplied with electric current. The rubber seals are used to prevent leakage of the liquid from the damper gap. The ends of the coil windings are connected in such way that the current in each of them flows in the opposite direction.

The body of the damper, its rings, the bearing and the shaft are made of steel having relative permeability 2 000. Further it is assumed that relative permeability of the magnetorheological liquid is 5 and of the air and of all other mechanical parts of the damper is equal to 1. Each coil has 240 turns of a copper conductor of 0.63 mm in diameter. This enables the maximum current of 2 A.

The magnetostatic analysis of the damper was performed by means of a finite element code COMSOL Multiphysics. Because the length to diameter ratio of the damper is small, the flow in the thin film of the magnetorheological liquid prevails in the axial direction. This enables to consider it in the radial cross section of the damper gap as planar and therefore also the distribution of the magnetic induction in the film can be investigated by means of a 2D magnetostatic analysis. Dependence of the magnetic induction on intensity of the magnetic field is assumed

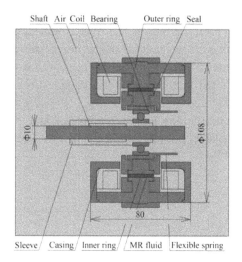

Fig. 4. Scheme of the investigated MR damper

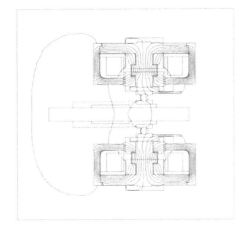

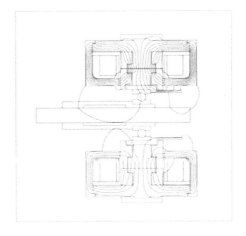

Fig. 5. The magnetic field distribution,
(2.5–2.5) mm, 1 A

Fig. 6. The magnetic field distribution,
(0.25–4.75) mm, 2 A

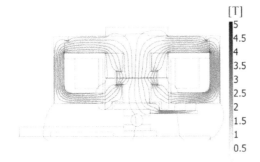

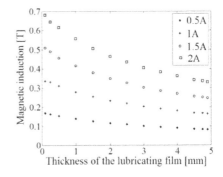

Fig. 7. The magnetic field, 0.25 mm, 2 A

Fig. 8. The flux density – thickness relationship

to be linear and isotropic for all materials. Magnetic saturation and material hysteresis are neglected. The source of the electric current is defined by a current density at locations of the electric coils ($1.76 \cdot 10^6$ Am^{-2} for the current of 1 A). In sufficient distance from the damper, the boundary condition of the magnetic insulation is defined.

The area was discretized in approximately 20 000 triangular elements with Lagrange-quadratic shape functions. Calculation of the magnetic quantities in the individual nodes arrived at solving a set of linear algebraic equations.

Fig. 5 and fig. 6 show a distribution of the magnetic flux lines for concentric and eccentric positions of the inner damper ring relative to the outer one. Inside the lubricating film the magnetic field is almost homogeneous (fig. 7) and magnitude of its induction is strongly effected by the thickness of the lubricating film.

The dependence of the mean value of the magnetic induction calculated by means of a finite element method in the damper gap (slight variations along the length of the damper have been averaged) on the thickness of the layer of the magnetorheological liquid for several magnitudes of the electric current in the coils is drawn in fig. 8. As evident the magnetic induction is with sufficient accuracy proportional to the current in the coils. Its dependence on the thickness of the lubricating film was approximated by relationship (19)

$$B = \frac{1}{X_1 + X_2 h} I \qquad (19)$$

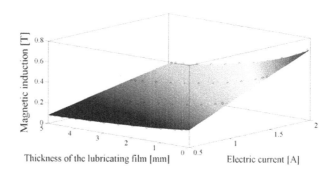

Fig. 9. Approximation of the flux density

where X_1 and X_2 are constants. Employing a least square method, one obtains the values of both constants $X_1 = 0.343\,1$ AT^{-1} and $X_2 = 0.668\,1$ AT^{-1}m^{-1}. Fig. 9 shows that application of relationship (19) approximates dependence of the magnetic induction in the damper gap on the current in the coils with good accuracy.

5. Example

The investigated rotor (fig. 10) is supported by two rolling element bearings mounted with cage springs which are coupled with the casing. The damping in the supports is realized by magnetorheological squeeze film dampers placed between the cage springs and the housing. The rotor rotates at a constant angular speed of 50 rad/s. At a specified moment of time it starts to accelerate (a sine ramp) and when the desired speed of 400 rad/s is reached it continues to turn at constant revolutions (fig. 11). The rotor is loaded by its weight and in addition it is excited by its imbalance. To eliminate deformation caused by the rotor weight, the cage springs are prestressed. The task was to investigate the influence of the dampers on the rotor vibration and on the force transmitted into the foundations.

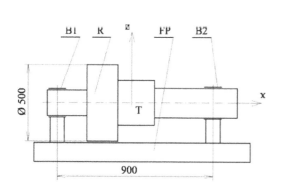

Fig. 10. Scheme of the rotor

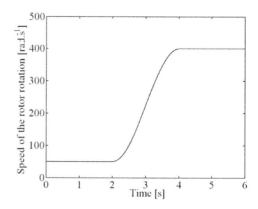

Fig. 11. Time history of the rotor revolutions

The Campbell diagram (fig. 12) shows that the rotor should pass the critical speeds during the acceleration once, maybe twice.

Time history of horizontal vibration of the rotor centre and of the damping force transmitted via damper B2 for two magnitudes of the electric current in the dampers coils are drawn in fig. 13, 14, 15 and 16. It is evident that the higher current produces magnetic field of higher

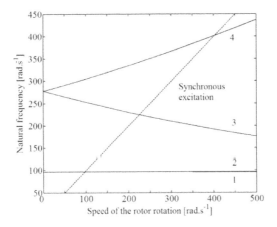

Fig. 12. Campbell diagram

intensity and this results in larger reduction of the rotor vibration in the neighbourhood of the critical revolutions. On the other hand it increases magnitude of the force transmitted into the foundations. The counter-rotating critical speed has no influence on the rotor vibration.

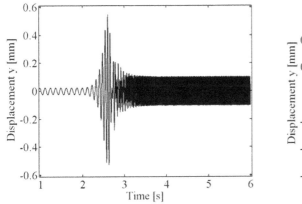

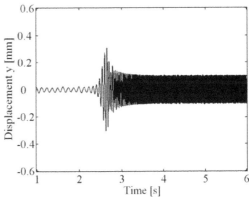

Fig. 13. Horizontal displacement of the rotor (1 A)   Fig. 14. Horizontal displacement of the rotor (2 A)

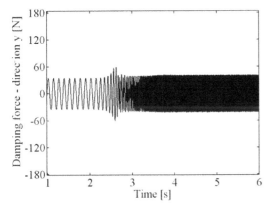

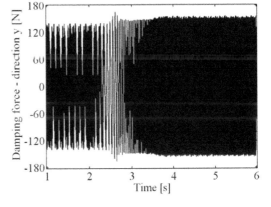

Fig. 15. Force transmitted to the foundations (1 A)   Fig. 16. Force transmitted to the foundations (2 A)

To achieve optimum performance of the damping device, the damping effect can be controlled by the current in the coils. The current is risen only during passing the critical speed and then it is decreased again (fig. 17). Maximum amplitude of the vibration is reduced (fig. 18) and increase of the damping force occurs only for a short time interval when the rotor overcomes the critical revolutions.

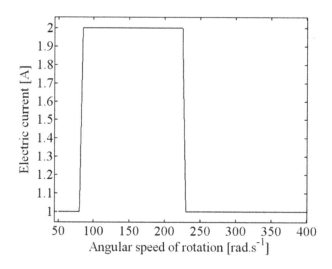

Fig. 17. The current – speed of rotation relationship

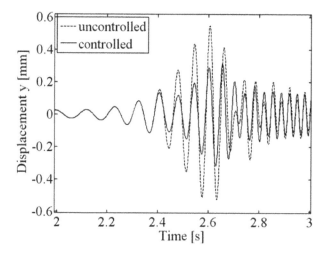

Fig. 18. The rotor horizontal displacement (controlled)

6. Conclusion

The developed numerical procedure represents a computational method for investigation of lateral vibration of rigid rotors that are supported by nonlinear short magnetorheological squeeze film dampers and that rotate at variable angular speed. The change of the yield shear stress of magnetorheological liquid by application of the magnetic field enables to control magnitude of the damping force and thus to achieve optimum performance of the damping device. The procedure is intended for determination of the rotor system response on force and kinematic excitation of a general time history and especially for investigation of the rotor vibration during its passing over the critical revolutions. The results of the carried out computer simulations showed that the damping effected both amplitude of the vibration and the force transmitted into the stationary part and that it was most efficient in the neighbourhood of the critical speeds. The dependence of magnitude of the damping force on magnitude of the electric current which produces the magnetic field has been also proved.

Acknowledgements

This work has been supported by the research project AVO Z20760514. The support is gratefully acknowledged.

References

[1] Ishida, Y., Yasuda, K., Murakami, S., Nonstationary oscillation of a rotating shaft with nonlinear spring characteristics during acceleration through a major critical speed (A discussion by the asymptotic method and the complex-FFT method), ASME Journal of Vibration and Acoustics 119 (1) (1997) 31–36.

[2] Ishida, Y., Yamamoto, T., Murakami, S., Nonstationary vibration of a rotating shaft with nonlinear spring characteristics during acceleration through a critical speed (A critical speed of a 1/3 – order subharmonic oscillation), JSME International Journal III 35 (3) (1992) 360–368.

[3] Ishida, Y., Yamamoto, T., Ikeda, T., Murakami, S., Nonstationary vibration of a rotating shaft with nonlinear spring characteristics during acceleration through a critical speed (A critical speed of a summed-and-differential harmonic oscillation, Nonlinear Dynamics 1 (5) (1990) 341–358.

[4] Ishida, Y., Ikeda, T., Yamamoto, T., Transient vibration of a rotating shaft with nonlinear spring characteristics during acceleration through a major critical speed, JSME International Journal 30 (261) (1987) 458–466.

[5] Yamamoto, T., Ishida, Y., Linear and nonlinear rotordynamics. A modern treatment with applications, John Wiley & Sons, New York, 2001.

[6] Lalanne, M., Ferraris, G., Rotordynamics prediction in engineering, John Wiley & Sons, Chichester, 1990.

[7] Blanco-Ortega, A., Silva-Navarro, G., Gómez-Mancilla, J. C., Dynamic stiffness control and acceleration scheduling for the active balancing control of a Jeffcott-like rotor, Proceedings of the 10th International Congress on Sound and Vibration, ICSV10, P098, Stockholm, Sweden, 2003, p. 227.

[8] Wang, J., Meng, G., Hahn, E. J., Experimental study on vibration properties and control of squeeze mode MR fluid damper-flexible rotor system, Proceedings of the 2003 ASME Design Engineering Technical Conference & Computers and Information in Engineering Conference, Chicago, Illinois, ASME, 2003, p. 955–959.

[9] Forte, P., Paterno, M., Rustighi, E., A magnetorheological fluid damper for rotor applications, International Journal of Rotating Machinery 10 (3) (2004) 175–182.

[10] Wang, G. J., Feng, N., Meng, G., Hahn, E. J., Vibration control of a rotor by squeeze film damper with magnetorheological fluid, Journal of Intelligent Material Systems and Structures 17 (4) (2006) 353–357.

[11] Zapoměl, J., Ferfecki, P., Mathematical modelling of a short magnetorheological damper, Transactions of the VŠB – Technical University of Ostrava, Mechanical Series 55 (1) (2009), 289–294.

[12] Kordonsky, W., Elements and devices based on magnetorheological effect, Journal of Intelligent Material Systems and Structures 4 (1) (1993) 65–69.

7

Crack path modelling in railway wheel under rolling contact fatigue

M. Kotoul[a,*]

[a] Brno University of Technology, Faculty of Mechanical Engineering, Technická 2, 616 69, Brno, Czech Republic

Abstract

A computational model of crack path for two-dimensional primary crack situated in a railway wheel rim is designed. The railway wheel rim is placed on the wheel disc of railway wheel with interference fit. Crack behaviour is analysed in the case of rectilinear ride of a train under rolling contact fatigue. Plank and Kuhn criterion is used to decide whether crack will either kink and follow mode I controlled (tensile mode) path, or it will propagate coplanar mode II controlled (shear mode). If mode I controlled crack growth is more probable then a direction of crack propagation is predicted using the maximum tensile stress range criterion. In this way a relationship between stress intensity factors and crack geometry is obtained. For comparison, crack behaviour in a solid railway wheel which is not subjected to pre-stress loading is also analysed. In the latter case the contact forces in the wheel-rail contact are considered to have i) only normal part ii) both the normal part and tangential part.

Keywords: rolling contact fatigue crack, non-proportional loading, mixed mode, railway wheel, FEM

1. Introduction

It is a matter of fact that fatigue crack growth in railway wheels may lead to the loss of a part of the wheel (spalling) or to radial crack extension. The result can be damage of rails and sleepers or vehicle wheel (spalling) or a radial crack extension. The result can be damage of rails and sleepers or vehicle components or even derailment. Obviously, with increasing train speed and axle load, the rolling contact fatigue will grow in importance. There is a great number of papers devoted to the problem of wheel-rail interaction. A reader is referred to the overviews [2, 5, 10, 11, 14, 20, 28, 31, 32, 34, 36].

Fatigue cracks tend to initiate at the wheel tread [10] near the contact between wheel and rail where plastic deformation develops. Due to ratcheting of surface material fatigue cracks are initiated. Such an initiation is promoted by the occurrence of material defects. It was observed [12] that ratcheting-induced surface cracks initially propagate at a shallow angle which soon deviates into almost radial direction. Depending upon the applied loading, the crack can later deviate into a circumferential direction. Another mechanism of crack initiation at the wheel thread is connected with formation of wheel flats when the wheel slides on the rail. After extreme thermal loading due to friction between rail and wheel, rapid cooling takes place when the wheel is released and the heat is conducted into surrounding cold wheel area. As a consequence, high surface tensile stresses develop and may cause crack initiation at microscopic notches. Moreover, a brittle zone of martensite may form and, consequently, cracks are initiated. They can further propagate as fatigue cracks.

---

*Corresponding author. e-mail: kotoul@fme.vutbr.cz.

Nomenclature

a	crack depth	$\Delta K_I = K_{I\max} - K_{I\min},$	stress intensity factor
b	lateral dimension of contact patch	$\Delta K_{II} = K_{II\max} - K_{II\min}$	ranges for modes I and II
c	width of contact patch	$\Delta K_I^*, \Delta K_{II}^*$	cyclic stress intensity range at the
p	contact pressure		short supplementary crack kink
$v_{rel,x}$	relative velocity at the contact patch		under non-proportional mixed
x_L, y_L	local coordinate system		mode loading
x_G, y_G	global coordinate system	$\overline{K_{II}}$	mean value of K_{II} during the
A_{ij}^{IJ}, B_{ij}^{IJ}	influence matrices		mode I cycle
E	Young's modulus	ΔK_{IIeff}	effective mode II range
G	shear modulus	K_{eq}	equivalent stress intensity factor
ν	Poisson's ratio	ΔK_{th}	threshold of fatigue crack growth
N_c	normal force		for the cyclic mode I
R	wheel radius	ΔK_{IIth}	threshold of fatigue crack growth
T	tangential force		for the cyclic mode II
V	rolling velocity	N	number of cycles
ΔT	time interval of the examined load	$\Delta \sigma_{n,\max}$	maximum tensile stress range
	cycle	α_1, α_2	contact position angle
f	friction coefficient between the	α_3	contact position at the start of
	wheel and rail		mode I cycle
μ	friction coefficient between crack	α_4	contact position at the end of
	faces		mode I cycle
K_I, K_{II}	stress intensity factors for modes I	φ	crack deviation angle
	and II	$\Delta\varphi$	range of crack deviation angle

The rolling contact fatigue is characterized by non-proportional mixed loading. Both shear stress controlled and normal stress controlled crack growth was reported. An existing pre-crack will either kink and will follow mode I controlled (tensile mode) path, or will propagate coplanar mode II controlled (shear mode) [26]. The general conclusion is drawn stating that non-proportional superposition of modes clearly affects the propagation behaviour of fatigue cracks. Both the crack growth rate and the direction of propagation are influenced by this. Maximum growth rate criterion proposed by Hourlier and Pineau [16] can be used to decide between tensile mode and co-planar shear mode crack growth. According to the experimental data, see e.g. [15, 37], a phase shift from proportional loading to non-proportional loading leads to an increase in fatigue life if the test is performed in a stress or load controlled condition. This increase may be explained by a smaller local cyclic plastic deformation when load maxima do not coincide.

Crack propagation rates in tensile mode often appear to be significantly lesser than the coplanar growth rates. Plank and Kuhn [26] suggested that for initiating coplanar crack growth the effective mode II range (i.e. the mode II range reduced due to a possible crack surface friction) must exceed a material-specific threshold value

$$\Delta K_{IIeff} > \Delta K_{IIth} \qquad (1)$$

and, additionally

$$|\Delta K_{II}| > \Delta K_I^* (\Delta\varphi), \qquad (2)$$

where ΔK_{II} denotes the mode II range on the starter crack and $\Delta K_I^*(\Delta\varphi)$ stands for the range of stress intensity on the infinitesimally short supplementary crack and $\Delta\varphi$ is the range of crack deviation angle φ. The range $\Delta\varphi$ is calculated from supplementary crack positions satisfying the local symmetry criterion $\Delta K_{II}^* = 0$. Namely, $\Delta\varphi = \varphi_{max} - \varphi_{min}$, where $\varphi_{max}, \varphi_{min}$ are two extreme angular positions for which the K_I^* reaches its maximum value under maximum and/or minimum load. A stress intensity range on the infinitesimally short supplementary crack is then as follows

$$\Delta K_I^*(\Delta\varphi) = K_{I\,max}^*(\varphi_{max}) - K_{I\,max}^*(\varphi_{min}). \tag{3}$$

As pointed out by Doquet and Pommier [9], it is questionable whether SIFs or their combinations are sufficient to describe crack growth rates under non-proportional loading because they cannot capture the complex interactions in terms of crack tip plastic flow that are likely to be loading path-dependent and to vary with the material behaviour. On the other hand, as long as the linear fracture mechanics is valid, crack growth behaviour should be explained exclusively in terms of linear elastic parameters. The aforementioned interactions could be captured by crack path criteria and a suitably modified Paris law. However, some solutions of stress intensity factor for the surface crack subjected to the simple tensile or shear stress have been found unavailable, because rolling contact fatigue (RCF) cracks experience a complex non-proportional mixed-mode loading and complicated boundary conditions [25]. Recently lot of work was devoted to modelling of rolling contact fatigue cracks in rails, see e.g. [3, 13, 29, 35]. The reason for that is quite clear and is connected with the increasing number of failures of rails contrary to decreasing number of failures of wheel and axles. More specifically, while failures of wheels and axles have been reduced by a factor of 20 over the last century, failure of rails per train kilometre have increased by a factor of more than 2 [30]. Fatigue cracks in rails initiate in the direction of wheel motion with a shallow angle of 20–30 degrees to the surface. They may branch down under repeated contact loading and propagate with a larger inclined angle to the rail surfaces, and finally lead to rail failure. For an efficient rail maintenance is it important to understand all factors that influence the fatigue propagation of short surface braking cracks. Apparently numerical tools such as FE modelling of crack growth can shed light upon this problem. Bower [7] developed a two-dimensional numerical model of surface initiated rolling contact fatigue cracks to study mode I and mode II stress intensity factors. Bogdanski et al. [2,4,5] have used the finite element method to examine the growth of rolling contact fatigue cracks and to predict crack tip stress intensity factors, increasing the understanding of mixed mode stress intensity factors. According to [3], the most promising models for RCF crack stress analyses are those which include liquid entrapment mechanism as it gives a considerable enhancement of the Mode I crack loading. Models developed by Kaneta et al. [23–25] included fluid pressure, which was assumed to decrease linearly along the length of the crack, being equal to the contact pressure at the crack mouth (e.g. at a railway wheel rail contact) and falling to zero at the crack tip. Stress intensity factors were calculated for circular and elliptical contact patches and semi-elliptical cracks. Most often Hertzian contact pressure distribution moving with respect to crack mouth is prescribed in FE analysis.

In this paper, we focus on FE modelling of rolling contact fatigue cracks in railway wheels. The goal is to simulate rolling contact fatigue crack growth for a two-dimensional (2D) case using FEM and taking into account a non-proportional mixed-mode loading. A parametric analysis is performed examining the influence of a friction of crack faces, presence of the tangential part of contact force and its orientation and the crack direction criterion. The analysis starts with an examination of whether a coplanar crack growth or tensile mode controlled crack growth, respectively, is more probable. It is assumed that fatigue crack growth starts, if the equivalent cyclic stress intensity ΔK_{eq} exceeds ΔK_{th}. Both, the radial crack extension and spalling are predicted and it is shown how the crack path depends on model parameters.

2. Numerical model

The starting point is the evaluation of contact forces in the wheel-rail rolling contact. The contact forces can be evaluated as an integral part of the FE analysis of rolling contact fatigue crack growth. However, such approach is extremely time- and memory-consuming one.

In order to reduce computational costs the following computational strategy consisting of two basic steps was suggested — in the first step the contact forces are evaluated using the CONTACT algorithm based on the boundary element method and developed by [21]. In the second step the FEM model is loaded with these contact forces to evaluate crack behaviour. The mentioned algorithm can be used for a contact of two bodies whose shapes cannot be replaced with a surface with a constant local curvature or for a contact of bodies which have different material properties. The algorithm treats separately the normal and tangential parts of the contact. The expected contact area is discretised and the influence matrix accordingly to the representation of Boussinesq and Cerruti [22] is calculated for each element.

By Kalker, the influence matrix of the element I in position $\boldsymbol{x_I}(x_I, y_I)$ generated by the element J is

$$\mathbf{A}^J(x_I, y_I) \equiv \mathbf{A}^{IJ} =$$

$$= \frac{1}{\pi \cdot G} \cdot \int\limits_{x_J - \Delta x}^{x_J + \Delta x} \int\limits_{y_J - \Delta y}^{y_J + \Delta y} \begin{bmatrix} \frac{1-\nu}{\rho} + \frac{(x'-x_I)^3}{\rho^3} & \frac{\nu \cdot (x'-x_I) \cdot (y'-y_I)}{\rho^3} & \frac{K \cdot (x'-x_I)}{\rho^2} \\ \frac{\nu \cdot (x'-x_I) \cdot (y'-y_I)}{\rho^3} & \frac{1-\nu}{\rho} + \frac{(y'-y_I)^2}{\rho^3} & \frac{K \cdot (y'-y_I)}{\rho^2} \\ -\frac{K \cdot (x'-x_I)}{\rho^2} & -\frac{K \cdot (y'-y_I)}{\rho^2} & \frac{1-\nu}{\rho} \end{bmatrix} \mathrm{d}x' \, \mathrm{d}y', \qquad (4)$$

where ρ is defined as $\rho = \sqrt{(x'-x_I)^2 + (y'-y_I)^2}$ and G, ν and K are combined material properties $\frac{1}{G} = \frac{1}{2 \cdot G^{(1)}} + \frac{1}{2 \cdot G^{(2)}}$, $\nu = G \cdot \left(\frac{\nu^{(1)}}{2 \cdot G^{(1)}} + \frac{\nu^{(1)}}{2 \cdot G^{(2)}} \right)$, $K = \frac{G}{4} \cdot \left(\frac{1-2 \cdot \nu^{(1)}}{G^{(1)}} + \frac{1-2 \cdot \nu^{(2)}}{G^{(2)}} \right)$, where G stands for the shear modulus, ν is Poisson's ratio and the superscripts (1) or (2) refer to the wheel or rail respectively. The x-axis of the contact patch is identical with the direction of the rolling velocity.

The deformation of the influence area is considered to be very small compared to the size of the wheel or the rail. The relation between the element displacement $u_i(x_I, y_I) \equiv u_i^I$ and the load acting on the contact patch is written as

$$u_i^I = \sum_{J=1}^{N} \sum_{j=1}^{3} A_{ij}^{IJ} \cdot p_j^J, \qquad (5)$$

where p_j^J is the j-component of load acting on the element J of the contact patch and the summation is performed over all elements of the contact patch.

The normal contact pressures are found from the solution of the system of equations

$$e^I = h^I + u_3^I = h^I + \sum_{J=1}^{N} \sum_{j=1}^{3} A_{3j}^{IJ} \cdot p_j^J,$$

$$e^I = 0 \text{ if the element } I \text{ lies inside the contact patch}, \qquad (6)$$

$$p_j^J = 0 \text{ if the element } I \text{ lies outside the contact patch},$$

where e^I is the deformed distance and h^I is the undeformed distance. The normal force is calculated as

$$N_c = \sum_{I \in C} p_3^I \cdot \mathrm{d}S_I. \qquad (7)$$

Tangential forces depend on the velocity of the vehicle, on relative velocities in the contact patch, on the normal forces and on the coefficient of adhesion. The tangential forces can be calculated similarly like the normal tractions. The basic presumption is to evaluate the influence matrices A_{ij}^{IJ} (current influence) and B_{ij}^{IJ}, (influence of the previous time step). Then the following system of equations is solved:

$$s_\tau^I = c_\tau^I + \frac{\sum_{J=1}^{N}\sum_{j=1}^{3} A_{\tau j}^{IJ} \cdot p_j^J(t) - B_{\tau j}^{IJ} \cdot p_j^J(t - \mathrm{d}t)}{\mathrm{d}t},$$

$$s_\tau^I = 0 \text{ if element is in the adhesion area,} \tag{0}$$

$$s_\tau^I = -S_I \cdot \frac{p_\tau^I}{f \cdot p_3^I} \text{ and } \sqrt{p_1^{I2} + p_2^{I2}} = f \cdot p_3^I \text{ if element is in the slip area } S_I,$$

τ denotes the tangential direction on the contact surfaces, c_τ^I is the rigid slip of an element, and s_τ^I is a virtual slip of an element. The time difference $\mathrm{d}t$ depends on the boundary element size $2\mathrm{d}x$ and rolling velocity V, $\mathrm{d}t = \frac{2 \cdot \mathrm{d}x}{V}$. In the first step of the algorithm it is considered that the adhesion area correspond to the whole contact patch, hence the slip area is an empty set. Accordingly, the linear set of equations is solved in the first step:

$$0 = c_\tau^I + \frac{\sum_{J=1}^{N}\sum_{j=1}^{3} A_{\tau j}^{IJ} \cdot p_j^J(t) - B_{\tau j}^{IJ} \cdot p_j^J(t - \mathrm{d}t)}{\mathrm{d}t}, \tag{9}$$

The solution of (9) for the contact patch of elliptical shape corresponds to the numerical solution of Kalker's linear theory of rolling contact. Tangential forces are defined as:

$$T_x = \sum_I p_1^I \cdot \mathrm{d}S_I, \quad T_y = \sum_I p_2^I \cdot \mathrm{d}S_I. \tag{10}$$

The distribution of contact pressures [19] along the direction parallel to the wheel axis is shown in Fig. 1.

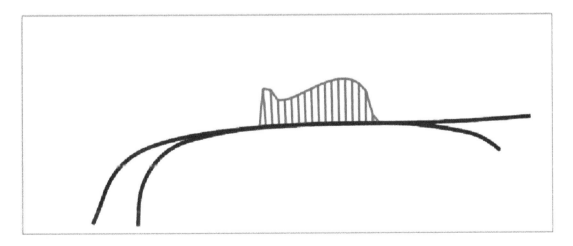

Fig. 1. Distribution of contact pressures along the direction parallel to the wheel axis

Fig. 2 shows the shape of half of the contact patch with distribution of contact pressures calculated by Hertz algorithm (upper part of figure) and by the CONTACT algorithm (lower part of figure) [19]. Apparently, the shape of the contact patch calculated using the CONTACT

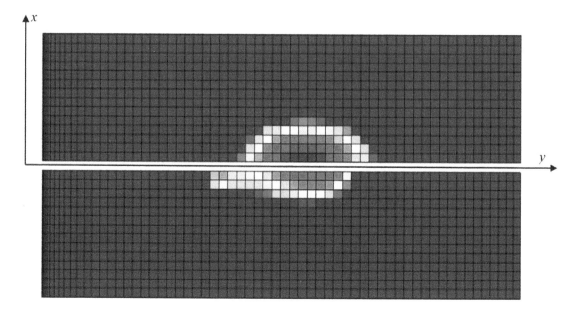

Fig. 2. Shape of half of the contact patch with distribution of contact pressures calculated by Hertz algorithm (upper part of figure) and by the CONTACT algorithm (lower part of figure)

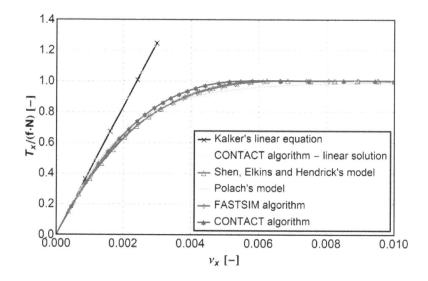

Fig. 3. Longitudinal tangential force as a function of the relative longitudinal creepage $v_x = v_{\mathrm{rel},x}/V$

algorithm differs from the Hertzian elliptic contact patch. Fig. 3 shows the longitudinal tangential force as a function of the relative longitudinal creepage $v_x = v_{rel,x}/V$ calculated by various methods ($v_{rel,x}$ is the relative velocity at the contact patch). Except of linear solutions, the longitudinal tangential force saturates at the value $f N_c$.

Previous results provide a basis for transformation of 3D rolling contact to 2D rolling contact. The wheel rim is considered to be sufficiently wide so that the contact problem can be reduced to plane strain problem at least in the middle plane of the wheel. We proceed as follows — the contact area is considered to be a strip $x \in [-c, c]$ and the contact pressure is described by the

2D Hertz solution

$$p(x) = p_{\max}\sqrt{1 - \frac{x^2}{c^2}}, \quad c^2 = \frac{8N_c/b\,R(1-\nu^2)}{\pi E}, \quad p_{\max} = \frac{2N_c}{\pi cb}. \tag{11}$$

N_c/b characterizes the normal force per unit length. The value of b is taken as the lateral dimension of the contact patch (along the y-axis) calculated above, see Fig. 2 and approximately equals to 20 mm. Considering $N_c = 10^5$ N and the outer diameter of the wheel rim $2R = 920$ mm, we get a 2D Hertz contact loading prescribed within the sector of approximately 1.2°, see Fig. 4.

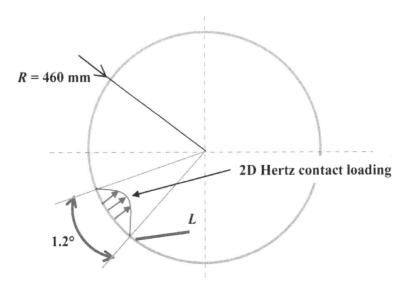

Fig. 4. 2D Hertz contact loading prescribed on the wheel rim within the sector approximately of 1.2°

Numerical model of crack was created in the system ANSYS version 14 (ANSYS Inc., Canonsburg, PA, USA). A rectilinear ride of a train with a constant speed is assumed and no geometric imperfections of rails and/or wheel tread are considered. An initial crack of depth of 2 mm is inclined to the tangential direction with shallow angle 20°, see Fig. 4. Such geometrical configuration is typical for railway wheels (RW) [36]. The depth of crack is increased by 0.03 mm after each loading step defined by the position of the crack mouth with respect to the contact point in the range limited by angles $\alpha_1 = -2°$ and $\alpha_2 = 5°$, see Fig. 5. As it will be shown later, outside this range both SIFs K_I and K_{II} are equal to zero if no static pre-stress is present. Note that virtually a number of cycles is required to propagate the crack of 0.03 mm. The number of cycles can be estimated for example using crack growth law developed by Bold and Brown [6]:

$$\Delta K_{eq} = \sqrt{\Delta K_I^2 + \left(\frac{614}{507}\Delta K_{II}^{3.21}\right)^{\frac{2}{3.74}}}, \tag{12}$$

$$\frac{\mathrm{d}a}{\mathrm{d}N} = 0.000\,507(\Delta K_{eq}^{3.74} - \Delta K_{th}^{3.74}),$$

where ΔK_{eq} is an equivalent stress intensity factor combining mode I and II even though the peaks of ΔK_I and ΔK_{II} are out of phase. The crack extension is performed for a wide range of deviation angle φ and the possibility of coplanar crack growth is tested using Eqs. (1) and (2).

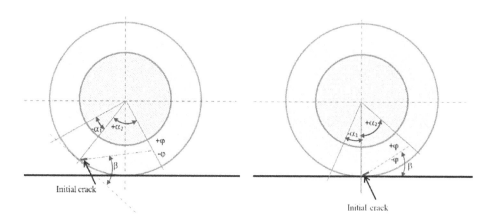

Fig. 5. Scheme of railway wheel geometry

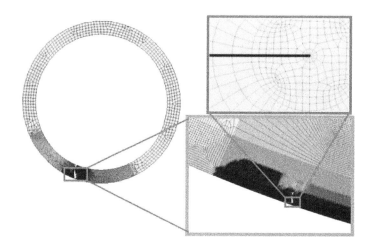

Fig. 6. FE mesh and size of discretization

Two basic configurations are considered: a crack on wheel rim fixed by an interference fit accompanied by a relative increase of the rim's inner diameter of about 1.44 % (amounting to approximately 1.11 mm), and a crack in a solid railway wheel. The outer diameter of the wheel rim is 920 mm and the thickness of the rim is 75 mm. The FE mesh consists of quadratic elements PLANE183, see Fig. 6. A sensitivity analysis of mesh has not revealed any substantial changes in the values of stress intensity factors during further mesh refinement.

The mesh was graded such that it exhibits high density near the contact and near the crack tip, see Fig. 6. It was shown elsewhere [32] that the concept of the linear elastic fracture mechanics is likely to be valid for crack modelling in rolling contact fatigue of railway wheels. Hence, a plastic zone ahead of the crack tip and related stress redistribution is not considered. The material of the wheel is assumed to be homogeneous, isotropic with the Young modulus $E = 2.1 \cdot 10^5$ MPa and Poisson's ratio $\nu = 0.3$.

The wheel is loaded by a distribution of contact pressures which correspond to the total contact force of 10 tons. The algorithm for Hertzian contact calculation was described above, for more details see e.g. [1, 17, 18]. The contact pressure data are prescribed in individual nodes of the quadratic element PLANE 183, see Fig. 7.

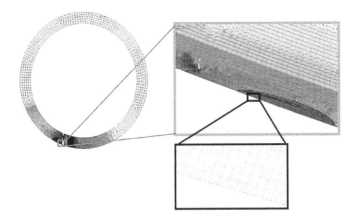

Fig. 7. Nodes of quadratic elements where the contact pressure data are prescribed

The stress intensity factors at a crack for a linear elastic fracture mechanics analysis were computed using the KCALC command in ANSYS. The analysis uses a fit of the nodal displacements in the vicinity of the crack. For full model the ANSYS software uses formulas for $\Theta = \pm 180°$ under plane strain conditions as follows:

$$K_I = \frac{1}{4}\sqrt{\frac{\pi}{2}\frac{E}{1-\nu^2}}\frac{|\Delta v|}{\sqrt{r}}, \quad K_{II} = \frac{1}{4}\sqrt{\frac{\pi}{2}\frac{E}{1-\nu^2}}\frac{|\Delta u|}{\sqrt{r}}, \quad K_{III} = \frac{1}{4}\sqrt{\frac{\pi}{2}\frac{E}{1-\nu^2}}\frac{|\Delta w|}{\sqrt{r}},$$

where u, v, w are displacements, r, Θ — coordinates in local cylindrical coordinate system, see Fig. 8 below.

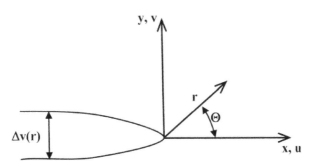

Fig. 8. Scheme of the crack and the local cylindrical coordinate system

The nodal displacements are fitted by a linear approximation like e.g. $|\Delta v|/\sqrt{r} = A + B \cdot r$. If r approaches to zero, one obtains $\lim_{r \to 0} |\Delta v|/\sqrt{r} = A$. Then equation

$$K_I = \frac{1}{4}\sqrt{\frac{\pi}{2}\frac{E}{1-\nu^2}}\frac{|\Delta v|}{\sqrt{r}}$$

will become

$$K_I = \frac{1}{4}\sqrt{\frac{\pi}{2}\frac{E}{1-\nu^2}}A.$$

Collapsing quadratic quarter-point elements and nodes were used for computing stress intensity factors at the crack tip.

3. Results and discussion

3.1. Fatigue cracks in a wheel rim

As the first, a possibility of coplanar crack growth is examined. To this purpose, the Plank and Kuhn criteria (1), (2) are tested. The K^*-factors on the short supplementary crack (0.03 mm) are calculated during one loading cycle for a different crack deviation angles aiming to look for the situation when K_I^* becomes maximum/minimum while K_{II}^* disappears. Hereafter fatigue crack growth is modelled for two cases of surface friction between the crack faces: i) without friction and ii) with friction prescribing the coefficient of friction $\mu = 0.5$. The results are shown in Fig. 9 and Fig. 10. Note that the interference fit generates a static pre-stress and, consequently, static K-factors. It is particularly seen for the mode II loading. As pointed out by Plank and Kuhn, the superposed static mode II loading may influence only the deviation and the crack propagation rate, but does not influence the crack propagation mode. Hence, ΔK_I^*, ΔK_{II}^* and also ΔK_{II} are referred to the static value which can be easily read far from the contact position with respect to crack mouth, see Fig. 9. By inspection of results in Fig. 9 one can see that the condition (2) is not fulfilled.

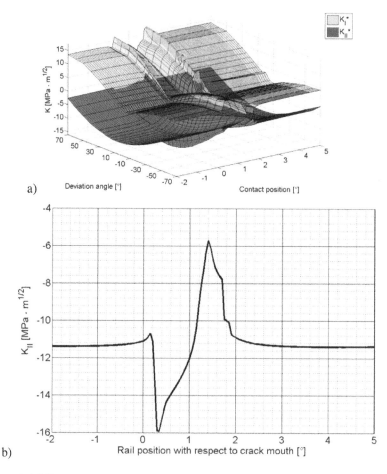

Fig. 9. a) ΔK_I^* and ΔK_{II}^* on the short supplementary crack for a wide range of crack deviation angles as functions of rolling contact position with respect to crack mouth; b) ΔK_{II} on the starter crack as a function of rolling contact position with respect to crack mouth. Friction between the crack faces is not considered

Specifically, ΔK_{II} for the starter crack takes the value of about $10\,\mathrm{MPa\,m^{1/2}}$, see Fig. 9b. From Fig. 9a, it can be further deduced that $\Delta K_I^*(\Delta\varphi)$ takes also the value of about $10\,\mathrm{MPa\,m^{1/2}}$ when $K_{I\,\max}^*(\varphi_{\max}) \cong 15\,\mathrm{MPa\,m^{1/2}}$ and $K_{I\,\max}^*(\varphi_{\min}) \cong 5\,\mathrm{MPa\,m^{1/2}}$ for $\varphi_{\max} \cong 70°$ and $\varphi_{\min} \cong 50°$, respectively, see also Eq. (3). The situation is even more pronounced when the surface friction between crack faces is considered, see Fig. 10. Observe in Fig. 10b that K_{II} takes the value of about $-8.5\,\mathrm{MPa\,m^{1/2}}$ far from the contact position with respect to crack mouth due to static pre-stress. The maximum value of K_{II} approaches zero due to superposed cyclic contact loading, hence $\Delta K_{II} \cong 8.5\,\mathrm{MPa\,m^{1/2}}$. The results shown in Fig. 10a indicate that $K_{I\,\max}^*(\varphi_{max}) \cong 18\,\mathrm{MPa\,m^{1/2}}$ for $\varphi_{max} \cong 70°$ and $K_{I\,\max}^*(\varphi_{min}) \cong 2\,\mathrm{MPa\,m^{1/2}}$ for $\varphi_{min} \cong -30°$, hence $\Delta K_I^*(\Delta\varphi)$ takes value of about $16\,\mathrm{MPa\,m^{1/2}}$. To conclude, mode II controlled crack growth is not likely to be initiated and the crack deviates tensile mode controlled path.

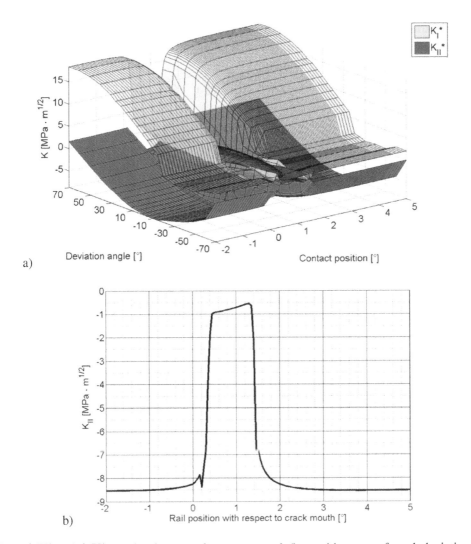

a)

b)

Fig. 10. a) ΔK_I^* and ΔK_{II}^* on the short supplementary crack for a wide range of crack deviation angles as functions of rolling contact position with respect to crack mouth; b) ΔK_{II} on the starter crack as a function of rolling contact position with respect to crack mouth. Surface friction between the crack faces with the coefficient of friction $\mu = 0.5$

The procedure of fatigue crack path prediction under non proportional loading is based on the assumption that the crack propagates in the direction perpendicular to the direction of the maximum tensile stress range $\Delta\sigma_{n,max}$. Note that $\Delta\sigma_{n,max}$ criterion predicts well the crack path in polymodal fatigue in structural steels. The crack deviation angle, φ, is given by the maximum tensile stress range criterion as [8]

$$\Delta\sigma_{n,\mathrm{max}} = \max_{\varphi}\left(\max_{t\in\Delta T}(\Delta\sigma_n(\varphi,t))\right), \tag{13}$$

where t is the time, ΔT is the time interval of the examined load cycle and

$$\sigma_n(\varphi,t) = \frac{1}{4\sqrt{2\pi r}}\left[K_I(t)\left(3\cos\frac{\varphi}{2}+\cos\frac{3\varphi}{2}\right)-K_{II}(t)\left(3\sin\frac{\varphi}{2}+3\sin\frac{3\varphi}{2}\right)\right]+O(r).$$

Surprisingly, the crack deviation angle, φ, calculated from Eq. (13) differs by a few percents from the angle calculated from Richard's criterion [27]

$$\varphi = \mp\left[155.5°\cdot\frac{|K_{II}|}{K_I+|K_{II}|}-83.4°\cdot\left(\frac{|K_{II}|}{K_I+|K_{II}|}\right)^2\right], \tag{14}$$

where for K_I and K_{II} their mean values during the mode I cycle are substituted. The deviation angle $\varphi < 0$ for $K_{II} > 0$ and $\varphi > 0$ for $K_{II} < 0$. The mean value of K_{II} during the mode I cycle is calculated as

$$\overline{K_{II}} = \frac{1}{\alpha_4-\alpha_3}\cdot\int_{\alpha_3}^{\alpha_4}K_{II}(x)\,\mathrm{d}x, \tag{15}$$

where α_3, α_4 correspond to contact positions when mode I cycle starts and finishes, respectively.

In the subsequent loading step the calculated kinking angle φ is used to rotate the local coordinate system x_L, y_L, see Fig. 11, and the constant crack increment of the length of 0.03 mm is then imposed.

Fig. 12 shows a predicted crack path in the global coordinate system depicted in Fig. 11, for the case when friction is not considered and for the case when the coefficient of friction between crack faces $\mu = 0.5$.

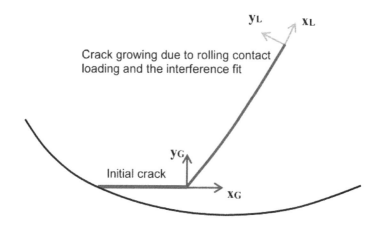

Fig. 11. Scheme of the crack configuration

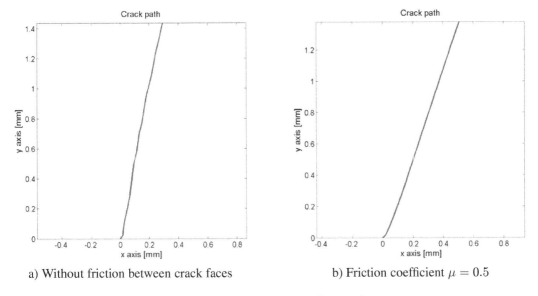

a) Without friction between crack faces   b) Friction coefficient $\mu = 0.5$

Fig. 12. Predicted crack path in RW rim

Apparently, due to the interference between the rim and the wheel a radial crack extension is a preferred mode of fracture. In the case of friction between crack faces, the crack path somewhat diverts from the radial direction in comparison to the case without friction. This behaviour can be easily explained by decrease of the effective mode II stress intensity factor due to friction. As can be seen from Fig. 13, a small change of K_{II} within the range $0 \div 3K_I$ leads to a significant change of the deviation angle φ.

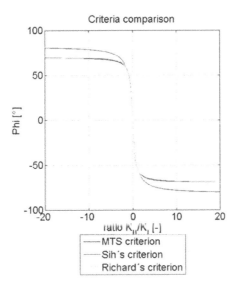

Fig. 13. Comparison of different criteria for prediction of the crack path

3D graphs in Fig. 14 show how K_I and K_{II} depend on the contact position, cf. Fig. 11, and on the crack depth. The calculations are performed for the case when the coefficient of friction between crack faces $\mu = 0.5$. Very similar results are obtained if no friction between crack faces is considered. Apparently, the amplitudes of K_I and K_{II} grow with the crack depth.

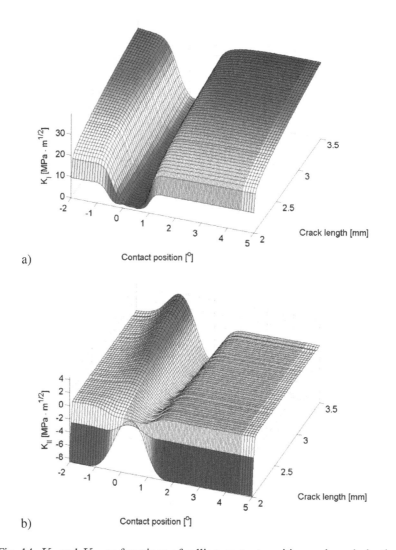

Fig. 14. K_I and K_{II} as functions of rolling contact position and crack depth

3.2. *Fatigue crack path in a solid railway wheel*

It is a matter of interest to compare the crack growth in the RW rim with a crack behaviour in a solid railway wheel which is not subjected to pre-stress loading.

The initial geometry of the solid railway wheel containing a crack is the same as in the case of rim wheel. Also boundary conditions and the computation algorithm are identical.

Analogously to the case of the RW rim we start examining a possibility of coplanar crack growth. Consider frictionless contact between crack faces. By inspection of the results in Fig. 15 one can see that contrary to the RW rim the condition (2) is fulfilled in the case of the solid railway wheel. Evidently, while $\Delta K_{II} \cong 9$ MPa m$^{1/2}$, $K_{I\,\mathrm{max}}^*(\varphi_{\mathrm{max}})$ is approximately equal to 3.5 MPa m$^{1/2}$ for $\varphi_{max} \cong 70°$ and $K_{I\,\mathrm{max}}^*(\varphi_{\mathrm{min}}) \cong 2$ MPa m$^{1/2}$ for $\varphi_{min} \cong -50°$, hence $\Delta K_I^*(\Delta\varphi) \cong 1.5$ MPa m$^{1/2}$. However, this is only a necessary condition, in addition, the effective mode II range must exceed a material-specific threshold value for initiating coplanar crack growth, see the condition (1). Note that a very similar result is obtained if the friction between crack faces is included.

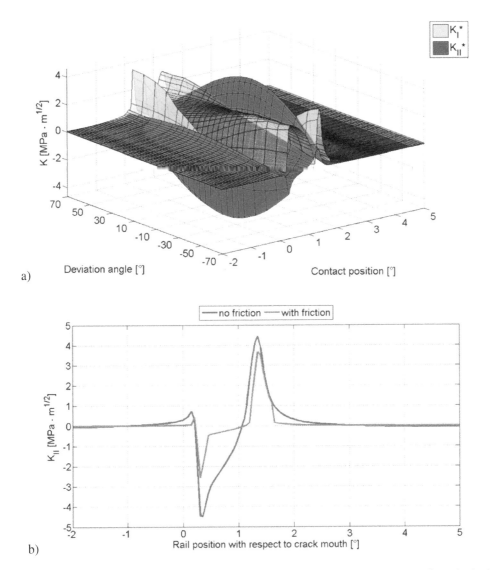

a)

b)

Fig. 15. a) $\Delta K_{I}*$ and $\Delta K*_{II}$ on the short supplementary crack for a wide range of crack deviation angles as functions of rolling contact position with respect to crack mouth; b) ΔK_{II} on the starter crack as a function of rolling contact position with respect to crack mouth

If mode II controlled crack growth is not likely to be initiated because the condition (1) is not fulfilled, the crack deviates tensile mode controlled path. Using the same methodology as in the case of RW rim, the crack path was predicted. Fig. 16a shows predicted crack path in the solid railway wheel for the case when friction is not considered while Fig. 16b pertains to the case when the coefficient of friction between crack faces $\mu = 0.1$. Apparently, crack path simulations in a solid railway wheel show that while without friction the crack follows a radial path shown in Fig. 16a, spalling is preferred mode of fracture if friction of crack faces is considered.

3D graphs in Fig. 17a, and Fig. 17b, which display the way how K_I and K_{II} depend on the contact position and on the crack depth, provide an explanation of such behaviour. Namely, while K_I changes only slightly with increasing friction between crack faces, cf. Fig. 17a and Fig. 17b, the range of K_{II} is reduced due to the crack surface friction, cf. Fig. 15b, Fig. 18a and Fig. 18b.

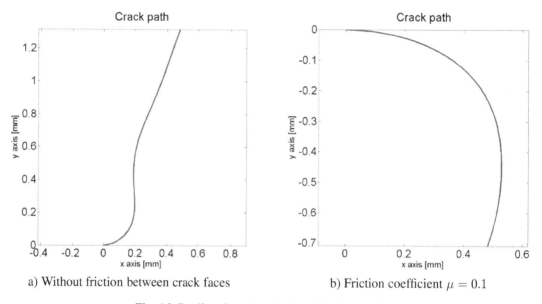

a) Without friction between crack faces   b) Friction coefficient $\mu = 0.1$

Fig. 16. Predicted crack path in solid railway wheel

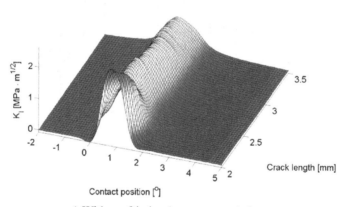

a) Without friction between crack faces

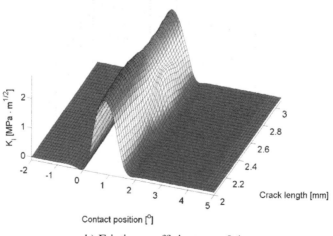

b) Friction coefficient $\mu = 0.1$

Fig. 17. K_I as a function of rolling contact position and crack depth

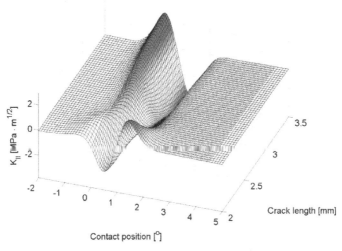

a) Without friction between crack faces

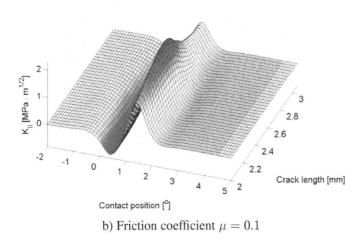

b) Friction coefficient $\mu = 0.1$

Fig. 18. K_{II} as a function of rolling contact position and crack depth

Specifically, for the initial crack without friction between crack faces $\Delta K_{II} \cong 9$ MPa m$^{1/2}$ but already with the friction coefficient $\mu = 0.1$ the mode II range ΔK_{II} decreases to 6 MPa m$^{1/2}$. Further, in the case when friction is not assumed between crack faces, the negative values of K_{II} prevail during the mode I cycle.

By contrast, the positive values of K_{II} during the mode I cycle are more dominant when the friction coefficient $\mu = 0.1$ is considered, see Fig. 15b. As a result, the maximum tensile stress range criterion predicts a positive value of crack deviation angle when friction is not assumed and crack propagates towards the wheel centre, see Fig. 16a. On the other side, a negative value of crack deviation angle is predicted in the latter case, and as a consequence, spalling may occur.

So far only normal contact forces in the wheel-rail contact were considered. However, the contact forces generally have also tangential part. According to the linear theory of rolling contact [21] the tangential force T exhibits a linear dependence on creepage, as it is also shown in Fig. 3. However, in reality it saturates at value $T = fN_c$, where $f = 0.2$ stands for the coefficient of friction between the wheel and rail, see e.g. [33] and N_c is the resulting normal contact force. Next, let us consider a saturated tangential force acting in the rolling contact. Two mutual configurations of crack and tangential contact force depicted in Fig. 19 are considered.

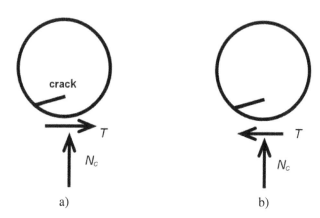

Fig. 19. Two mutual configurations of crack and tangential contact force

First, let us start with the configuration in Fig. 19a. Consider that the friction coefficient between crack faces $\mu = 0.1$. By inspection of Fig. 20 one can see that the loading of crack is very complex and it is not easy to examine the condition (2). Nevertheless, it is apparent that in the stage of rolling contact specified by the range of angles $\alpha \in (-1°; 1.4°)$ is K_I* always smaller than K_{II}, so the coplanar crack growth is possible if also the condition (1) is fulfilled. It is not true in the last stage of rolling contact specified by the range of angles $\alpha \in (-1.4°; 3°)$, where the condition (2) is not fulfilled. (Very similar result is obtained if the friction between crack faces is not considered.) It means that mode I controlled crack growth can be initiated during the latter stage. Fig. 21 shows predicted crack path in the solid railway wheel when the tangential part of contact force acts in the direction shown in Fig. 19a. The case when friction is not considered is shown in Fig. 21a while Fig. 21b pertains to the case when the coefficient of friction between crack faces $\mu = 0.1$ is prescribed. Crack path simulations indicate that crack follows a nearly radial path. Contrary to the calculations when the contact force is purely normal one, see Fig. 16, the presence of friction does not significantly influence the crack path.

Finally, the configuration shown in Fig. 19b is investigated. Consider that the friction coefficient between crack faces $\mu = 0.1$. By inspection of results in Fig. 23 one can see that contrary to the configuration shown in Fig. 19a the condition (2) is not fulfilled in the first stage of rolling contact, i.e. in the range of the contact position angle $\alpha \in (-2°, 1°)$. Note that a similar result is obtained if the friction between crack faces is included. It means that crack will deflect in this stage and the coplanar crack growth is not possible.

The predicted crack path in the solid railway wheel, when the tangential part of contact force acts in the direction shown in Fig. 19b, is displayed in Fig. 22. Apparently, crack path simulations show that spalling is preferred mode of fracture regardless of the presence of friction between crack faces.

Apparently, all presented results depend on the calculated variations of the stress intensity factors during rolling contact loading. It would be desirable to compare the calculated SIFs towards the results in literature. The authors carried out very careful check of available literature, however for specified boundary conditions no results for crack in rail wheels were found. However, there are many results for cracks in rails. Perhaps closest to the results from the point of view of boundary conditions are the results presented in Xiangyuan Xu et al. [35] in their Fig. 5, where boundary conditions including the friction coefficients are very close to the conditions used for the obtaining of results shown in Fig. 23a and Fig. 23b. Though the variations of SIFs differ significantly, their maximum values differ by 5 % in case of the results in Fig. 23 and by 33 % in case of the results in Fig. 23.

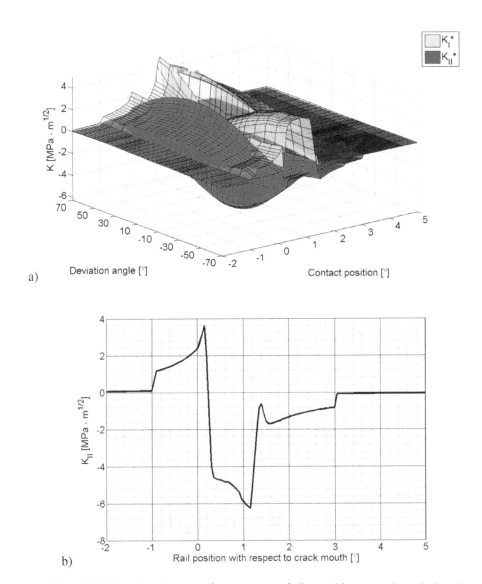

Fig. 20. a) ΔK_I^* and ΔK_{II}^* on the short supplementary crack for a wide range of crack deviation angles as functions of rolling contact position with respect to crack mouth; b) ΔK_{II} on the starter crack as a function of rolling contact position with respect to crack mouth. Tangential contact force is considered according to the scheme in Fig. 19a. The friction coefficient between crack faces $\mu = 0.1$

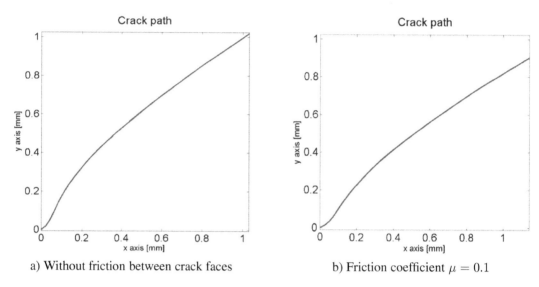

a) Without friction between crack faces   b) Friction coefficient $\mu = 0.1$

Fig. 21. Predicted crack path in solid railway wheel. The tangential part of contact force acts in the direction shown in Fig. 19a

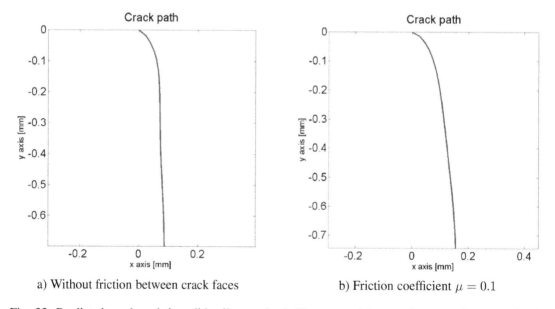

a) Without friction between crack faces   b) Friction coefficient $\mu = 0.1$

Fig. 22. Predicted crack path in solid railway wheel. The tangential part of contact force acts in the direction shown in Fig. 19b

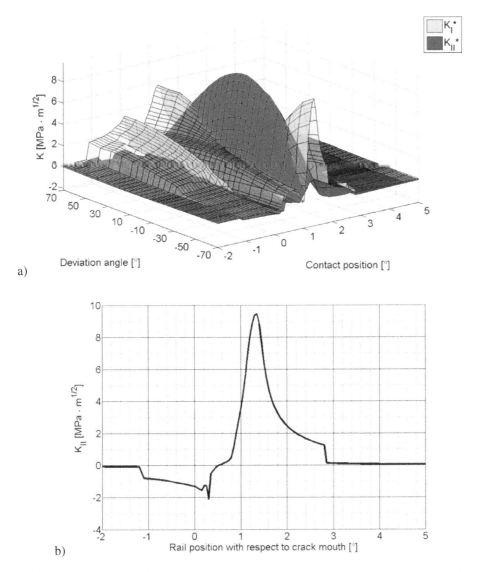

Fig. 23. a) ΔK_I* and $\Delta K_{II}*$ on the short supplementary crack for a wide range of crack deviation angles as functions of rolling contact position with respect to crack mouth; b) ΔK_{II} on the starter crack as a function of rolling contact position with respect to crack mouth. Tangential contact force is considered according to the scheme in Fig. 19b. The friction coefficient between crack faces $\mu = 0.1$

4 Concluding remarks

A computational 2D analysis of crack path for crack in a railway wheel rim was performed. Two basic configurations were considered: a crack on wheel rim fixed by an interference fit and a crack in a solid railway wheel. Plank and Kuhn criterion was used to decide whether crack would either kink and follow mode I controlled (tensile mode) path, or it will propagate coplanar mode II controlled (shear mode). If mode II controlled crack growth is not likely to be initiated, the crack deviates tensile mode controlled path. In the latter case the procedure of fatigue crack path prediction under non proportional loading was based on the assumption that the crack propagates in the direction perpendicular to the direction of the maximum tensile stress range $\Delta \sigma_{n,max}$.

The computational analysis based upon the linear fracture and contact mechanics approach allows drawing the following conclusions:

Crack path simulations in the RW rim show that the interference between the rim and the wheel influences significantly the crack path. Radial crack extension is preferred mode of fracture and the fatigue crack accelerates significantly with increasing crack depth. The friction between crack faces seems to support shear dominated fatigue crack growth, nevertheless the crack path does not change notably with friction. Hence, it may be stated that RW rim always failures in radial direction and coplanar crack growth is not probable.

Crack path simulations in solid railway wheel show that, under assumption of pure normal contact forces in the wheel-rail contact, spalling is preferred mode of fracture if the friction of crack faces is considered while a radial path occurs if the friction is zero. Nevertheless, in both cases coplanar crack growth is also possible mode of fracture. If also tangential part of contact force is taken into account, then it is shown that orientation of the tangential part of contact force matters. Specifically, the orientation illustrated in Fig. 19a promotes a radial crack path regardless of presence of the friction between crack faces. A coplanar crack growth may occur but mode I controlled crack growth is more probable. On the contrary, the orientation of the tangential part of contact force illustrated in Fig. 19b promotes spalling regardless of presence of the friction between crack faces and the coplanar crack growth does not occur.

Acknowledgements

The work has been supported by the NETME Centre established thanks to a financial support of the European Regional Development Fund under the Operational Program Research and Development for Innovation. The presented results have been obtained within NETME CENTRE PLUS (LO1202) project co-funded by the Czech Ministry of Education, Youth and Sports within the support program National Sustainability Program I.

Reference

[1] Andersson, C., Johansson, A., Prediction of rail corrugation generated by three-dimensional wheel-rail interaction, Wear 257 (2004) 423–434.

[2] Bogdański, S., Brown, M. W., Modelling the three-dimensional behaviour of shallow rolling contact fatigue cracks in rails, Wear 253 (2002) 17–25.

[3] Bogdański, S., Lewicki, P., 3D model of liquid entrapment mechanism for rolling contact fatigue cracks in rails, Wear 265 (2008) 1 356–1 362.

[4] Bogdański, S., Olzak, M., Stupnicki, J., Numerical modelling of a 3D rail RCF 'squat'-type crack under operating load, Fatigue & Fracture of Engineering Materials & Structures 21 (1998) 923–935.

[5] Bogdański, S., Olzak, M., Stupnicki, J., Numerical stress analysis of rail rolling contact fatigue cracks, Wear 191 (1996) 14–24.

[6] Bold, P. E., Brown, M. W., Allen, R. J., Shear mode crack growth and rolling contact fatigue, Wear 144 (1991) 307–317.

[7] Bower, A. F., The influence of crack face friction and trapped fluid on surface initiated rolling contact fatigue cracks, Journal of Tribology 110 (1988) 704–711.

[8] Dahlin, P., Olsson, M., The effect of plasticity on incipient mixed-mode fatigue crack growth, Fatigue & Fracture of Engineering Materials & Structures 26 (2003) 577–588.

[9] Doquet, V., Pommier, S., Fatigue crack growth under non-proportional mixed-mode loading in ferritic-pearlitic steel, Fatigue & Fracture of Engineering Materials & Structures 27 (2004) 1 051–1 060.

[10] Ekberg, A., Kabo, E., Fatigue of railway wheels and rails under rolling contact and thermal loading — an overview, Wear 258 (2005) 1 288–1 300.

[11] Ekberg, A., Kabo, E., Nielsen, J. C. O., Lundén, R., Subsurface initiated rolling contact fatigue of railway wheels as generated by rail corrugation, International Journal of Solids and Structures 44 (2007) 7 975–7 987.

[12] Ekberg, A., Sotkovszki, P., Anisotropy and rolling contact fatigue of railway wheels, International Journal of Fatigue 23 (2001) 29–43.

[13] Fletcher, D. I., Smith, L., Kapoor, A., Rail rolling contact fatigue dependence on friction, predicted using fracture mechanics with a three-dimensional boundary element model, Engineering Fracture Mechanics 76 (2009) 2 612–2 625.

[14] Guagliano, M., Sangirardi, M., Vergani, L., Experimental analysis of surface cracks in rails under rolling contact loading, Wear 265 (2008) 1 380–1 386.

[15] Hoffmeyer, J., Döring, R., Seeger, T., Vormwald, M., Deformation behaviour, short crack growth and fatigue livesunder multiaxial nonproportional loading, International Journal of Fatigue 28 (2006) 508–520.

[16] Hourlier, F., Pineau, A., Propagation of fatigue cracks under polymodal loading, Fatigue & Fracture of Engineering Materials & Structures 5 (1982) 287–302.

[17] Jacobson, B., Kalker, J. J., Rolling contact phenomena, Springer-Verlag Wien GmbH, New York, 2000.

[18] Jandora, R., Modelling of the railway wheelset movement considering real geometry, Engineering Mechanics 1 (2007) 105–106.

[19] Jandora, R., Numerical simulations of dynamic loads in wheel-rail contact with shape irregularities, Doctoral Thesis, Brno Univesity of Technology, 2012.

[20] Kabo, E., Ekberg, A., Fatigue initiation in railway wheels — a numerical study of the influence of defects, Wear 253 (2002) 26–34.

[21] Kalker, J. J., Paper I (iii) Elastic and viscoelastic analysis of two multiply layered cylinders rolling over each other with coulomb friction, Tribology Series 17 (1990) 27–34.

[22] Kalker, J. J., Three-dimensional elastic bodies in rolling contact, Springer – Science + Business Media, B.V., Waterloo, 1990.

[23] Kaneta, M., Murakami, Y., Propagation of semi-elliptical surface cracks in lubricated rolling/sliding elliptical contacts, Journal of Tribology 113 (1991) 270–275.

[24] Kaneta, M., Murakami, Y., Suetsugu, M., Mechanism of surface crack growth in lubricated rolling/sliding spherical contact, Journal of Applied Mcchanics 53 (1986) 354–360.

[25] Kaneta, M., Yatsuzuka, H., Murakami, Y., Mechanism of crack growth in lubricated rolling/sliding contact, A S L E Transactions 28 (1985) 407–414.

[26] Plank, R., Kuhn, G., Fatigue crack propagation under non-proportional mixed mode loading, Engineering Fracture Mechanics 62 (1999) 203–229.

[27] Richard, H. A., Fulland, M., Sander, M., Theoretical crack path prediction, Fatigue & Fracture of Engineering Materials & Structures 28 (2005) 3–12.

[28] Richard, H. A, Sander, M., Fulland, M., Kullmer, G., Development of fatigue crack growth in real structures, Engineering Fracture Mechanics 75 (2008) 331–340.

[29] Ringsberg, J. W, Bergkvist, A., On propagation of short rolling contact fatigue cracks, Fatigue & Fracture of Engineering Materials & Structures 26 (2003) 969–983.

[30] Smith, R. A., Fatigue in transport: problems, solutions and future threats, Process Safety and Environmental Protection 76 (1998) 217–223.

[31] Taraf, M., Zahaf, E. H., Oussouaddi, O., Zeghloul, A., Numerical analysis for predicting the rolling contact fatigue crack initiation in a railway wheel steel, Tribology International 43 (2010) 585–593.

[32] Wallentin, M., Bjarnehed, H. L., Lundén, R., Cracks around railway wheel flats exposed to rolling contact loads and residual stresses, Wear 258 (2005) 1 319–1 329.

[33] Weber, R. L., Manning, K. V., White, M. W., College Physics, 4th Edition, USA, McGraw-Hill, 1965.

[34] Wong, S. L., Bold, P. E., Brown, M. W., Allen, R. J., A branch criterion for shallow angled rolling contact fatigue cracks in rails, Wear 191 (1996) 45–53.

[35] Xu, X., Cho, D.-H., Chang, Y.-S., Choi, J.-B., Kim, Y.-J, Jun, H.-K., Seo, J.-W., Kim, D.-S., Evaluation of slant crack propagation under RCF in railway rail, Journal of Mechanical Science and Technology 25 (2011) 1 215–1 220.

[36] Zerbst, U., Mädler, K., Hintze, H., Fracture mechanics in railway applications — an overview, Engineering Fracture Mechanics 72 (2005) 163–194.

[37] Zerres, P., Brüning, J., Vormwald, M., Fatigue crack growth behavior of fine-grained steel S460N under proportional and non-proportional loading, Engineering Fracture Mechanics 77 (2010) 1 822–1 834.

8

Use of electromyography measurement in human body modeling

L. Valdmanová[a], H. Čechová[b,*]

[a] *Department of Mechanics, Faculty of Applied Sciences, University of West Bohemia, Univerzitní 8, 306 14 Plzeň, Czech Republic*
[b] *New Technologies — Research Centre, University of West Bohemia, Univerzitní 8, 306 14 Plzeň, Czech Republic*

Abstract

The aim of this study is to test the use of the human body model for the muscle activity computation. This paper shows the comparison of measured and simulated muscle activities. Muscle active states of biceps brachia muscle are monitored by method called electromyography (EMG) in a given position and for given subsequently increasing loads. The same conditions are used for simulation using a human body model (Hynčík, L., Rigid Body Based Human Model for Crash Test Purposes, Engineering Mechanics, 5 (8) (2001) 1–6). This model consists of rigid body segments connected by kinematic joints and involves all major muscle bunches. Biceps brachia active states are evaluated by a special muscle balance solver. Obtained simulation results show the acceptable correlation with the experimental results. The analysis shows that the validation procedure of muscle activities determination is usable.

Keywords: Hill-type model, muscle activity, EMG measurement

1. Introduction

Currently safety studies play one of the main roles in the automobile industry development. The crash tests usually performed with standard crash test dummies are very expensive in general and moreover dummies are not able to simulate the "real" life issues as vein pressure, tissues ruptures, muscles pre-stress etc. However experiments with biological tissues or even full scale cadavers are governed by ethical issues. Hence human body models become a powerful tool for a human-friendly and safe vehicles computer aided design. Recently automobile industry focuses on human body models which become more biofidelic as the computing techniques develop.

Previous works published by many authors described the influence of the pre-crash muscular activity on the impact for various body regions, i.e. [6].

The main aim of the study is to present a procedure of validation of a specific human body model using an electromyography (EMG) measurement. In particular the study determines the biceps brachia muscle forces of a previously developed human body model [4] and compares them to experimental results. For this purpose the static test with isometrically contracting biceps brachia muscle is performed. Measured EMG responses are compared to the muscle activity determined by a muscular balance solver [5]. Simulations are done in the computational environment of the PAM software [13]. The comparison of the obtained results of the simulation to the experiment is discussed.

---

*Corresponding author. e-mail: hcechov@ntc.zcu.cz.

2. Experiment

2.1. EMG theoretical base

EMG is the clinical measuring method based on the analysis of the electrical signal closely associated with muscle activations. The EMG is related to tension in such a way that the amplitude of the signal grows with the force generated by the muscle [14]. Muscle contraction is a muscle response to the electrical potential changes. Muscle fibers contract when the action potentials of the motor nerve achieve a depolarization threshold. This action generates an electromagnetic field and the potential is measured as the voltage [7].

The EMG signal is usually measured with two kinds of electrodes — surface or fine wire. Measuring by surface electrodes enables global examination of muscular electrical activity while fine wire electrodes monitor the signal of only several muscle fibers close to the electrode. Advantages of the surface electrodes are painless, easy application and a global response of a monitored muscle. Hence surface electrodes are used for the presented experiment.

2.2. The experimental setup

The static test is performed by measuring the EMG activity on the biceps brachia muscle when carrying a given load. The biceps brachia muscle is the biggest muscle of the upper arm. It starts with two heads (caput longum and caput breve) on the scapula near by the limb and finish by the main tendon on the radius. The main function of this muscle is the elbow flexion and it also contributes to the elbow supination [10]. It is situated nearly under the skin so it could be very clearly touched. Therefore, it is suitable for the monitoring using surface electrodes.

Fig. 1 shows the test setup. The biceps brachia is not the main elbow flexor in this position, however it is a large surface muscle suitable for surface EMG monitoring without cross talks. The volunteer holds his right hand flexed in the elbow such that the upper arm and the forearm form the right angle. The palm is turned to the body. This very simple position is chosen to eliminate possible inaccuracies.

The weight is hung in the supposed palm center of gravity to eliminate voluntary muscle contractions caused by holding the load. Such load placement is chosen with regard to following simulation since each rigid body segment of the model can by loaded only in its gravity centre.

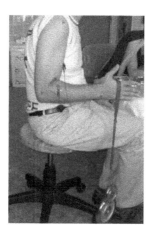

Fig. 1. EMG measurement, signal recording while carrying imposed load

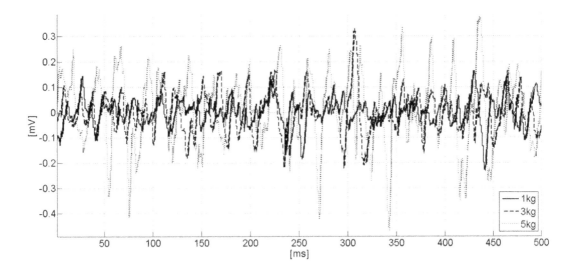

Fig. 2. Raw EMG signal; comparison of EMG biceps brachia response to different loads

The electrodes are stuck on the skin and the EMG signal of isometric muscle contraction for various loads is monitored. The active electrode is situated upon the muscle bunch, reference electrode upon the tendon. The third electrode supports the grounding. The resulting EMG signal is the difference between the active and reference electrode. The hand is subsequently loaded by the weights from 0.5 kg to 5 kg stepwise increased with the increment 0.5 kg. Each case is four times repeated with sufficient rest period.

2.3. Signal processing

The raw EMG output is the EMG activity-time relation as shown in Fig. 2. In general the EMG amplitude increases with the increasing contraction force and contraction velocity [3]. However there is no clear dependency between the force and EMG amplitude. Presented test analyzes isometric contractions hence the influence of contraction velocity is eliminated. Simultaneously the particular measurements are also isotonic thus the mean value of the EMG signal corresponds to the muscle force generated to keep the given loaded position [14].

Firstly, the raw EMG signal has to be processed. During recording all signals are filtered by the low pass filter with the cut-off frequency of 10 kHz and the high pass filter with the cut-off frequency of 20 Hz as recommended in [14]. To obtain the muscle activity generated during performed contraction the mean value of the full-wave rectified signal is calculated. The full-wave rectification equals the absolute value of EMG usually with a positive polarity. The original EMG has a mean value of zero but the full-wave rectified signal does not cross through zero. Hence, it has an average that fluctuates with the strength of the muscle contraction [14]. The full-wave rectified signals with their mean values are shown in Fig. 3. Described process is applied on each measurement and computed mean values for each load are averaged. The computed average activities of biceps brachia muscle are displayed in Table 1.

Usually the measured EMG signal is normalized by the EMG signal generated by the maximal isometric muscle contraction, see [1], [2] or [3]. The main question now is how to exactly determine the maximal isometric contraction. To avoid inaccuracies and to ensure the measurement reproducibility instead of maximal isometric contraction the quantities of the maximal applied loads are taken. Hence each obtained mean value of the EMG amplitude is normalized

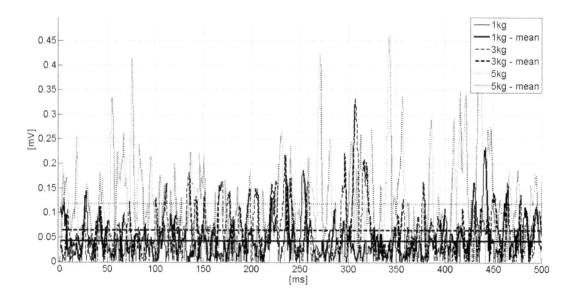

Fig. 3. Full–wave rectified EMG signal with its mean value; comparison for different loads

Table 1. The average EMG values for each load

No.	Load [kg]	Mean EMG values [mV] $mean\_r\_EMG$	
		Average value	Standard deviation
1	0.5	0.028 6	0.005 3
2	1.0	0.040 2	0.003 3
3	1.5	0.049 8	0.003 3
4	2.0	0.062 1	0.004 7
5	2.5	0.068 3	0.012 8
6	3.0	0.069 9	0.005 9
7	3.5	0.078 1	0.006 7
8	4.0	0.094 2	0.008 8
9	4.5	0.095 1	0.011 9
10	5.0	0.118 1	0.005 1

by the maximal measured mean value of the EMG amplitude which corresponds to the case of 5 kg load. The same normalization is then applied as well in simulation presented bellow.

3. Computer reconstruction

The experimental test is performed in the environment of the PAM software.

3.1. Human body model

The used rigid body based human model is called Robby and it has been developed during the long time cooperation with the ESI Group company. The Robby's development and validation

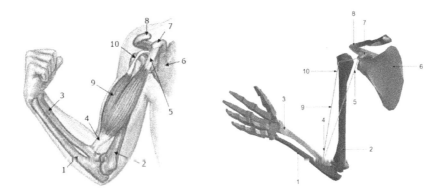

Fig. 4. The biceps brachia muscle structure: 1 – ulna, 2 – humerus, 3 – radius, 4 – tendon, 5 – caput breve, 6 – scapula, 7 – coracoid apex, 8 – coracoid process, 9 – biceps, 10 – caput longum

is described in [4]. The model is designed mainly for automotive safety application. This articulated rigid body model represents a 50th percentile human male with anthropometry according to [8]. It is implemented in the PAM software. The rigid body segments are connected by kinematic joints. The human body model accommodates all major muscles. Each skeletal muscle is modeled by bar elements (one or a set) connected to bones in order to perform a correct muscle function. Muscle behavior is defined according to a Hill-type model [16]. Muscle physiological properties as pennation angle, maximal isometric force, and optimal length are set according to published sources [12] and [9]. Separated upper arm model with the biceps brachia muscle is shown in Fig. 4 in comparison with the real anatomical architecture.

3.2. Skeletal muscle model

The Hill-type muscle model consists of the active and passive parts (see Fig. 5). The active part is represented by the contractile element (CE), which substitutes the contractile mechanism. The parallel connected passive part is modeled by the visco-elastic element (VE) and substitutes the collagen and elastin network of the muscle tissue.

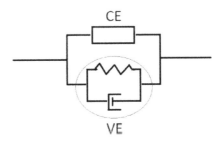

Fig. 5. Schema of Hill-type model

The resultant force of the whole muscle element is computed as the sum of forces of its elements

$$F_{mus} = F_{CE} + F_{VE}, \tag{1}$$

where F_{CE} is the active force of the muscle and F_{VE} is the passive force. The active force is defined as

$$F_{CE} = N_a(t) \cdot F_L(l) \cdot F_v(v), \tag{2}$$

where $N_a(t)$ is the muscle active state, $F_L(l)$ is the force-length characteristic and $F_v(v)$ is the force-velocity characteristic. The dependencies $N_a(t)$, $F_L(l)$, $F_v(v)$ are driven by relations mentioned below or can be directly defined by the user.

The muscle active state, $N_a(t)$, is interpreted as the ratio of a current value of muscle active force to the maximal force that can be exerted by a given muscle at a given length and elongation/shortening rate. Then $N_a(t)$ is dimensionless quantity ranging from its minimal possible value A_{min} to its maximum activation equal to 1. Based on the literature [13] it can be estimated that in vivo $A_{min} = 0.005$. The state where $N_a = 1$ corresponds to fully tetanized muscle. Active muscle state dynamics is driven by a set of two ordinary differential equations

$$T_{ne}\frac{\mathrm{d}N_e}{\mathrm{d}t} = u - N_e, \tag{3}$$

$$T_a\frac{\mathrm{d}Na}{\mathrm{d}t} = N_e - N_a, \tag{4}$$

where N_e is the neuromuscular excitation, T_{ne} is the time constant of excitation, and T_a is the time constant of activation and u is the neuro-controller output signal [13].

The active force-length characteristic function $F_L(l)$ depends on the instantaneous muscle length l and respects the relation

$$F_L(l) = F_{\max}\exp\left(-\left(\frac{\frac{l}{l_{opt}} - 1}{C_{sh}}\right)^2\right), \tag{5}$$

where C_{sh} is the shape parameter that determines the concavity of the muscle force-length characteristic [13].

The muscle force-velocity characteristic function has different forms for muscle elongation and shortening

$$F_v(v_n) = \begin{cases} 0 & v_n \leq -1 \\ \frac{C_{short}(1+v_n)}{C_{short}-v_n} & -1 < v_n \leq 0, \\ \frac{C_{leng}+C_{mvl}v_n}{C_{leng}+v_n} & v_n > 0 \end{cases} \tag{6}$$

where v_n is the muscle elongation/shortening rate normalized to the maximum shortening velocity v_{max}, $v_n = v/v_{max}$; C_{short} and C_{leng} are the Hill-type shape parameters for muscle shortening and lengthening, respectively, and C_{mvl} is the parameter which determines the ratio of ultimate force during active lengthening to the isometric force at full activation [13].

In the presented test the unknown muscle active force F_{CE} is searched. Since the test is a static isometric problem, $F_v = 1$, $F_L = \text{const}$ and $F_{CE} = N_a \cdot \text{const}$. Hence it can be said that the active muscle force is proportional to the muscle active state.

3.3. Muscular balance solver

The musculo-skeletal system is overdetermined. It means that from the mechanical point of view it is possible to get the actual position by activation of different muscles. Hence it is necessary to solve the problem by an optimization method. The question now is which cost function to choose. In [11] the summary of various cost functions is published. In the presented study a special muscular balance solver is used [5]. It includes the cost function that minimizes muscular discomfort while respecting the main muscle role, i.e. if the muscle belongs to a group of agonists or antagonists. Agonists are the main actors of a movement while antagonists oppose the movement. The resultant muscle active force is also influenced by the parameter involving a voluntary muscle contraction. A human subject can carry a given load in a given posture under more or less overall voluntary muscle contraction (0–100 %). So the voluntary contraction can be expressed as an ability of human being to willingly tense its muscles without carrying any load. The level of voluntary contraction is the input parameter defined by the user.

The muscular balance solver [5] evaluates the activations for all particular muscles to keep a given loaded position involving the cost function which can be represented as the least possible muscle energy that should be expended for the given task. Constrains are represented by force and momentum equilibrium equations of all body segments. As the output the muscle active forces (F_{CE}) are obtained. Further the active forces are using the Hill muscle model, described in the previous paragraph, converted to muscle active states (N_a).

3.4. Simulation setup

The human body model Robby is positioned in accordance to the experiment. The right upper arm is right angled in the elbow and the hand canter of gravity is loaded. The Robby's right upper arm including muscle elements is displayed in Fig. 6. All joint elements except the elbow and the wrist are locked to keep the same position during the loading of the hand as in the experiment. No voluntary contraction is assumed. Since the volunteer's physical proportions correspond to a 50th male as well as the Robby no model scaling is applied.

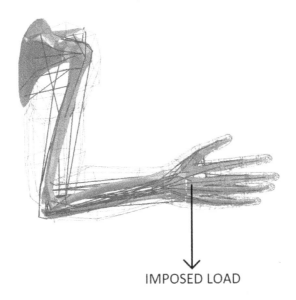

IMPOSED LOAD

Fig. 6. Loaded Robby's right upper extremity

4. Results

Whether the relationship between EMG signal and muscle tension is linear, it has been the subject of many studies. Despite that, the EMG signal is often used as an estimate of the active state defined in the Hill-type muscle element [2]. In general, the relation $N_a(t)$ describes the muscle response to the neurocontroller input signal, and the output of this process is similar to a rectified, normalized, and slightly filtered EMG [15].

In presented case of isometric and isotonic contraction the muscle active state is constant in time and corresponds to the normalized mean value of the full-wave rectified EMG signal, $mean\_r\_EMG$. As described above all measured and processed EMG signals are normalized by the maximum measured case, $mean\_r\_EMG_{max}$, i.e. the one with the 5 kg load.

Further using the muscular balance solver the values of biceps brachia active muscle states, N_a, are computed for ten different loads. Obtained values determine muscle activities that are exerted by the biceps brachia to keep the hand loaded by the weights from 0.5 kg to 5 kg in the given position. All computed cases are normalized by N_{amax}, i.e. N_a computed for the load of 5 kg. The ratio of the computed normalized muscle activations then corresponds to measured normalized EMG responses and can be compared:

$$\frac{mean\_r\_EMG_i}{mean\_r\_EMG_{max}} \approx \frac{N_{ai}}{N_{amax}}, \tag{7}$$

where $i = 1, \ldots, 10$. The measured and computed results are summarized in Table 2.

Table 2. The comparison of the measured and computed active muscle states of biceps brachia muscle; all measured/computed cases are normalized by the measured/computed cases with 5 kg of load

No.	Weight [kg]	Normalized active muscle state [–]		Difference [%]
		Measurement $\frac{mean\_r\_EMG}{mean\_r\_EMG_{max}}$	Simulation $\frac{N_a}{N_{amax}}$	
1	0.5	0.242	0.266	9.0
2	1.0	0.340	0.300	11.8
3	1.5	0.421	0.358	14.9
4	2.0	0.526	0.450	14.4
5	2.5	0.578	0.559	3.3
6	3.0	0.591	0.671	11.9
7	3.5	0.661	0.783	15.6
8	4.0	0.798	0.893	10.6
9	4.5	0.805	1.000	19.6
10	5.0	1.000	1.000	0.0

5. Conclusion

The paper introduces the procedure of the human model Robby validation using the EMG measurement. The comparison of measured and simulated muscle activities of biceps brachia, the greatest muscle of the upper arm is shown. The paper presents as well the method of EMG application in human body modeling using Hill muscle model in general.

Firstly, muscle activations were monitored by clinical electromyography in a given unchanging position and for given loads. While keeping still the same upper arm position for the various loads the biceps brachia muscle responses were recorded. Each case was four times repeated to get relevant statistical data set. The EMG signal was monitored by the surface electrodes and processed. Then the same conditions were simulated using the human body model Robby. The Robby's right arm is positioned according to the experiment. The hand center of gravity is subsequently loaded by the forces corresponding to the used weights. Using the muscular balance solver the activations of the arm muscle are calculated for each case based on the optimization method.

Normalized measured and computed muscle activations of the biceps brachia muscle show an acceptable correlation. The procedure presents a possible way of validation of muscle activity determination in the Robby model. Robby model can be used for the muscle activity computation without bigger falsities.

The numerical human body models used this way bring the possibility to simulate the "real" life in contrast to dummies. Presented method enables to involve for example pre-crash muscle activities into computer simulations and contribute to development in passive safety.

Acknowledgements

The work is supported by the internal grant project SGS-2010-077. Special thanks belong to prof. MUDr. Zdeněk Ambler, DrSc., from FN Plzeň.

References

[1] Bogey, R. A., Perry, J., Gitter, A. J., An EMG-to-Force Processing Approach for Determining Ankle Muscle Forces During Gait. IEEE Transactions on Neural Systems and Rehabilitation Engineering, 10 (3) (2005) 302–310.

[2] Craik, R. L., Oatis, C. A., Gait analysis, Mosby, 1994.

[3] Electromyography, Kompendium, (in Czech)
http://biomech.ftvs.cuni.cz/pbpk/kompendium/biomechanika/experiment_metody_emg.php.

[4] Hynčík, L., Rigid Body Based Human Model for Crash Test Purposes, Engineering Mechanics, 5 (8) (2001) 1–6.

[5] PAM-Muscle Solution — Dedicated to Muscular Balance Calculation, Reference Manual, ESI Group, France, 2009.

[6] Pithioux, M., Chavet, P., St-Onge, N., Nicol, C., Influence of muscle preactivation of the lower limb on impact dynamics in case of frontal collision, International Journal of Crashworthiness, 10 (2005) 557–565.

[7] Rash, G. S., Electromyography Fundamentals, Western Washington University.
http://myweb.wwu.edu/ chalmers/EMGfundamentals.pdf.

[8] Robbins, D. H., Anthropometric Specifications for Mid sized Male Dummy, The University of Michigan, 1983.

[9] Seireg, A., Biomechanicaal Analysis of Musculoskeletal Structure for Medicin and Sports, Hemisphere Publishing Corporation, 1989.

[10] Sinělnikov, R. D., Atlas of human anatomy I., AVICENUM, Praha, 1980 (in Czech).

[11] Tsirakos, D., Baltzopoulos, V., Bartlett, R., Inverse optimization: functional and physiological considerations related to the force-sharing problem, Critical Reviews in Biomedical Engineering (25) (1997) 371–407.

[12] Valenta, J., Konvičková, S., Valerián, D., Biomechanics of human sceletal articulations, ČVUT, Praha, 1999 (in Czech).

[13] Virtual Performance Solution-Solver Notes Manual, ESI Group, France, 2009.

[14] Winter, D. A., Biomechanics and Motor Control of Human Movement, Willey & Sons, INC, Waterloo, 2005.

[15] Winters, J. M., Stark, L., Estimated mechanical properties of synergistic muscles involved in movements of a variety of human joints, Journal of Biomechanics 21 (12) (1988) 1 027–1 041.

[16] Wittek, A., Mathematical Modeling of the Muscle Effects on the Human Body Responses under Transient Loads, Chalmers University of Technology, Sweden, 2000.

9

A model of Engineering Materials Inspired by Biological Tissues

M. Holeček[a], F. Moravec[a,*], J. Vychytil[a]

[a] *Faculty of Applied Sciences, University of West Bohemia, Univerzitní 22, 306 14 Plzeň, Czech Republic*

Abstract

The perfect ability of living tissues to control and adapt their mechanical properties to varying external conditions may be an inspiration for designing engineering materials. An interesting example is the smooth muscle tissue since this "material" is able to change its global mechanical properties considerably by a subtle mechanism within individual muscle cells. Multi-scale continuum models may be useful in designing essentially simpler engineering materials having similar properties. As an illustration we present the model of an incompressible material whose microscopic structure is formed by flexible, soft but incompressible balls connected mutually by linear springs. This simple model, however, shows a nontrivial nonlinear behavior caused by the incompressibility of balls and is very sensitive on some microscopic parameters. It may elucidate the way by which "small" changes in biopolymer networks within individual muscular cells may control the stiffness of the biological tissue, which outlines a way of designing similar engineering materials. The 'balls and springs' material presents also prestress-induced stiffening and allows elucidating a contribution of extracellular fluids into the tissue's viscous properties.

Keywords: living tissues, smooth muscles, prestressed cytoskeleton, tissues viscoelasticity, control of stiffness

1. Introduction

Living organisms are far more complex than the most complicated engineering structures. Namely they provide many different functions such as metabolism, growth, remodeling, reproduction as well as control, sensing and communication allowing them to react to a wide spectrum of changing physical conditions. The fact that the structure of living tissues has been "designed" during hundred millions of years of evolution indicates that it must be optimized in a way that cannot be expected in engineering structures being evolved for hundreds or even tens of years. May we learn some "tricks" that has been used by Nature in construction of such effective structures? The problem is that the detailer study of the living tissues is done, the more complicated details and connections are found out. The picture becomes very complex and some features that may be important for our engineering inspiration remain unnoticed. Here, the role of oversimplified physical and mechanical models may be very important. Namely, they may discover some "right" views that neglect many complications and details and highlight only certain features that may be an inspiration how designing novel engineering solutions.

In this contribution we look for an inspiration in the structure of smooth muscle tissues that have remarkable mechanical properties. Their ability to adapt to the whole scale of external conditions by rapid changes of their mechanical properties is enormous. They are able to undergo extremely large deformations without damaging their structure and return back. Special mechanisms in the cytoskeleton (a protein fiber network that spans living cells) are able

---

*Corresponding author. e-mail: fanny@kme.zcu.cz.

to change mechanical properties of this tissue in several orders. There is no doubt about the usefulness of materials with such properties in the industry. How are they designed?

From a strictly chemical viewpoint, the basic structure of living tissues is formed from complex conglomerates of various polymer fibers saturated by several kinds of liquid solutions [1]. Mechanical properties of this kind of condensed matter are given both by mechanical behavior of arrangements of elaborately linked and entanglement fibers as well as the presence of liquids. Generally, such structures are soft and practically *incompressible*. The fact differentiating living tissues from other kinds of such soft matter structures is their *special arrangement* in the form of living cells (at sizes of tens or hundreds micrometers) delimited by thin (~ 7 nm) *membranes* that are highly sophisticated structure of phospholipid and protein molecules – see Fig. 1. There are many reasons why living tissues are designed in such a manner. The cell structure indeed allows organisms to perform many tasks very effectively (e.g. metabolism or reproduction). We notice, above all, how such arrangement may be important in explaining special mechanical properties of smooth muscle tissues.

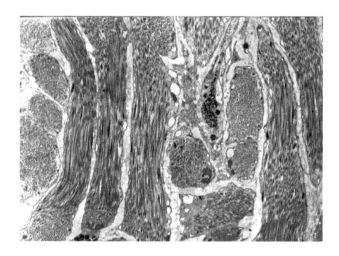

Fig. 1. Section through the smooth muscle cells of a gastropod (scale 5 μm), [8]

At macroscopic scales, living tissues may be understood as viscoelastic materials. Their viscoelasticity is, however, determined by other mechanisms than that of pure polymeric materials. Again the special structure of living tissues plays the important role. Namely, the polymeric viscosity is supplemented by effects connected with the flow of extracellular fluids around individual cells. We study this effect in our simplified model. The results may be also interesting when designing special engineering materials with a similar structure.

The paper is organized as follows. In the second paragraph we present a simple model material, motivated by basic features of a tissue structure, consisting of incompressible but flexible balls connected mutually by linear linkages. We show briefly some interesting properties of such a structure that is highly nonlinear, especially when the stiffness of balls is essentially smaller than that of their links. The third paragraph is devoted to the situation when the balls are prestressed. We show how the effect of prestress-induced stiffening, that occurs in living tissues, may be easily explained by this simple model material. The fourth paragraph deals with involving the viscoelasticity of the structure caused by movement of the fluid around balls during its deformations. Paper finishes with concluding remarks in the fifth paragraph.

2. Balls and springs

Let us imagine an incompressible structure consisting of identical flexible (very soft) balls filled with a fluid and joined mutually by elastic linkages. Because the balls are very soft, the deformation of the structure is realized predominantly by changes of their shapes so that the extracellular springs deform only a little. As a result, the material is very soft too as evidenced by a simple estimation of the stiffness

$$k_{est} \approx \left(k_s^{-1} + k_b^{-1}\right)^{-1} , \tag{1}$$

where k_s, k_b is the linkage and the ball stiffness respectively, see also Fig. 2. If k_b is very small in comparison with k_s, the structure stiffness k_{est} is near to k_b, i.e. $k_{est} \sim k_b$. It means that if balls become perfectly soft, i.e. $k_b \sim 0$, the structure is infinitely soft too. It, however, cannot happen if there exist some constraints on the balls' deformation preventing cases where none of all extracellular springs is deformed. Such a constraint adds some correction to the formula (1) and the structure becomes stiffer.

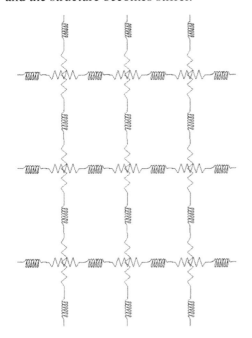

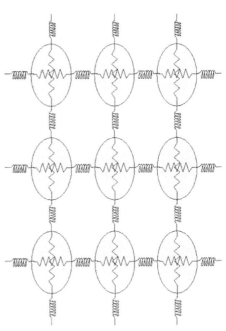

Fig. 2. The idealized 'balls and springs' material (without constraint on the balls) behaves as an arrangement of springs (with no coupling between the different space directions)

Fig. 3. The studied 'balls and springs' material includes a constraint on the balls' volume

A typical constraint of this kind is realized when the balls keep their volume to be *constant*, i.e. the balls are incompressible. Then, the formula (1) ceases to be valid if k_b is small regarding to k_s. Some nonlinear "structural effects" appear that correct the effective stiffness of the material. To estimate them, we define the simplest form of the *'balls and springs' material* (a continuum limit of the structure presented in Fig. 3) [2]: the structure is regular, the springs connecting the balls are linear and the balls are reinforced by some linear springs that define the balls stiffness. The strain-energy function of this material, W_{BS}, consists of two parts,

$$W_{BS} = W_{spring} + W' , \tag{2}$$

where W_{spring} is the strain-energy function of a structure in which the balls are fully compressible (i.e. the arrangement of linear springs shown in Fig. 2 which stiffness is expressed by (1)). The part W' corresponds to the structural effect caused by the incompressibility of balls. It is a nonlinear function that has to be determined numerically [2]. If the stiffness of balls is comparable with the stiffness of linkages or larger, the term W' is negligible. If the balls are essentially softer, the term W' is dominant and defines the mechanical properties of the structure (see Fig. 4).

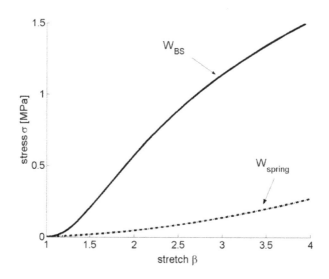

Fig. 4. Stresses resulting from the energies W_{BS} and W_{spring} in dependence on the stretch if the balls are essentially softer than the linkages ($k_i \approx 10^{-4}$), [2]

The most important result coming from the analysis of the 'balls and springs' material is as follows. Let β_i represent *principal stretches* at a point in a deformed state. The incompressibility of the material guarantees that

$$\beta_1 \beta_2 \beta_3 = 1 . \tag{3}$$

We define some "effective stretches" as

$$\beta_i^{eff} = \frac{1 + \delta_i}{1 + k_i}(\beta_i - 1) + 1 , \tag{4}$$

where k_i represents the ratio of stiffness of balls to stiffness of linkages in the i-th direction and δ_i is the ratio of the size of gap between balls to the ball dimension in the i-th direction. (Notice that $\beta_i^{eff} = 1$ whenever $\beta_i = 1$.) The study of the 'balls and springs' material shows [2] that if

$$\beta_1^{eff} \beta_2^{eff} \beta_3^{eff} = 1 , \tag{5}$$

the energy W' vanishes. At the point where (5) is valid the strain-energy function has a deep local minimum (see Fig. 5).The effective stretches (4) depend also on parameters of the structure, k_i and δ_i. When changing slightly these parameters, we leave the minimum and the stiffness of the material may considerable increase.

Might it be the essence of a "trick" of Nature allowing smooth muscle to change very effectively its overall stiffness by certain processes within the cellular cytoskeleton? The smooth muscle cells are usually (in normal conditions) considerably softer than the extracellular matrix,

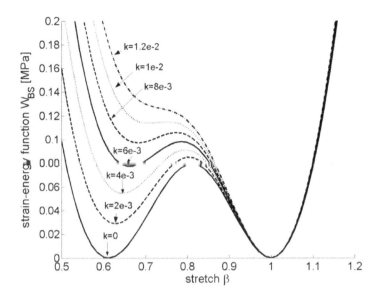

Fig. 5. The occurrence of a deep energy minimum in a (numerical) compression test of the 'balls and springs' material in dependence on the stretch ($\beta = 1$ represents the reference configuration), [2]

i.e. k_i are very small. Similarly, the gap between cells is very small compared to their size (in Fig. 1, the gap is about 250 nm) [9]. It means that β_i^{eff} are near to β_i that implies that the local state of the tissue is not far from the local minimum defined by (5) (since $\beta_1\beta_2\beta_3 = 1$). Small changes of cell stiffness (varying k_i) or their spatial dimensions (varying δ_i) thus may drive the material from/to the minimum and hence cause essential changes in its stiffness. In real smooth muscle cells, the molecular motors causes changes in strength of protein fibers that influence both the cells stiffness and their dimensions (i.e. all parameters k_i and δ_i may be varied in various manners).

3. The constant volume of cells as a control principle?

But smooth muscle cells are *not* balls with an impermeable surface filled with a constant amount of a fluid guaranteeing constancy of their volumes. The cell is an *open* system and there is a permanent exchange of the matter with its surrounding (a variable permeability of membrane lipid bilayers allows water to move across the plasma membrane if the osmotic strength of the extracellular space changes even by a small amount). Nevertheless, cells employ both short- and long-term strategies to *maintain a constant volume* by some mechanisms that compensate volume changes caused by flows through the membrane (e.g. cells respond to loss of water by activating ion pumps that bring ions into the cell and water follows, returning the cell to its original volume in minutes). These mechanisms are well defined, but how cells sense volume changes or trigger these responses is less clear [6].

Another question is *why* do cells sustain complicated mechanisms to keep their volumes constant upon any terms? The results obtained by studying a toy model of cellular structure – the 'balls and spring' material – might outline a partial answer. Namely, the maintenance of a constant volume may be explained as a simple *control mechanisms* allowing cells to tune and govern their mechanical properties. In a highly complicated structure of complex protein fibers, many deformable bodies, fluids carrying many chemical components, etc., the constant volume may serve as a "fix point" enabling cells to use complicated chemical mechanisms on polymer networks to produce *effectively* various macroscopically meaningful effects (forces, change of stiffness, movement etc.).

To support this idea we notice an interesting phenomena well-known in cellular mechanics. Namely, it is an experimental evidence that the cytoskeleton carries the pre-existing tension, the so-called prestress. Even at states with no outer load, the fibers are not relaxed. Since the cytoskeleton is responsible for the mechanical behavior of the whole cell, the prestress consequently plays an important role.

At the cellular level, the effect called prestress-induced stiffening is experimentally observed [13]. It means that with increasing prestress within cytoskeleton, the stiffness of the cell increases. This dependence is almost linear, as depicted in Fig. 6. The prestress is thus an important mechanism how cell controls its mechanical response. By increasing prestress, the stiffness increases and thus the cell actively resists deformation.

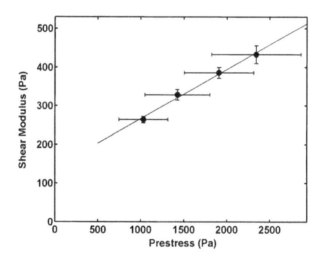

Fig. 6. The relation between prestress and shear modulus in smooth muscle cells [13]

Nevertheless, the prestress of a structure (e.g. a guitar with a tight string) may or may not mean the increase of the structure stiffness. If the stress in the guitar string depends linearly on its strain, for instance, the stiffening cannot occur. To find this effect in linear structures we have to suppose the existence of some elements – "bars" being able to carry a compression, that are combined with other elements in a special arrangement. It is popular to "sight" such structures (called the tensegrity, see e.g. [13]) as formed within the cellular cytoskeleton. Nevertheless, it is less clear how such complicatedly designed structures could be formed by spontaneous processes in cellular polymer networks, how their stability could be guaranteed, and so on.

When accepting the idea that cells control their volume to be constant, we can define the prestress simply by the assumption that the value of the volume maintained by a cell differs from that in which the cell might reach the minimum of energy [12]. In the case of the 'balls and springs' structure, the constant cell's volume is proportional to

$$V \equiv c_1^{ref} c_2^{ref} c_3^{ref} , \qquad (6)$$

where c_i^{ref} is the size of an individual ball in the i-th direction at the reference state (state with no external load). On the other hand, the volume vanishing the cell's energy is proportional to

$$V_0 \equiv c_1^{(0)} c_2^{(0)} c_3^{(0)} , \qquad (7)$$

where $c_i^{(0)}$ are the rest lengths of the cell's reinforcement (linear springs). The important assumption allowing us to incorporate the prestress into the 'balls and springs' structure is that V differs from V_0. For simplicity, let us suppose that

$$V \geq V_0 . \tag{8}$$

In the case of equality, there is no prestress within the structure. When the sharp inequality holds, the inner springs must be stretched to $c_i^{ref} > c_i^{(0)}$ to span the volume of V. In other words, constant volume works as a constraint which does not allow the inner springs to relax. For convenience, we introduce the (dimensionless) numbers

$$P_i = 1 - \frac{c_i^{(0)}}{c_i^{ref}} , \tag{9}$$

which values range from 0 (no prestress in the i-th direction) to 1 (limit value of prestress), to quantify the level of prestress.

The effect of prestress on the mechanical response of the corresponding 'balls and springs' material is determined via the strain-energy function [11]. To emphasize its dependence on prestress, the strain-energy function is denoted with W_{BS}^p. Analogous to (2), it can be divided into two contributions (both depending on prestress),

$$W_{BS}^p = W_{spring}^p + W_p' , \tag{10}$$

where W_{spring}^p is the "averaged" elasticity of springs and W_p' is the contribution due to the arrangement of microstructure. Analogous to the section 2, the "effective stretches" can be introduced as

$$^p\beta_i^{eff} = \frac{1+\delta_i}{1+k_i}(\beta_i - 1) + 1 - \frac{k_i}{1+k_i}P_i . \tag{11}$$

Compared to (4) an additional term appears due to prestress, see [11] for details. It is worth stressing that for zero prestress ($P_i = 0$, $\forall i$), the prestress-dependent quantities coincide with those defined in section 2,

$$W_{BS}^p \to W_{BS}, \quad W_{spring}^p \to W_{spring}, \quad W_p' \to W', \quad {}^p\beta_i^{eff} \to \beta_i^{eff} . \tag{12}$$

Prestress-induced stiffening of the 'balls and springs' material can be shown by determining the Young's modulus. It is defined as

$$Y_{BS} = \left. \frac{d^2 W_{BS}^p}{d\varepsilon^2} \right|_{\varepsilon=1} , \tag{13}$$

where ε is a small deformation ($\beta_1 = 1 + \varepsilon$, $\beta_2 = \beta_3 = (1+\varepsilon)^{-1/2}$ in the case of transverse isotropy). Unfortunately, it is not possible to determine the analytical solution of (13) in general. However, if

$$^p\beta_1^{eff}\, {}^p\beta_2^{eff}\, {}^p\beta_3^{eff} \approx 1 , \tag{14}$$

it is possible to find an approximative formula,

$$Y_{BS}(P_1) \approx Y_0 \left[1 + f \cdot P_1\right] , \tag{15}$$

where Y_0 is the Young's modulus of the structure with no prestress, and f is a function of material parameters [10, 11]. Notice that the condition (14) is fulfilled for any stretch and any prestress if $k_i \ll 1$ and $\delta_i \approx k_i$. It means that the approximative formula is accurate for the case of smooth muscles (cells are considerably softer than the extracellular matrix and gaps between neighbouring cells are very small compared to their sizes).

The result shows the linear dependence of the stiffness on the level of prestress for the 'balls and springs' material. In fact, it corresponds to the mechanical behavior of a single microscopic element that is composed of an individual ball (representing the smooth muscle cell) surrounded by extracellular matrix [10]. It is in qualitative agreement with the so-called prestress-induced stiffening that is observed for living cells (see Fig. 6). By increasing a pre-tension (caused by shortening the rest lengths of cytoskeletal fibers) the stiffness of the cell grows. The prestress can thus be understood as a mechanism by which the living cells control their overall mechanical response.

As the numerical simulations illustrate, the similar effect of the prestress-induced stiffening is exhibited for the 'balls and springs' material also at the macroscale. In Fig. 7, the uniaxial traction test with the macroscopic sample (sizes in the order of at least millimeters) is depicted. The level of prestress is set at the microscale since it corresponds to the change of rest lengths of fibres within individual balls (sizes of the order of micrometers). From the figure it is clear that by increasing the prestress the overall mechanical response is stiffer and the material thus resists deformation.

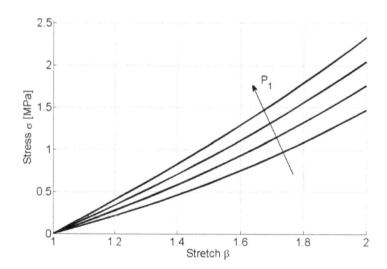

Fig. 7. Uniaxial traction test with the 'balls and springs' material. With an increasing prestress the material stiffens

4. Tissues' viscoelasticity

The 'balls and springs' model has been build on the hypothesis of elasticity. However a slight modification of the 'balls and springs' model allows us to catch a specific viscoelastic property that is also observed in biological tissues. Namely, when straining the tissue, the fluid filling the space between cells has to move. The reason is that the gap between neighbouring cells slightly varies and the fluid has to fill or drain the spaces. This movement is connected with some viscous forces that may be introduced in our model. The resulting continuum limit describes a material with internal variables.

In the continuum description, the thermodynamic state of elastic materials is fully deter-mined by two variables distributed in space, $\mathbf{F}$ and Θ, the deformation gradient and the tem-perature distribution, respectively. Concerning dissipative materials, other state variables are necessary to characterize the inelastic behavior of the material. Such variables usually cannot be defined as some macroscopic quantities. Nevertheless, we suppose a set of some "hidden" ones that are not directly accessible by experimental measurements at the macroscopic level. We call them the *internal variables*.

Let us suppose an occurrence of n scalar internal variables, α_i, $i = 1, \ldots, n$. If all processes are isothermal, an explicit dependence on the temperature may be omitted. The fact that the internal variables are state parameters implies that the Helmholtz free-energy function may be written in the form $\Phi = \Phi(\mathbf{F}, \boldsymbol{\alpha})$ (where $\boldsymbol{\alpha}$ represents the set of all internal variables α_i). Following [3], we assume the dissipation in the material to be characterized by functions Ξ_i such that the internal dissipation, D_{int}, is described as

$$D_{int} = \sum_{i=1}^{n} \Xi_i(\mathbf{F}, \dot{\mathbf{F}}, \boldsymbol{\alpha}, \dot{\boldsymbol{\alpha}}) \, \dot{\alpha}_i \,, \tag{16}$$

where the dot denotes the time derivative of the state variables. The second law of thermody-namics claims the validity of the Clausius-Planck inequality, namely

$$D_{int} = w_{int} - \dot{\Phi} \geq 0 \,, \tag{17}$$

where $w_{int} \equiv \Pi : \dot{\mathbf{F}}$ is the rate of internal work and Π is the first Kirchhoff stress measure. Applying the chain rule for the time derivative of the free-energy function, we obtain from (17) that

$$D_{int} = \left(\Pi - \frac{\partial \Phi}{\partial \mathbf{F}} \right) : \dot{\mathbf{F}} - \sum_{i=1}^{n} \frac{\partial \Phi}{\partial \alpha_i} \dot{\alpha}_i \geq 0 \,. \tag{18}$$

To fulfill the inequality (18) in all admissible processes the constitutive law,

$$\Pi = \frac{\partial \Phi(\mathbf{F}, \boldsymbol{\alpha})}{\partial \mathbf{F}} \,, \tag{19}$$

has to be valid. With (16), it implies that the time evolution of the n internal variables α_i is governed by n differential equations,

$$\Xi_i(\mathbf{F}, \dot{\mathbf{F}}, \boldsymbol{\alpha}, \dot{\boldsymbol{\alpha}}) + \frac{\partial \Phi(\mathbf{F}, \boldsymbol{\alpha})}{\partial \alpha_i} = 0 \,. \tag{20}$$

In absence of dissipation (i.e. if $\Xi_i - 0$) the differential equations (20) reduce to a system of non-linear equations

$$\frac{\partial \Phi(\mathbf{F}, \boldsymbol{\alpha})}{\partial \alpha_i} = 0, \tag{21}$$

fixing the internal variables to their expressions $\boldsymbol{\alpha}^*(\mathbf{F})$ minimizing the energy at a given macro-deformation, and the free-energy function reduces to the strain-energy function, i.e.

$$\Phi(\mathbf{F}, \boldsymbol{\alpha}^*(\mathbf{F})) = W_{BS}(\mathbf{F}). \tag{22}$$

On the contrary, the expression of the internal variables (solution of 20) are time-dependent, i.e. $\boldsymbol{\alpha}(t)$, when the dissipation is taken into account.

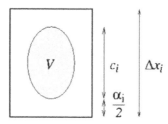

Fig. 8. Used notation in the RVE cross-section

With the 'balls and springs' structure, it is natural to associate the internal variables with some parameters characterizing the 'microstructure' as, for instance, the three principal dimensions of the gap separating neighboring balls. The balls dimensions c_i are functions of α_i and $\mathbf{F}$. Namely, they are given by the differences between the RVE dimensions, say Δx_i, and the distances α_i separating neighboring balls (see Fig. 8), i.e.

$$c_i(\mathbf{F}, \boldsymbol{\alpha}) = \Delta x_i(\mathbf{F}) - \alpha_i = \beta_i \Delta x_i^{ref} - \alpha_i \,, \tag{23}$$

where $\Delta x_i^{ref} = c_i^{ref} + \alpha_i^{ref}$ is the dimension of the RVE in the reference configuration. Since we consider the only dissipation involved by the extracellular fluid movement, the dissipation D_{int} is defined as the power of viscous forces necessary to fill or drain fluid in the gap between balls. Using the dimensional analysis we obtain [5] the expression

$$\Xi_i(\mathbf{F}, \dot{\mathbf{F}}, \boldsymbol{\alpha}, \dot{\boldsymbol{\alpha}}) = \frac{\dot{\alpha}_i}{\alpha_i^3} \frac{\tau G(c_j c_k)^2}{V^{rve}}, \quad j \neq k, \ i \neq j, \ i \neq k \,, \tag{24}$$

where G is a characteristic energy per volume (it is a function of the material stiffness), V^{rve} is the characteristic material size (volume of the Representative Volume Element of tissue) and $\tau \equiv \eta \kappa / 2G$ is a characteristic time of the problem (η is the viscosity of the extracellular fluid and κ is a dimensionless number).

The effect of the extra-cellular fluid viscosity on material behavior is clearly illustrated by the occurrence of hysteresis during cycles of loading/unlaoding tests, see Fig. 10. The loading and unloading branches differ, forming a loop which inner area measures the energy dissipation. A permanent loop (preconditioning) is reached after more or less cycles depending on material parameters.

5. Inspiration for engineering materials?

The 'balls and springs' material shows the way in which macroscopic mechanical properties of a specially designed material may be tuned by small changes within its structure. The main "trick" consists in occurrence of very soft cells within the material that are, however, firmly connected with surrounding (stiff) material. The incompressibility of cells then realizes a special linkage between deformations in different spatial directions. The tuning of the material stiffness consists in defining a measure of *how much* the stiff matrix has to deform in other directions to obtain the demanded deformation in a chosen direction. The existence of deep local minimum in the energy "landscape" means that small changes in material structure may influence the material stiffness essentially.

In engineering practice there are various materials (metals, wood, plastics, polymer composites and many others) whose mechanical properties depend on their structure and are governed

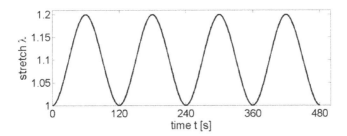

Fig. 9. Loading/unloading cycles. a strain oscillating between the values 0 and 20 % in a run of 60 s (as a polynomial of third degree) is applied to the material sample

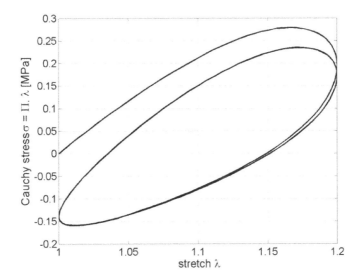

Fig. 10. The relationship between stress and stretch draws hysteresis loops when the loading process shown in Fig. 9 is applied. (The softening at the hysteresis angles results from the slowing of the stretch rate near the stretch peak $\lambda = 1$ or 1.2 due to the polynomial approximation.)

by different mechanisms in which the intermolecular forces play an important role. These forces also realize bindings among deformations in individual spatial directions so that they contribute to the material stiffness. The cellular structure of living tissues, however, allows tissues to use such bindings effectively so that the tissue may change its mechanical properties in a large extent. It may be an inspiration for designing some "smart" engineering materials – similar effects might arise, for example, in some special multi-phase polymer materials which materials sample manufacture is the object of our further efforts.

Another inspiration comes from a special "interaction" of fluids and the inclusions ("balls") within the structure. This special arrangement contributes in a special way to the structure viscous properties. This contribution has different properties than that coming only from the polymeric viscosity and depends on the structural parameters of the material. As a result, the viscous behavior of such a material might be also tuned by some microstructural changes.

Acknowledgements

The work has been supported by the grant project GAČR 106/09/0734.

References

[1] Alberts, B., Johnson, A., Lewis, J., Raff, M., Roberts, K., Walter, P., Molecular Biology of the Cell, Garland Science, New York, 2002.

[2] Holeček, M., Moravec, F., Hyperelastic model of a material which microstructure is formed by 'balls and springs', Int. J. Solids and Structures 43 (2006) 7 393–7 406.

[3] Holzapfel, G. A., Nonlinear Solid Mechanics. John Wiley & Sons, LTD (2001).

[4] Kochová, P., Tonar, Z., 3D reconstruction and mechanical properties of connective and smooth muscle tissue, in proceedings of Human Biomechanics, Congress of the Czech Society of Biomechanics, 1–9 (2006).

[5] Moravec, F., Holeček, M., Modelling the smooth muscle tissue as a dissipative microstructured material, in J.–F. Ganghoffer, F. Pastrone (Eds.), Mech. of Microstru. Solids, LNACM 46 (2009) 101––108.

[6] Pollard, T. D., Earnshaw, W. C., Cell Biology, W. B. Saunders Company, Philadelphia, 2004.

[7] Storm, C., Pastore, J. J., MacKintosh, F. C., Lubensky, T. C., Janmey, A. P., Nonlinear elasticity in biological gels, gels, Nature 435 (2005) 191–194.

[8] Tonar, Z., Markoš, A., Microscopy and morphometry of integument of the foot of pulmonate gastropods Arion rufus and Helix pomatia, Acta Veterinaria Brno 73 (2004) 3–8.

[9] Tonar, Z., Kochová, P., Janáček, J., Orientation, anisotropy, clustering, and volume fraction of smooth muscle cells within the wall of porcine abdominal aorta, Applied Comput. Mechanics 1 (2008) 145–156.

[10] Vychytil, J., Moravec, F., Holeček, M., Prestress in 'balls and springs' model, Applied Comput. Mechanics 1 (2007) 363–370.

[11] Vychytil, J., Holeček, M., Two-scale hyperelastic model of a material with prestress at cellular level, Applied Comput. Mechanics 2 (2008) 167–176.

[12] Vychytil, J., Holeček, M., The simple model of cell prestress maintained by cell incompressibility, Math. and Comput. in Simulations (in press).

[13] Wang, N., et al, Mechanical behavior in living cells consistent with the tensegrity model, PNAS 98 (2001) 7 765–7770.

10

Modal properties of the flexural vibrating package of rods linked by spacer grids

V. Zeman[a,*], Z. Hlaváč[a]

[a] *Faculty of Applied Sciences, University of West Bohemia, Univerzitní 22, 306 14 Plzeň, Czech Republic*

Abstract

The paper deals with the modelling and modal analysis of the large package of identical parallel rods linked by transverse springs (spacer grids) placed on several level spacings. The rod discretization by finite element method is based on Rayleigh beam theory. For the cyclic and central symmetric package of rods (such as fuel rods in nuclear fuel assembly) the system decomposition on the identical revolved rod segments was applied. A modal synthesis method with condensation is used for modelling of the whole system. The presented method is the first step for modelling the nuclear fuel assembly vibration caused by excitation determined by the support plate motion of the reactor core.

Keywords: package of rods, spacer grids, modelling of vibration, modal values, modal synthesis method

1. Introduction

Dynamic properties of nuclear fuel assembly (FA) are usually investigated using global models, whose properties are gained experimentally, as it was shown e.g. in [3, 6] and in several research reports elaborated mainly in OKB Gidropress Podolsk in Russia. Experimentally gained eigenfrequencies and eigenvectors serve as initial data for parametric identification of the American nuclear VVANTAGE6 FA [7] and Russian TVSA-T FA in nuclear power plant (NPP) Temelín [1]. These models, however, do not enable investigation of dynamic deformations and load of FA components, such as the fuel rods, guide thimbles, angle pieces, spacer grids and other.

Nuclear fuel assemblies are in term of mechanics very complicated systems of beamed type, whose basic structure is formed from large number of parallel rods linked by transverse spacer grids (Fig. 1). The spacer grids inside the every segment (gray) are shown by solid lines and within the segments by dashed lines. All springs at the level of one spacer grid are the same ones. All the rods are identical including boundary conditions. The goal of the paper is a development of analytical method for modelling and modal analysis of large package of parallel rods linked by spacer grids placed on several transverse planes.The variable modifying mathematical model of this large system will be in future used for modelling the nuclear FA vibration caused by pressure pulsations [9] and seismic excitation [1] in terms of fuel rods deformation and abrasion of fuel element coating [4]. The developed methodology and software can be used for vibration analysis of the different large parallel beam systems.

---

*Corresponding author. e-mail: zemanv@kme.zcu.cz.

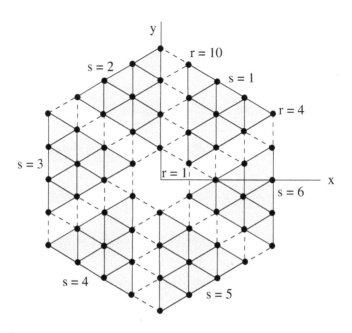

Fig. 1. The rod package cross-section with six segments linked by spacer grids

2. Mathematical model of the system

2.1. Modelling of the rod

The creation of a model is divided into three steps. The *first step* is the modelling of one isolated rod r in the segment s (see segment $s = 1$ in Fig. 2) by means of 1D beam finite elements [5] in the coordinate system

$$q_{r,s} = [\ldots, \xi_{r,g}^{(s)}, \eta_{r,g}^{(s)}, \vartheta_{r,g}^{(s)}, \psi_{r,g}^{(s)}, \ldots]^T, \quad g = 1, \ldots, G, \tag{1}$$

where $\xi_{r,g}^{(s)}$, $\eta_{r,g}^{(s)}$ are mutually perpendicular lateral displacements and $\vartheta_{r,g}^{(s)}$, $\psi_{r,g}^{(s)}$ are bending angles of rod cross-section in contact nodal point g on the level of grid g (in Fig. 3 $g = 1, 2, 3$). The directions of $\xi_{r,g}^{(s)}$ displacements are radial with respect to vertical axis of the package (nuclear fuel assembly).

The detailed model of the rod created by FEM is replaced by alternate rod devided into $G + 1$ prismatic beam elements in contact nodal points with grids. Every beam element is determined by parameters ρ (mass density), A (cross-section area), J (second moment of the cross-section area), l (length) and E (Young's modulus) for concrete material. Mathematical model of the beam element of the alternate rod in coordinate system with different displacement arrangement in comparison with (1)

$$q_{r,s}^* = [\ldots, \xi_{r,g}^{(s)}, \psi_{r,g}^{(s)}, \eta_{r,g}^{(s)}, \vartheta_{r,g}^{(s)}, \ldots]^T, \quad g = 1, \ldots, G, \tag{2}$$

which is more suitable for the beam element modelling, has the form [5]

$$M_e^* = \begin{bmatrix} S_1^{-T}(I_1 + I_2)S_1^{-1} & 0 \\ 0 & S_2^{-T}(I_1 + I_2)S_2^{-1} \end{bmatrix}; K_e^* = \begin{bmatrix} S_1^{-T}I_3S_1^{-1} & 0 \\ 0 & S_2^{-T}I_3S_2^{-1} \end{bmatrix}, \tag{3}$$

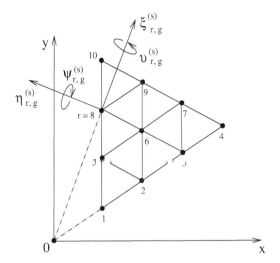

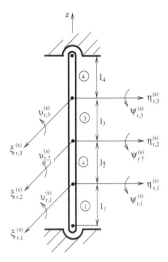

Fig. 2. Displacements of rod r of segment $s = 1$ in contact points with spacer grid g

Fig. 3. The displacements of rod r in segment s at the level of spacer grids

where

$$
\boldsymbol{I}_1 = \rho Al \begin{bmatrix} 1 & \frac{l}{2} & \frac{l^2}{3} & \frac{l^3}{4} \\ \frac{l}{2} & \frac{l^2}{3} & \frac{l^3}{4} & \frac{l^4}{5} \\ \frac{l^2}{3} & \frac{l^3}{4} & \frac{l^4}{5} & \frac{l^5}{6} \\ \frac{l^3}{4} & \frac{l^4}{5} & \frac{l^5}{6} & \frac{l^6}{7} \end{bmatrix}, \quad
\boldsymbol{I}_2 = \rho Jl \begin{bmatrix} 0 & 0 & 0 & 0 \\ 0 & 1 & l & l^2 \\ 0 & l & \frac{4l^2}{3} & \frac{3l^3}{2} \\ 0 & l^2 & \frac{3l^3}{2} & \frac{9l^4}{5} \end{bmatrix},
$$

$$
\boldsymbol{I}_3 = EJl \begin{bmatrix} 0 & 0 & 0 & 0 \\ 0 & 0 & 0 & 0 \\ 0 & 0 & 4 & 6l \\ 0 & 0 & 6l & 12l^2 \end{bmatrix}, \quad
\boldsymbol{S}_1 = \begin{bmatrix} 1 & 0 & 0 & 0 \\ 0 & 1 & 0 & 0 \\ 1 & l & l^2 & l^3 \\ 0 & 1 & 2l & 3l^2 \end{bmatrix}, \quad
\boldsymbol{S}_2 = \begin{bmatrix} 1 & 0 & 0 & 0 \\ 0 & -1 & 0 & 0 \\ 1 & l & l^2 & l^3 \\ 0 & -1 & -2l & -3l^2 \end{bmatrix}.
$$

For model transposition into general coordinates $\boldsymbol{q}_{r,s}$ defined in (1) mass and stiffness matrices must be transformed in the form

$$
\boldsymbol{X}_e = \boldsymbol{P}^T \boldsymbol{X}_e^* \boldsymbol{P}, \quad \boldsymbol{X} = \boldsymbol{M}, \boldsymbol{K}, \tag{4}
$$

where permutation matrix is

$$
\boldsymbol{P} = \begin{bmatrix} 1 & 0 & 0 & 0 & 0 & 0 & 0 & 0 \\ 0 & 0 & 0 & 1 & 0 & 0 & 0 & 0 \\ 0 & 0 & 0 & 0 & 1 & 0 & 0 & 0 \\ 0 & 0 & 0 & 0 & 0 & 0 & 0 & 1 \\ 0 & 1 & 0 & 0 & 0 & 0 & 0 & 0 \\ 0 & 0 & 1 & 0 & 0 & 0 & 0 & 0 \\ 0 & 0 & 0 & 0 & 0 & 1 & 0 & 0 \\ 0 & 0 & 0 & 0 & 0 & 0 & 1 & 0 \end{bmatrix}.
$$

By FE summation we get the mass and stiffness matrices of the alternative rod (subscript R) in the block diagonal form

$$
\boldsymbol{X}_R = [x_{ij}^{(R)}] = \sum_{e=1}^{G+1} \text{diag}\,[0, \boldsymbol{X}_e, 0], \quad \boldsymbol{X} = \boldsymbol{M}, \boldsymbol{K}, \quad x = m, k, \tag{5}
$$

with block matrices $\boldsymbol{X}_e$ determined in (4). Matrices in (5) must be arranged in accordance with boundary conditions. The modal behaviour of the conservative mathematical model of the alternate rod is determined by the matrix equation of motion

$$\boldsymbol{M}_R \ddot{\boldsymbol{q}}_{r,s} + \boldsymbol{K}_R \boldsymbol{q}_{r,s} = \boldsymbol{0}. \qquad (6)$$

Eigenfrequencies Ω_ν and eigenvectors $\boldsymbol{v}_\nu$ of one isolated alternate rod depend on global material parameters ρ, E and local geometrical parameters A_e, J_e ($e = 1, \ldots, G+1$) of the beam elements. The aim of tuning of the mathematical model (6) is to change the values of the above-mentioned parameters to new values to achieve required modal values. Global material and local geometrical parameters, that will be changed, constitute a vector of tuning parameters $\boldsymbol{p} = [p_j]$. The selected tuned modal values — eigenfrequencies and eigenvectors coordinates — form the vector of tuning $\boldsymbol{l} = [\ldots, \Omega_\nu, \ldots, \boldsymbol{v}_\nu, \ldots]^T$ and the desired vector of tuning $\boldsymbol{l}^* = [\ldots, \Omega_\nu^*, \ldots, \boldsymbol{v}_\nu^*, \ldots]^T$, where Ω_ν^* and $\boldsymbol{v}_\nu^*$ are eigenfrequencies and eigenvectors calculated from the detailed finite element model or experimentally obtained. The tuning problem of the alternate rod model can be formulated as an optimization problem with the objective function

$$\psi(\boldsymbol{p}) = \sum_i g_i \left[1 - \frac{l_i(\boldsymbol{p})}{l_i^*} \right], \qquad (7)$$

where g_i is a weighted coefficient corresponding to i-th coordinate of vectors $\boldsymbol{l}(\boldsymbol{p})$ and $\boldsymbol{l}^*$. The tuning parameters are constrained by lower and upper limits

$$\boldsymbol{p}_L \leq \boldsymbol{p} \leq \boldsymbol{p}_U. \qquad (8)$$

2.2. Modelling of the rod segment

The *second step* is the modelling of the rod segment s (see segment $s = 1$ in Fig. 1) in which the rods are linked by transverse springs with small prestressing placed on several level spacings $g = 1, \ldots, G$. The stiffnesses k_g of the springs in one lateral horizontal plane are identical. The generalized coordinates of the segment s are

$$\boldsymbol{q}_s = [\boldsymbol{q}_{1,s}^T, \boldsymbol{q}_{2,s}^T, \ldots, \boldsymbol{q}_{r,s}^T, \ldots, \boldsymbol{q}_{R,s}^T]^T, \qquad (9)$$

where R is number of the rods in the segment. The deformation $d_{q,g}^{(s)}$ of the spring k_g between two rods u and v of the segment s (see Fig. 4), modelling the coupling q by means of spacer grid g, is

$$d_{q,g}^{(s)} = \xi_{v,g}^{(s)} \cos \gamma_q + \eta_{v,g}^{(s)} \sin \gamma_q + \xi_{u,g}^{(s)} \cos \beta_q - \eta_{u,g}^{(s)} \sin \beta_q. \qquad (10)$$

The stiffness matrix $\boldsymbol{K}_{qg}$ corresponding to this coupling results from identity

$$\frac{\partial E_{q,g}^{(s)}}{\partial \boldsymbol{q}_s} = \boldsymbol{K}_{qg} \boldsymbol{q}_s, \qquad (11)$$

where $E_{q,g}^{(s)} = \frac{1}{2} k_g (d_{q,g}^{(s)})^2$ is potential (deformation) energy of latter coupling. This matrix has the form

$$\boldsymbol{K}_{qg} = k_g \begin{bmatrix} & \vdots & & \vdots & \\ \cdots & \boldsymbol{A}_q & \cdots & \boldsymbol{B}_q & \cdots \\ & \vdots & & \vdots & \\ \cdots & \boldsymbol{B}_q^T & \cdots & \boldsymbol{C}_q & \cdots \\ & \vdots & & \vdots & \end{bmatrix}, \quad g = 1, \ldots, G, \quad q = 1, \ldots, Q, \qquad (12)$$

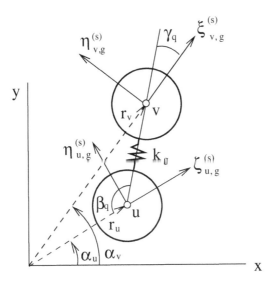

Fig. 4. The spring between two rods replacing the stiffness of the spacer grid g

where

$$A_q = \begin{bmatrix} \cos^2 \beta_q & -\sin \beta_q \cos \beta_q \\ -\sin \beta_q \cos \beta_q & \sin^2 \beta_q \end{bmatrix}, \quad B_q = \begin{bmatrix} \cos \beta_q \cos \gamma_q & \sin \gamma_q \cos \beta_q \\ -\sin \beta_q \cos \gamma_q & -\sin \beta_q \sin \gamma_q \end{bmatrix},$$

$$C_q = \begin{bmatrix} \cos^2 \gamma_q & \sin \gamma_q \cos \gamma_q \\ \sin \gamma_q \cos \gamma_q & \sin^2 \gamma_q \end{bmatrix} \tag{13}$$

and angles β_q, γ_q (see Fig. 4) are determined by polar coordinates r_u, α_u and r_v, α_v of the linked rods [2]. The blocks A_q, B_q, C_q in (12) are localized at positions corresponding to coordinates $\xi_{v,g}^{(s)}$, $\eta_{v,g}^{(s)}$ and $\xi_{u,g}^{(s)}$, $\eta_{u,g}^{(s)}$ in the vector of generalized coordinates q_s in (9). The conservative mathematical model of the arbitrary rod segment s is

$$M_s \ddot{q}_s + (K_s + \sum_{q=1}^{Q} \sum_{g=1}^{G} K_{qg})q_s = 0, \quad s = 1, \ldots, S, \tag{14}$$

where Q is the number of the transverse springs inside one segment. The mass M_s and stiffness K_s matrices of the all identical parallel uncoupled identified rods in the segment are block diagonal

$$X_s = \text{diag}\,[X_R, \ldots, X_R], \quad X = M, K. \tag{15}$$

2.3. Modelling of the rod segment package

The *third* and *final step* is the rod segment package model assembly (below system), that contains the number of S identical revolved rod segments linked by transverse springs between outer rods (in Fig. 1 marked with dashed line). The mass and stiffness matrices of the segments (see Eq. (14)) modelled in radial and circumferential displacements of rod nodal points are identical. Therefore the conservative model of the system in the configuration space

$$q = [q_1^T, \ldots, q_s^T, \ldots, q_S^T]^T \tag{16}$$

can be written as

$$M\ddot{q} + (K + K_C)q = 0, \tag{17}$$

where mass M and stiffness K matrices of the mutually isolated segment package are block diagonal matrices

$$M = \text{diag}\,[M_S,\ldots,M_S]\,,\quad K = \text{diag}\,[K_S^*,\ldots,K_S^*]\,,\tag{18}$$

where

$$K_S^* = K_S + \sum_{q=1}^{Q}\sum_{g=1}^{G} K_{qg}\,.$$

The number of the block matrices M_S and K_S^* in global matrices M, K corresponds to number of segments. The structure of the coupling matrix K_C between segments is analogical to the coupling matrix between rods inside the segment.

2.4. Condensed model of the system

The global model (17) has too large DOF number $n = 4RGS$ for calculation of the dynamic response excited by different sources of excitation. Therefore we compile the condensed model of the large package of rods using the modal synthesis method [5]. After the modal analysis of one isolated rod segment with $n_S = 4RG$ number of DOF we choose a set of its m_S master eigenvectors normed by M-norm which will be arranged in modal submatrix $^mV_S \in R^{n_S,m_S}$ corresponding to spectral submatrix $^m\Lambda_S \in R^{m_S,m_S}$. A set of other eigenmodes of each segment will be neglected. We introduce the transformation of rod segment generalized coordinates

$$q_s = {}^mV_S x_s\,,\quad s = 1,\ldots,S\,.\tag{19}$$

The condensed mathematical model of the system has the form [5]

$$\ddot{x} + ({}^m\Lambda + {}^mV^T \cdot K_C \cdot {}^mV)x = 0\,,\tag{20}$$

where $x = [x_1^T,\ldots,x_s^T,\ldots,x_S^T]^T$ and

$$^m\Lambda = \text{diag}\,[^m\Lambda_s] \in R^{m,m}\,,\quad {}^mV = \text{diag}\,[^mV_s] \in R^{n,m}\,,\quad s = 1,\ldots,S$$

are block diagonal matrices, whereas $^m\Lambda_s = {}^m\Lambda_S$, $^mV_s = {}^mV_S$ are spectral and modal submatrices of the isolated rod segment (14). Eigenfrequencies Ω_ν and eigenvectors

$$x_\nu = [x_{1,\nu}^T,\ldots,x_{s,\nu}^T,\ldots,x_{S,\nu}^T]^T\,,\quad \nu = 1,\ldots,m$$

of the system are obtained from the modal analysis of the condensed model (20). Subvectors $x_{s,\nu}$, corresponding to rod segment s ($s = 1,\ldots,S$), can be transformed according to (19) from the space of master modal coordinates of the condensed model (20) to the original configuration space of the generalized coordinates of rod segments by

$$q_\nu = {}^mV x_\nu\quad \text{or}\quad q_\nu^{(s)} = {}^mV_S x_{s,\nu}\,,\quad s = 1,\ldots,S\,.\tag{21}$$

The eigenvalues calculated using the condensed model (20) are tested with respect to noncondensed model (17) for different number m_S of applied rod segment master eigenvectors on the basis of the cumulative relative error of the eigenfrequencies and the normalized cross orthogonality matrix [8].

3. Example

Let us consider the central symmetric package of rods with six rod segments (Fig. 5) linked by three identical spacer grids uniformly located between fixed ends of rods ($l_e = 1$ m, $e = 1, \ldots, 4$, see Fig. 3). Each segment has ten lines of rods and consists of $R = 55$ identical rods with fully restrained ends in the form of steel tube ($\rho = 7800$ kgm^{-3}, $E = 2 \cdot 10^{11}$ Pa) with outer radius 4.55 mm and inner radius 4.25 mm. The rod spacing is 13 mm. Eigenfrequencies f [Hz] of one *isolated rod* (without grid springs) are presented in Table 1. The eigenfrequencies of the isolated axially symmetric rod are double-frequencies

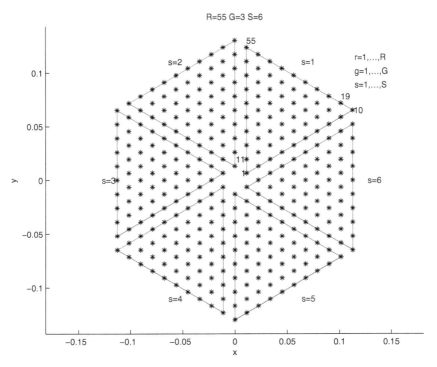

Fig. 5. The cross-section of the system with six rod segments and ten rods inline in one segment

Table 1. Rod eigenfrequencies

ν	1.2	3.4	5.6	7.8	9.10	11.12
f_ν^R	3.513	9.76	19,361	36,627	60.546	97.436

Let use consider the *isolated first rod segment* with spacer grids characterized by two different transverse springs $k_g = 100$ and $k_g = 200$ N/m for $g = 1, 2, 3$ between adjacent rods. Eigenfrequencies of these rod segments are bounded bellow by triple of eigenfrequencies $f_1^S = f_2^S = f_3^S$ equal to the lowest rod eigenfrequency pair $f_1^R = f_2^R = 3.513$ Hz. Highest rod segment triple eigenfrequencies $f_{658}^S = f_{659}^S = f_{660}^S = 97.84$ Hz for $k_g = 100$ N/m and $f_{658}^S = f_{659}^S = f_{660}^S = 98.27$ Hz for $k_g = 200$ N/m only little exceed the highest rod eigenfrequency pair $f_{11}^R = f_{12}^R = 97.436$ Hz. The spacer grids influence the spectrum of eigenfrequencies between values presented in Table 1. The number of segment eigenfrequencies between lower values in Table 1 is smaller for stiffer grids and for softer grids vice versa. As an illus-

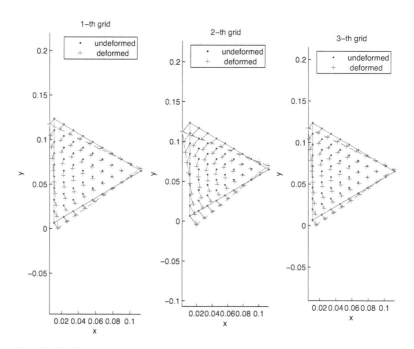

Fig. 6. The first mode shape of the spacer grids of the isolated rod segment

tration, the mode shapes of the rod segment with springs $k_g = 200$ N/m corresponding to the lowest eigenfrequency $f_1^S = 3.513$ Hz at the level of grids is shown in Fig. 6.

It follows from the figures that the spacer grids are not deformed and only transfer to new positions in consequence of different rod deformations. Analogous to the mode shapes corresponding to the first triple of eigenfrequencies, spacer grids are not deformed on mode shapes corresponding to other triples of rod segment eigenfrequencies presented in Table 1. All other eigenfrequencies and mode shapes of the rod segment from set of $n_S = 4RG = 4 \cdot 55 \cdot 3 = 660$ eigenvalues depend on spacer grid stiffnesses k_g.

The complex *package of rods* under consideration (see Fig. 5) has $n = S \cdot n_S = 3960$ DOF. The spectrum of eigenfrequencies for $k_g = 200$ N/m is distributed between values $f_1 = f_2 = f_3 = 3.513$ Hz and $f_{3958} = f_{3959} = f_{3960} = 98.334$ Hz. The lowest triple of eigenfrequencies is the same as with one segment and the highest triple of eigenfrequencies is slightly different. The spectrum is very crowded, especially for higher frequencies.

As an illustration, the mode shapes of the system at the level of the second (central) spacer grid corresponding to lowest three identical eigenfrequencies are shown in Fig. 7, 8, 9. The spacer grids are not deformed and appropriate eigenfrequencies do not depend on spacer grid stiffnesses k_g. Analogous to the isolated rod segment the mode shapes corresponding to other triples of eigenfrequencies (values are in Table 1) are characterized by transfer of undeformed spacer grids.

The condensed mathematical model (20) was applied to the calculation of eigenfrequencies $f_\nu(m_S)$ for different number of rod segment master eigenvectors m_S included in modal submatrix $^m V_S$. An accuracy of condensed model was tested in terms of *relative errors* of lowest eigenfrequencies defined in the form

$$\varepsilon_\nu = \frac{|f_\nu(m_S) - f_\nu|}{f_\nu},$$

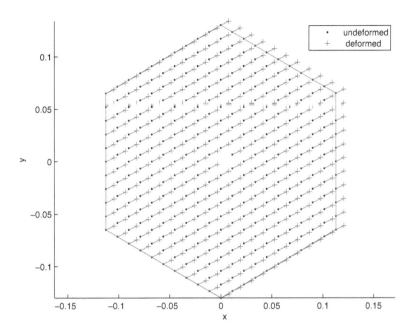

Fig. 7. The first mode shape of the second (central) spacer grid of the complex package of rods

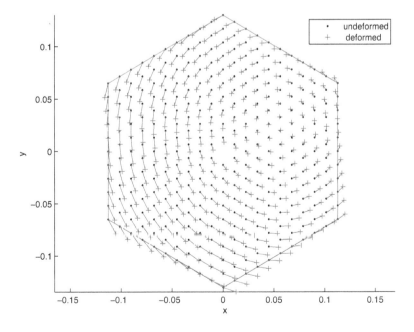

Fig. 8. The second mode shape of the second (central) spacer grid of the complex package of rods

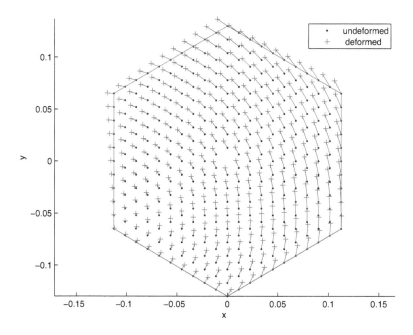

Fig. 9. The third mode shape of the second (central) spacer grid of the complex package of rods

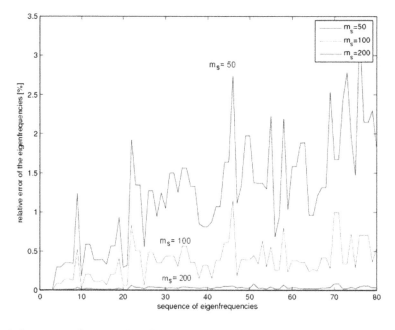

Fig. 10. The relative errors of lowest eigenfrequencies of the complex package of rods condensed model for different number of rod segment master eigenvectors m_S

where f_ν are eigenfrequencies of the full (noncondensed) model with 3960 DOF. The relative errors of 50 lowest eigenfrequencies of the condensed model for different number $m_S = 50, 100, 200$ is shown in Fig. 10. The frequency lower eigenmodes corresponding to condensed model with $m_s = 200$ segment master eigenvectors practically have no deviations from eigenmodes of the condensed model. It stands to reason that condensed model with number of DOF $m = Sm_S = 6 \cdot 200 = 1\,200$ is suitable for next phases of package rods dynamic analysis.

4. Conclusion

The described method enables to investigate effectively the flexural vibration of the large package of parallel rods linked by spacer grids. The special coordinate system of radial and orthogonal rod displacements makes possible to separate the complex package of rods into several identical revolved rod segments characterized by identical mass and stiffness matrices. This approach to modelling makes possible to significantly stream-line the computing program assemblage, modal analysis in Matlab code and to save the computer memory.

   This new approach, based on the system decomposition into more rod segments and modal synthesis method with reduction of DOF number, was applied to the test package of rods which is structurally conformable to nuclear fuel assembly. In future this methodology will be used for modelling the nuclear fuel assembly vibration caused by kinematic excitation determined by the support plate motion of the reactor core.

Acknowledgements

This work was supported by the research project MSM 4977751303 of the Ministry of Education, Youth and Sports of the Czech Republic.

References

[1] Hlaváč, Z., Zeman, V., The seismic response affection of the nuclear reactor WWER1000 by nuclear fuel assemblies, Engineering Mechanics, (17) (2010) (in the press).

[2] Hlaváč, Z., Zeman, V., Flexural vibration of the package of rods linked by lattices, Proceedings of the 8-th conference Dynamic of rigid and deformable bodies 2010, Ústí nad Labem, 2010 (in Czech).

[3] Lavreňuk, P. I., Obosnovanije sovmestnosti TVSA-T PS CUZ i SVP s projektom AES Temelín, Statement from technical report TEM-GN-01, Sobstvennosť OAO TVEL (inside information of NRI Řež, 2009).

[4] Pečínka, L., Criterion assessment of fuel assemblies behaviour VV6 and TVSA T at standard operating conditions of ETE V1000/320 type reactor, Research report DITI 300/406, NRI Řež, 2009.

[5] Slavík, J., Stejskal, V., Zeman, V., Elements of dynamics of machines, ČVUT, Praha, 1997 (in Czech).

[6] Smolík, J. and coll., VVANTAGE 6 Fuel Assembly Mechanical Test, Technical Report No. Ae 18018T, Škoda, Nuclear Machinery, Pilsen, Co. Ltd., 1995.

[7] Zeman, V., Hlaváč, Z., Pašek, M., Parametric identification of mechanical systems based on measured eigenfrequencies and mode shapes, Zeszyty naukowe nr. 8, Politechnika Slaska, Gliwice, 1998, 95–100.

[8] Zeman, V., Hajžman, M., Usage of the generalized modal synthesis method in dynamics of machines, Engineering Mechanics, 1/2 (14) (2007), 45–54.

[9] Zeman, V., Hlaváč, Z., Dynamic response of VVER1000 type reactor excited by pressure pulsations, Engineering Mechanics, 6 (15) (2008), 435–446.

11

Ductile-brittle behavior at blunted cavities in 3D iron crystals uncovered and covered by copper atoms

V. Pelikán[a,*], P. Hora[a], O. Červená[a], A. Spielmannová[b], A. Machová[b]

[a] *Institute of Thermomechanics of the ASCR, v.v.i., Veleslavínova 11, 301 14 Plzeň, Czech Republic*
[b] *Institute of Thermomechanics of the ASCR, v.v.i., Dolejškova 5, 182 00 Praha, Czech Republic*

Abstract

This paper is devoted to studies of the mechanical response of an atomically blunted cavity uncovered and covered by copper atoms by means 3D molecular dynamic (MD) simulations. The cavity is loaded uni-axially in tension mode I. Our question is how the copper atoms influence the ductile-brittle behavior at the crack front of the blunted cavity in comparison with the blunted cavity in pure bcc iron. We show that the dislocation emission is easier in the Fe–Cu system in comparison with pure bcc iron. However, stability of the blunted cavities seems to be weaker in copper region than in pure bcc iron.

Keywords: molecular dynamics, bcc iron crystal, blunted cavity, copper cover, ductile-brittle behavior

1. Introduction

Molecular dynamic (MD) simulation is a valuable tool in material science since it provides information on the micromechanics and kinetics of failure in materials, which is often not accessible from experiments. Much attention has been devoted to bcc (body centered cubic) iron and Fe–Cu system, both in experiments (see e.g. [9, 15, 16, 17, 19]) and theoretical studies [1, 8, 10, 11, 13, 14, 18] because of their importance in structural steel applications, including older reactor ferritic steels. While older experimental observations in the model Fe–Cu dilute alloys brought information concerning bcc Cu nano-particles [17, 19], recent experimental findings show [15] that vacancy-Cu complexes formed by irradiation aggregate into nano-voids where inner surface of the nano–voids is covered by Cu atoms.

Unlike our previous 3D crack simulations [7, 14, 18] where narrow cracks in bcc iron and in Fe–Cu system were studied by means of MD simulations, this paper is devoted to studies of the mechanical response of an atomically blunted cavity uncovered and covered by copper atoms, which was observed in mentioned experiments [15]. Our question is how the copper atoms influence the ductile-brittle behavior at the crack front in comparison with pure bcc iron.

The paper shows that the dislocation emission is easier in the Fe–Cu system in comparison with pure bcc iron. However, stability of the blunted cavities seems to be weaker in copper region than in pure bcc iron.

*Corresponding author. e-mail: pelikan@cdm.it.cas.cz.

2. MD simulations

Similar to [18], the bcc iron crystal has basic cubic orientation {100} and we use our MD code for parallel processing with Message Passing Interface. Interatomic interactions in bcc iron and in Fe–Cu system are described using semi-empirical many-body potentials presented in [1] that are based on tight binding model from quantum mechanics. We consider a pre-existing central Griffith (through) cavity loaded in tension mode I. The cavity was introduced by removing part of atoms in 3 planes, so its initial blunting corresponds to 2 a_0, where $a_0 = 2.866\,5$ Å is the lattice parameter of bcc iron. The cavity is relatively long, its half crack length is $l_0 = 100a_0$. The crystal consist of 1999 planes in the $x = [100]$ direction of the potential crack extension (width W), 99 planes along the crack front in the $y = [010]$ direction (thickness B) and 1999 planes in the $z = [001]$ direction (length L) of loading. The crystal contains about 100 million of atoms (more precisely, the number of atoms is $N = 98\,921\,249$). Since the interatomic potentials are short ranged, the cavity surfaces perpendicular to z-axis are free of forces. While inside the perfect unloaded lattice the resulting forces at individual atoms are zero, there are unresolved forces at free surfaces of the sample due to missing interatomic bonds. Therefore, surface relaxation was performed before loading to avoid its influence on crack tip processes.

Copper atoms are initially set on bcc iron lattice. It recalls internal stress in copper region since the lattice parameter in bcc copper is larger [1] than in bcc iron. The relaxation mentioned above decreases also the internal stress in copper region, which was studied in detail for the basic cubic orientation in [13].

Newtonian equations of motion for the individual atoms have been solved by a central difference method using time integration step $h = 1 \times 10^{-14}$ s. The samples were loaded symmetrically in the $\langle 001 \rangle$ directions by prescribing external forces distributed homogeneously at individual atoms lying on the lower and upper surface layer. Each time step $t = nh$ we monitored the total number of existing interactions and global energy balance in the system. The crystal was loaded by external forces gradually (linearly), according to the scheme for 0 K in [18, fig. 2] with loading rate 0.014 GPa/ps. Initial atomic velocities in simulations were zero and the further thermal atomic motion was not controlled, i.e. during loading no atomic velocities are prescribed and our computer experiments after loading represent low temperature simulations with low total kinetic energy in the system.

Three different configurations were studied without any periodic boundary conditions: i) the blunted cavity in pure bcc iron; ii) the blunted cavity covered by six copper layers; iii) the blunted cavity covered by two layers of copper atoms. These studies represent free 3D simulations.

In the fourth configuration, left corner of the cavity along the crack front was covered by a small Cu inclusion (of the area 8×8 atoms) and these simulations utilized a periodic boundary condition in the x-direction. Here, the total number of atoms is somewhat different, $N = 98\,921\,249$.

The crack tip processes in 3D are visualized along the crack front, i.e. in the atomic planes of the type (010), perpendicular to the crack front. It enabled 3D graphic output files representing a detail at the crack front with atomic coordinates, saved at prescribed time steps for further analysis. These files were relatively small due to a large memory and space requirements in further graphic treatments of the results. To recognize the slip patterns coming from the different slip planes, we also performed "block like shear" (BLS) simulations in 3D perfect bcc iron crystals.

3. Results and Discussions

We present results by means of details only at the left corner of the cavity since situation at the right corner is similar.

Each bond breakage or dislocation emission or etc. in the system leads to the stress relaxation at the crack front, which causes acoustic emission of the stress waves propagating in all directions toward free sample surfaces where the waves are reflected back to the interior of the crystal and may influence the situation at cavity region. Our 3D simulations after the first microscopic event are influenced soon by the back reflections due to small sample thickness B (after $90h$). As to lateral back reflections (along length L), the fastest longitudinal waves in the $\langle 001 \rangle$ directions ($C_L = 5\,550$ m/s) in our relatively large samples requires $5\,164$ time steps for the back stress wave reflections in the direction of loading, while 4648 time steps in the direction of potential crack extension (along width W). We are trying to present results that are not influenced by the lateral back wave reflections after dislocation emission or bond breakage at the crack front. Note that the back wave reflections influence the situation also in fracture experiments, but their influence is less intensive than in free 3D atomistic simulations. Here we are focused on comparison of 3D atomistic results in pure bcc iron and in Fe–Cu system. Since the atomistic samples have the same geometry in both cases, the most important influence on different behavior in the two systems plays the wave reflections from the Fe–Cu interfaces, which cannot be avoided, similar to scattering of the loading waves at the free cavity surfaces.

3.1. Blunted cavity in pure bcc iron

Fig. 1 shows the atomic configuration in the unloaded stage on two surface layers (distinguished by two different color atoms) where plane stress conditions must be fulfilled. In the middle of our thin crystal the stress state is neither plane strain nor plane stress but something between, with prevailing plane strain at the crack front. The Griffith stress needed for cleavage growth of our cavity corresponds to values $\sigma_G = 2.72$ GPa for plane strain and $\sigma_G = 2.64$ GPa for plane stress conditions, as follows from the analysis presented in [18]. The lower Griffith level is reached at the loaded borders at time step $18\,857h$ while at the plane placed in the middle of the crystal it is later due to flight time correction for the longitudinal loading waves, which

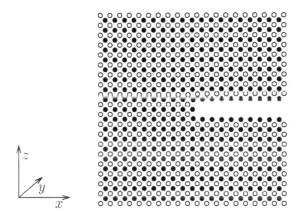

Fig. 1. Initial cavity blunting in pure bcc iron, a detail at left cavity corner

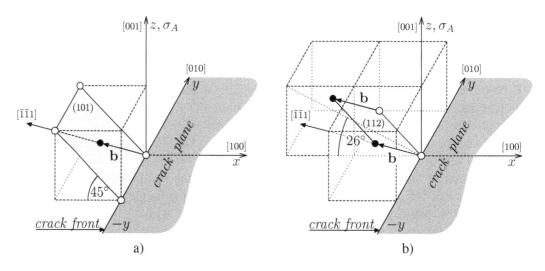

Fig. 2. Scheme of the inclined slip system $\langle 111 \rangle \{101\}$ a) and $\langle 111 \rangle \{112\}$ b) at the crack front

corresponds to $2\,582h$ [18]. It means that the critical stress concentration for cleavage in the middle of the crystal can be reached at time step by about $21\,439h$. Unlike [18], we did not observe brittle crack initiation in pure bcc iron in the present simulation with the atomically blunted cavity shown in fig. 1. It can be explained by the fact that a larger blunting decreases the stress concentration at the crack front. According to isotropic Goodier's continuum solution, presented e.g. in [4], it depends on the ratio of the initial half crack opening versus half crack length. This ratio in [18] corresponds to $c_0/l_0 = 1/200$, while here (see fig. 1) it is $c_0/l_0 = 1/100$. The larger blunting in the present paper decreases the concentration of the normal stress component at the crack front by a factor 2 according to Goodier's solution. More precise anisotropic solution by Savin [21] for our crystal orientation is presented in [22]. We observed the beginning of slip processes at time step 24 000 at the lower corner of our blunted cavity on free surface perpendicular to the crack front, which was identified as a dislocation emission on the inclined slip plane $\{101\}$ by means of BLS simulation mentioned above. This slip system is schematically shown in fig. 2a. It is visible that the $\langle 111 \rangle \{101\}$ slip system is inclined at the angle $45°$ with respect to the $x = [100]$ direction. The second available but oblique slip system $\langle 111 \rangle \{112\}$ is shown in fig. 2b. Note that the inclined slip systems contain the crack front, while the oblique slip systems intersect the crack front. As mentioned already in [18], these two slip systems have larger Schmid factor than the third possible slip system $\{123\}$ in bcc iron. Particularly in case of a perfect crystal with our orientation, the nominal shear stresses acting in the individual slip systems are:

$$\langle 111 \rangle \{110\} : \tau = 0.41\sigma_A,$$
$$\langle 111 \rangle \{112\} : \tau = 0.47\sigma_A,$$
$$\langle 111 \rangle \{123\} : \tau = 0.15\sigma_A.$$

In comparison with a perfect crystal where validity of the Schmid law is expected, the presence of a crack or cavity causes stress intensification at the crack front (including the shear stress) as discussed in detail in [18]. The slip processes in [18] start by emission of dislocations in the $\langle 111 \rangle \{101\}$ from the corner where the crack penetrates the free sample surfaces since the stress state here is more favorable than in the middle of the crystal [18]. It is in a qualitative agreement with the presented results. However, cross slip of the dislocations to $\langle 111 \rangle \{112\}$

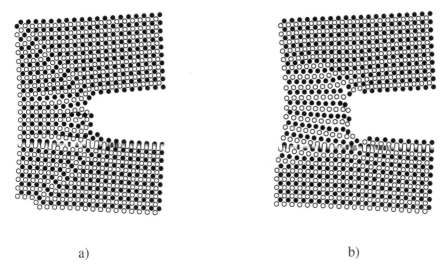

a)   b)

Fig. 3. Detail of the atomic configuration at the left corner of the cavity in pure bcc iron at time step 24 500h; a) dislocation emission in the $\langle 111 \rangle \{101\}$ inclined slip systems, the first two surface layers; b) situation in the layers 43–44 near the middle of the crystal

slip systems was monitored later in [18]. Here, until time step 25 000 when the simulation was terminated, the slip patterns from the $\langle 111 \rangle \{112\}$ slip system at the blunted cavity were not observed. We observed only the patterns from the inclined slip systems $\langle 111 \rangle \{101\}$ which illustrates fig. 3 at time step 24 500 where symmetric atomic configuration at the crystal surface (fig. 3a) and near the middle of the crystal (fig. 3b, layer 43–44) are shown under higher applied stress $\sigma_A = 3.429$ GPa. The slip patterns in fig. 3a containing three black and white atoms and starting from the cavity corners come from the double emission of dislocations on the $\langle 111 \rangle \{101\}$ slip systems, which follows from BLS simulations. These patterns disappear in the middle of the crystal since the dislocations emitted from the free surface perpendicular to the crack front may finish at the free cavity surface along the crack front, similar to what is illustrated in [18, fig. 9]. While the cavity in fig. 3a is blunted and stable due to dislocation emission, certain structural changes in front of the cavity are visible in the middle of fig. 3b, leading to a possibility of small crack deflections at the corners after the plastic deformation described above. Such a small crack deflection is observed in the middle of the crystal. Dislocation emission on $\{101\}$ planes occurs first, since the stress barrier for dislocation generation on $\{101\}$ planes $\tau_c = 14.5$ GPa is smaller [18] than $\tau_c = 16.3$ GPa on $\{112\}$ slip planes. This barrier can still be decreased due to the presence of the so-called T-stress acting parallel to crack plane similar to stress component σ_{xx}. For a narrow cavity and our basic cubic orientation $T = Re(\mu_1 \mu_2)\sigma_A$, where $Re(\mu_1 \mu_2) \sim -1$ [22], similar to isotropic continuum. By Rice [20], it may decrease the stress barrier according to a simple interchange $\tau_c \rightarrow \tau_c + T \sin \theta \cos \theta$.

In our case, the angular function occurring in the later relation should be replaced by Schmid factor for the $\langle 111 \rangle \{101\}$ slip system viewed in fig. 2a. It gives an estimate
$\langle 111 \rangle \{101\} : \tau_c = 14.5$ GPa $- 0.41\sigma_A$.

Note that the stress barriers given above correspond to a generation of straight edge dislocations in BLS simulations. In free 3D simulations, curved dislocations (see e.g. [18] or [7]) of mixed type (with screw and edge components) are emitted since they have lower net strain energy. It again decreases the stress barrier for dislocation generation in 3D.

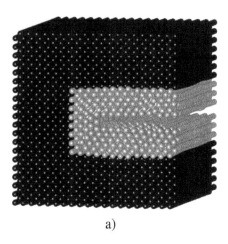

a)   b)

Fig. 4. a) 3D-detail of the initial configuration at the left corner. b) Detail of atomic configuration in the middle of the crystal, time step $19\,200h$

   In comparison with the results in [18] for 0 K and the narrow crack, in this study with the initially blunted cavity (fig. 1) under the same loading conditions, we detected the brittle→ductile transition caused by the initial blunting. The blunted cavity in fig. 3 is stable at the applied stress $\sigma_A \sim 1.3\,\sigma_G$, significantly above the Griffith level for plane stress. According to isotropic continuum predictions presented in [2, 5] this ductile behavior is theoretically possible in bcc iron at 0 K. The prediction in [5] is based on Peierls-Nabarro model and it depends on several dimensionless parameters e.g. $\gamma_{us}/2\gamma_s$, $\rho/c_0 = c_0/l_0$ and the angle θ . Here, $\gamma_{us} = 0.992\,4$ J/m^2 is the unstable stacking fault energy describing the energy barrier for dislocation generation in the slip system $\langle 111 \rangle \{101\}$, $2\gamma_s = 3.624$ J/m^2 is the surface formation energy [12] needed for cleavage between the $\{001\}$ planes. The parameters $\gamma_{us}/2\gamma_s = 0.274$ and $\theta = 45°$ are the same for this study and the paper [18]. The parameter c_0/l_0 is different: in [18] it is $c_0/l_0 = 0.005$, here it is $c_0/l_0 = 0.01$. It lies close to the borders for the brittle→ductile transition predicted in [5, fig. 8]. The different (more simple) prediction [2] predicts brittle behavior at sharp cracks in bcc iron, while ductile behavior for significantly blunted cavities in bcc iron and so, the agreement or disagreement with the continuum isotropic predictions cannot be decided. More precise analysis requires include into continuum models [2, 5] the effects given by anisotropy, T-stress and normal relaxation in the slip system [3] (which is accessible only at UCSB).

3.2. Blunted cavity covered by a thick film of copper atoms

Detail from the initial 3D configuration at the left corner is shown in fig. 4a, where the iron atoms are shown by black color and copper atoms by gray color. After loading, a small crack deflection in the middle of the crystal occurred already at time step $19\,200$ (fig. 4b) when the applied stress corresponded to $\sigma_A = 2.687$ GPa, which is about $1.02\,\sigma_G$. It happened probably after an attempt to emit dislocation from the upper cavity surface into $\langle 111 \rangle \{101\}$ slip systems, as the pairs of yellow and green copper atoms indicate at the upper corner. Dislocation emission in $\langle 111 \rangle \{101\}$ slip systems started from free sample surface between time steps $19\,600$–$19\,700$. In comparison with the cavity in pure bcc iron, the cavity covered a thick film of copper atoms is less stable. The reason of the asymmetry in fig. 4b is uncertain. It could be caused by the fact that the bcc copper with the used potential from [1] is metastable and dislocation generation

a)   b)

Fig. 5. Dislocations at the left corner of the cavity covered by a thin film of copper atoms at time step 20 900h; a) symmetric dislocation emission in the inclined slip systems $\langle 111 \rangle \{101\}$ on the first two surfaces layers; b) dislocations on the oblique slip planes 112 at the upper corner of the cavity in the middle of the crystal (layers 49–50)

may recall their structural instability, especially at a corner with higher stress concentration. It was observed also in 2D simulations presented in [19] and in 3D simulations [14] with different crack orientation. The second possibility for the asymmetry is different level of the residual stress at the corners after surface relaxation. Note that at time step 24 500 (comparable with pure bcc iron in fig. 3), the atomic structure in front of the crack front in this Fe–Cu system is more damaged and an asymmetric crack deflection is monitored. This situation can be already influenced by the back stress wave reflections and by absorption of the energy in the system via random thermal atomic motion, which is possible in nonlinear atomistic force models as in our case, unlike harmonic models with parabolic potentials that lead to linear force model and do not enable spontaneous thermal expansion and absorption in the atomic lattice.

3.3. Blunted cavity covered by a thin film of copper atoms

In this case the dislocation emission in the $\langle 111 \rangle \{101\}$ inclined slip systems was monitored at the crystal surface already at time step 19 800, unlike pure bcc iron where no traces of dislocation emission were detected at the same time step. Detail from atomic configuration on the surface and in the middle of the crystal is shown in fig. 5a and fig. 5b at time step 20 900 when $\sigma_A = 2.925$ GPa which corresponds to about 1.1 σ_G. While on the crystal surface (fig. 3a) one may see symmetric slip patterns coming from dislocation emission in the $\langle 111 \rangle \{101\}$ slip system, in the middle of the crystal at the upper corner one can see slip patterns (with empty atomic positions) coming from the slip of a dislocation on the oblique $\{112\}$ planes. Again, these patterns have been identified by means of BLS simulations in a small 3D iron crystal. As discussed in detail in [18], these patterns can arise after cross slip of screw dislocation from a $\{101\}$ plane to a $\{112\}$ plane (see [18, fig. 9]) or by direct dislocation emission from the crack front in the oblique $\langle 111 \rangle \{112\}$ slip system. Our output graphic files are too small in comparison with [18] to decide this question (arrival or emission of the dislocation). Nevertheless, it is well visible in fig. 5 that dislocation emission in the inclined slip systems $\langle 111 \rangle \{101\}$ leads

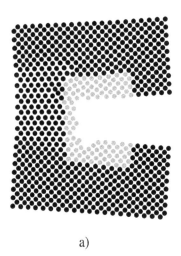 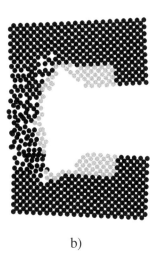

a)   b)

Fig. 6. Detail from the atomic configuration at the Cu nano-inclusion at the left cavity corner in the
middle of the crystal (layers 49–50) at time step a) $22\,400h$, b) $24\,500h$

to cavity blunting and its stability (fig. 5a), while an arrival or emission of dislocations from
the oblique slip systems $\langle 111 \rangle \{112\}$ (see fig. 2b) create a small jog in the crack front in fig. 5b.
It was observed also in pure bcc iron in [18]. At time step 24 500 the structure in front of the
cavity is more damaged after plastic deformation both from the $\{101\}$ and $\{112\}$ slip planes
but the cavity is stable, similar to bcc iron.

3.4. Cu nano-inclusion along the crack front

In this case plastic deformation started again via dislocation emission on the inclined $\{101\}$
planes from the free sample surface about at time step 22 900, which corresponds to $\sigma_A =
3.206$ GPa. It is below the applied stress needed for dislocation emission in pure bcc iron.
Before it, already time step 22 400 (fig. 6a) and $\sigma_A = 3.136$ GPa, the possibility of crack deflections is monitored in the middle of the crystal, probably after an attempt to emit dislocation.
The situation at time step 24 500 (comparable with pure bcc iron) in the middle of the crystal
is shown in fig. 6b where also slip patterns from the oblique slip systems $\langle 111 \rangle \{112\}$ at the
cavity corners and in front of the cavity are visible. The structure in front of the cavity is more
damaged after plastic deformation than in pure bcc iron, but the cavity is still stable similar as in
pure bcc iron. Crack deflections in at the corners (fig. 6b) and damage in copper are caused by
the emission of dislocations from the oblique slip systems $\langle 111 \rangle \{112\}$ after the jog formation
mentioned above.

The all presented results show that dislocation emission is easier in the Fe–Cu system in
comparison with pure bcc iron since the energy needed for dislocation emission in bcc copper
is lower [14] than in bcc iron. However, the stability of the blunted cavities in Fe–Cu systems seems to be weaker in copper region than in pure bcc iron, which could be related to the
metastable character of bcc copper, which is discussed in [1] and [14].

Presented results are in a qualitative agreement with the results in [14], where the interaction of Cu nano-particles with a narrow crack in iron crystals of different orientation was
investigated.

As follows from MD simulations [8, 10, 14], hindering of dislocations by Cu nanoprecipitate
can contribute to hardening and embrittlement in dilute Fe–Cu alloys which is in agreement with

experiments presented e.g. in [8, 19]. Damage at the blunted cavities covered by copper atoms presented here causes re-distribution of stress concentration which may leads to nucleation of new cracks at the cavities and contribute also to copper embrittlement observed in fracture experiments [6] with irradiated ferritic older reactor steels.

4. Summary

Our MD simulations show that the initially blunted cavity $(001)[010]$ in pure bcc iron at temperature of 0 K is stable after dislocation emission in the inclined systems $\langle 111 \rangle \{101\}$. Just a small crack deflection after the plastic deformation is observed in the middle of the crystal, well above Griffith level of loading. This ductile behavior is different from our previous 3D simulations [7, 14, 18] with the narrow cavity embedded in the crystal (of the same geometry and orientation under the same loading conditions at 0 K, where brittle crack initiation was monitored. It indicates that the brittle→ductile transition can be recalled in bcc iron also at 0 K due to an initial crack blunting, which is theoretically possible also according to continuum predictions.

All the presented results show that the dislocation emission is easier in the Fe–Cu system in comparison with pure bcc iron since the energy needed for dislocation emission in bcc copper is lower than in bcc iron. Here, slip processes are observed both on the inclined $\{101\}$ planes and as well on the oblique $\{112\}$ planes, unlike pure bcc iron. However, stability of the blunted cavities in Fe–Cu systems seems to be weaker in copper region than in pure bcc iron, which could be related to metastable character of bcc copper. Presented results are in a qualitative agreement with our previous MD results, where interaction of Cu nano-particles with an atomically sharp crack $(-110)[110]$ in iron crystals of different orientation was investigated.

The results presented here may contribute to a better understanding of the mechanisms leading to copper embrittlement observed in fracture experiments with irradiated ferritic older reactor steels.

Acknowledgements

The work was supported by the Institute Research Plan AV0Z20760514 and by the grants GA CR No 101/07/0789 and GA AS CR KJB200760802. The access to the MetaCentrum clusters provided under the research intent MSM6383917201 is highly appreciated.

References

[1] Ackland, G. J., et al., Computer simulation of point defect properties in dilute Fe–Cu alloy using a many-body interatomic potential, Phil. Mag. A 75 (1997) 713–732.

[2] Beltz, G. E., Lipkin, D. M., Fisher, L. L., Role of crack blunting in ductile versus brittle response of crystalline materials, Phys. Rev. Letters 82 (1999) 4 468–4 471.

[3] Beltz, G. E., Machová, A., Reconciliation of continuum and atomistic models for the ductile versus brittle response of iron, Modelling Simul. Mater. Sci. Eng. 15 (2007) 65–83.

[4] Dienes, G. J., Paskin, A., Molecular dynamic simulations of crack propagation, J. Phys. Chem. Solids 48 (1987) 1 015–1 033.

[5] Fisher, L. L., Beltz, G. E., The effect of crack blunting on the competition between dislocation nucleation and cleavage, J. Mech. Phys. Solids 49 (2001) 635–654.

[6] Herztberg, R. W., Deformation and fracture mechanics of engineering materials, John Wiley & Sons, Second edition (1983) 405–410.

[7]   Hora, P., Pelikán, V., Machová, A., Spielmannová, A., Prahl, J., Landa, M. and Červená, O., Crack induced slip processes in 3D, Engineering Fracture Mechanics 75 (2008) 3 612–3 623.

[8]   Kizler, P., Koehler, C., Binkele, P., Willer, D., Al-Kssab, T., Ageing of steels by nucleation and growth of Cu precipitates understood by a synopsis of various experimental methods, molecular dynamics and Monte-Carlo simulations of energy minimization, Conference Proceedings, Third International Conference on Multiscale Materials Modeling, Freiburg, Germany, (2006) p. 736.

[9]   Kočík, J., TEM microstructure after neutron irradiation (in Czech), Research Report MSM 267 224 4501(2005) Research center Řež (near Prague).

[10] Koehler, C., Kizler, P., Schmaudler, S., Atomistic simulations of precipitation hardening in α-iron: influence of precipitate shape and chemical composition, Modelling Simul. Mater. Sci. Eng. 11 (2005) 745–753.

[11] Lee, B. J., Wirth, B. D., Shim, J. H., Kwon, J., Kwon, S. C., Hong, J. H., Modified embedded-atom method interatomic potential for the Fe–Cu alloy system and cascade simulations on pure Fe and Fe–Cu alloys, Physical Review B 71 (2005) 184205-1-15.

[12] Machová, A., Ackland, G. J., Dynamic overshoot in α-iron by atomistic simulations, Modelling Simul. Mater. Sci. Eng. 6 (1998) 521–524.

[13] Machová, A., Residual stress in Fe–Cu alloys at 0 and 600 K, Computational Materials Science 24 (2002) 535–543.

[14] Machová, A., Spielmannová, A., Hora, P., 3D atomistic simulation of the interaction between a ductile crack and a Cu nanoprecipitate, Modelling Simul. Mater. Sci. Eng. 17 (2009) 035008 19 pp.

[15] Nagai, Y., Takadate, K., Tang, Z., Ohkubo, H., Sunaga, H., Takizawa, H., Hasegawa, M., Positron annihilation study of vacancy-solute complex evolution in Fe-based alloys, Physical Review B 67 (2003) 224202-6.

[16] Odette, G. R., On the dominant mechanism of irradiation embrittlement of reactor pressure vessel steels, Scripta Metall. 17 (1983) 1 183–1 188.

[17] Othen, P. J., Jenkins, M. L., Smith, G. D. W., Phythian, W. J., Transmission electron microscope investigations of the structure of copper precipitates in thermally-aged Fe–Cu and Fe–Cu–Ni, Philosophical Magazine Letters 64 (1991) 383–391.

[18] Pelikán, V., Hora, P., Machová, A., Spielmannová, A., Brittle-ductile behavior in 3D iron crystals, Czechoslovak Journal of Physics 55 (2005) 1 245–1 260.

[19] Phythian, W. J., Foreman, A. J., English, C. A., Buswell, J. T., Herington, M., Roberts, K., Pizzini, S., The structure and hardening mechanism of copper precipitation in thermally aged or irradiated Fe–Cu and Fe–Cu–Ni model alloys, Proc. 15th Int. Symp. On effects of radiation in Materials, Nashville, Tennessee, ASTM STP, 1990, also in AEA Technology Harwell Report AEA-TRS-2004.

[20] Rice, J. R., Limitation to the small scale yielding approximation for crack tip plasticity, J. Mech. Phys. Solids 22 (1974) 17–26.

[21] Savin, G. N., Stress Concentration Around Holes, New York: Pergamon Press, (1961).

[22] Spielmannová, A., Stress calculations at the crack front on atomistic level in 3D (in Czech), Research Study, ČVUT-FJFI-KMAT Prague (2004) 34 pp.

12

Design of the hydraulic shock absorbers characteristics using relative springs deflections at general excitation of the bus wheels

P. Polach[a,*], M. Hajžman[a]

[a] *Section of Materials and Mechanical Engineering Research, ŠKODA VÝZKUM s. r. o., Tylova 1/57, 316 00 Plzeň, Czech Republic*

Abstract

The air-pressure-controlled hydraulic shock absorbers of axles' air suspension are capable of changing their damping forces in dependence on air pressure in air springs. Due to the possibility of improving dynamic properties of all vehicles that use the axles' air suspension, BRANO a.s., the Czech producer of shock absorbers, developed semi-active air-pressure-controlled hydraulic telescopic shock absorbers. The force-velocity characteristics of the controlled shock absorbers were designed on the basis of relative deflections of the air springs. As a criterion for the design of the optimum characteristics of the controlled shock absorbers the maximum similarity of dynamic responses of multibody models of the SOR C 12 bus for all the considered weights to the dynamic response of the reference multibody model was chosen. Time histories of relative deflections of the axles' air springs determined during the simulations are compared. Simulations of running over an obstacle with all the wheels were originally chosen (symmetric kinematic excitation of wheels). Verification of the suitability of the designed force-velocity characteristics of the APCSA described in this paper is performed on the basis of the simulations of general kinematic excitation of wheels. Driving on the artificially created test track according to the ŠKODA VÝZKUM methodology was chosen.

Keywords: vehicle dynamics, multibody model, controlled shock absorber, air spring deflection, bus

1. Introduction

In 2003, in order to improve the dynamic properties of buses and heavy vehicles, BRANO a.s., the producer of shock absorbers for those types of vehicles, started to develop semi-active hydraulic telescopic shock absorbers controlled by air pressure (see fig. 1). The hydraulic telescopic shock absorber controlled by air pressure is capable of changing its damping force depending on the air pressure in air springs. If the air pressure in the springs rises with increasing vehicle load the shock absorber damping force increases, too. If the vehicle load decreases the pressure in the springs drops and causes a decrease in the damping forces of the shock absorbers. Thus the vehicle keeps a constant driving stability and comfort during various operational situations. This property of the air-pressure-controlled shock absorber (APCSA) can be advantageously used in a suspension design.

The SOR C 12 intercity bus (see fig. 2), produced by SOR Libchavy, spol. s r. o., was the reference vehicle, for which the research and development of the shock absorbers was done and on which the shock absorbers were verified. The main question was which force-velocity characteristics of the shock absorbers could be appropriate for different weights of the vehicle.

*Corresponding author. e-mail: pavel.polach@skodavyzkum.cz.

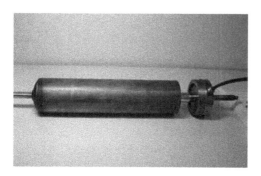 

Fig. 1. The air-pressure-controlled hydraulic shock absorber and its structural members

 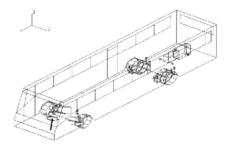

Fig. 2. The SOR C 12 intercity bus — the real vehicle and the multibody model visualization

The answer was found using the results of the computer simulations with the bus multibody models.

Multibody simulations had already been used for developing and improving damping properties of the vehicles' suspension. The influence of various control strategies on vehicle handling properties and a ride comfort are discussed and compared in [5]. Many articles deal with the optimum damping properties with respect to the ride comfort of a driver and passengers. The approximation concept [4] is proposed and used for the stroke-dependent damper design. The application to a military vehicle is shown in [9] and a so called vibration dose value based on the computation of accelerations is employed as the ride comfort criterion [10]. The ride comfort of a heavy truck is also improved in [6] using RMS values of accelerations as an objective function. The principles of the shape optimization were used for the suspension design with respect to the optimum ride comfort and riding safety in [2]. A real time damper system suitable for the optimum vehicle handling properties was proposed in [1]. A road friendliness is another criterion in the suspension design. For that purpose a dynamic load stress factor leading to the improvement of road-tire forces is used in [20].

In comparison with the above mentioned selected papers, in which the optimum behaviour was characterized by the minimization of some chosen variables, the optimum behaviour of the shock absorbers in case of the APCSA of the axles' air suspension of the SOR C 12 intercity bus was determined directly by the producer. On the basis of the shock absorbers producer's experience the operational situations in the field of vehicles vertical dynamics were chosen for the design of the optimum force-velocity characteristics of the shock absorbers. Operational situations in the field of a lateral dynamics (i.e. driving manoeuvres) or a longitudinal dynamics (i.e. start or braking) are influenced by the shock absorbers behaviour not as significantly as in the case of the vertical dynamics. For the design of the force-velocity characteristics of the APCSA (which should lead to the defined optimum dynamic behaviour of the vehicle) the objective function was proposed and used in [12, 13, 14, 15, 16] and [17].

As a criterion for the design of the optimum force-velocity characteristics of the semi-active APCSA (see fig. 1) the maximum similarity of dynamic responses of the multibody models of the SOR C 12 bus for various vehicle weights to the dynamic response of the multibody model of the bus of the reference vehicle weight was chosen. Time histories of the relative deflections of the axles' air springs determined during the simulations are compared [1]. Simulations of running over an obstacle (modified obstacle according to ČSN 30 0560 Czech Standard — see fig. 5) with all the wheels citepol1 were originally chosen (symmetric kinematic oxcitation of wheels). Verification of the suitability of the designed force-velocity characteristics of the APCSA described in this paper is performed on the basis of the simulations of general kinematic excitation of wheels. Driving on an artificially created test track according to the ŠKODA VÝZKUM methodology was chosen (e.g. [19]; see fig. 4).

Suitability of the designed force-velocity characteristics of the controlled shock absorbers of the axles' air suspension of the SOR C 12 intercity bus was evaluated according to other criteria (e.g., [3, 20]). Those criteria are the keeping of the acceleration of the sprung mass within the reasonable limits from the point of view of a driver and passengers (investigated in [13]), minimizing the relative displacement of the engine with respect to the chassis (investigated in [15]) or keeping the amplitude of the tire-road vertical contact forces within reasonable limits (investigated in [16]). But the criterion of the maximum similarity of time histories of the relative deflections of the axles' air springs was the best from the point of view of the APCSA design [13, 15, 16]. This criterion was used at the verification of the suitability of the designed force-velocity characteristics of the APCSA on the basis of the simulations of an asymmetric kinematic excitation of wheels [17] (determination of force-velocity characteristics of the APCSA at symmetric excitation of the wheels was evaluated as more suitable).

The aim of the work is to verify the originally designed force-velocity characteristics of the APCSA of the SOR C 12 intercity bus [12, 14].

2. Multibody models of the SOR C 12 intercity bus

Force-velocity characteristics of the APCSA of the axles' air suspension of the SOR C 12 intercity bus (see fig. 1) are designed on the basis of results of computer simulations with the bus multibody models (see fig. 2) created in the *alaska* simulation tool [7].

Multibody models of an empty (i.e., of the curb weight), a fully loaded (i.e., of the maximum weight) and three variants of a partly loaded vehicle were created. Two variants of multibody models of the partly loaded bus (20 % and 50 % of the maximum load) were created because of the design of the force-velocity characteristics of the APCSA for those states of the vehicle load. The third variant of multibody models of the partly loaded bus (71.5 % of the maximum load) corresponds to the weight of the real vehicle during the operational tests performed at the Hoškovice airport in September 2004. The optimum setting of the force-velocity characteristics of the non-controlled shock absorbers of the SOR 12 C bus loaded to 71.5 % of the maximum load was the result of operational tests. The vehicle load was realized using barrels filled with water, which were placed on the bus seats and floor. This optimum setting of the force-velocity characteristics of the non-controlled shock absorbers was performed taking into account the BRANO a.s. testing engineers' experience. On the basis of records of the experimental measurements documented in [8], the created multibody models of the SOR 12 C bus loaded to 71.5 % of the maximum load were verified at the same time. As a matter of fact, the

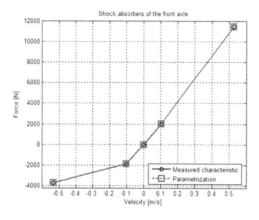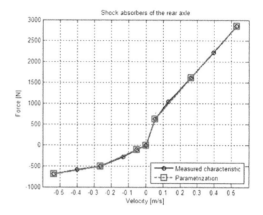

Fig. 3. The force-velocity characteristics of non-controlled shock absorbers of the front and rear axles of the SOR C 12 intercity bus and their parametrization

coordinates of the centre of mass of the bus body, which could not be determined more exactly due to discrete load realized by the barrels filled with water, were given in more detail.

The SOR C 12 intercity bus multibody models are described in [11, 12] or [14] in detail.

3. The methodology of the verifying the optimum force-velocity characteristics design of the controlled shock absorbers

As a criterion for the design and verifying the design of the optimum force-velocity character-istics of the semi-active APCSA the maximum similarity of time histories of the relative deflec-tions of the air springs of the SOR C 12 bus multibody models for various vehicle weights to the time histories of the relative deflections of the air springs of the bus multibody model of the reference vehicle weight was chosen. The reference multibody model was the bus model with the same load as during the experimental measurements with the real vehicle at the Hoškovice airport [8].

Simulations of running over an obstacle (a modified obstacle according to ČSN 30 0560 Czech Standard — see fig. 5) with all the wheels [1] were originally chosen (symmetric kine-matic excitation of wheels). The suitability of the designed force-velocity characteristics of the APCSA is evaluated on the basis of simulation of general kinematic excitation of wheels at driving on the artificially created test track according to the ŠKODA VÝZKUM road vehicles testing methodology (see fig. 4).

3.1. Parametrization of the problem

In the case of tuning the force-velocity characteristics of the shock absorbers it is evident that the design parameters are the quantities defining the course of the force-velocity characteristics. The force-velocity characteristics of the non-controlled shock absorbers of the SOR C 12 bus (see fig. 3) used in the computer simulations were obtained by measuring on a special test stand under specific operational conditions. After processing the measurement, dependence of damping force F in the shock absorbers on relative velocity v of the shock absorber rebound and compression was available.

The values of measured damping forces F_i, ($i = 1, 2, \ldots, N$, where N is the number of the force-velocity characteristic points), which will be changed during a tuning process, were chosen to be the design parameters (like in [12, 13, 14, 15, 16] and [17]). In practice it is

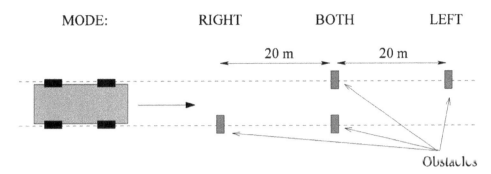

Fig. 4. Scheme of the track according to the ŠKODA VÝZKUM road vehicles testing methodology

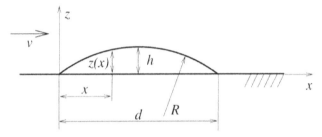

Fig. 5. The standardized artificial obstacle

not suitable to choose too many points because it is not possible to design a hydraulic shock absorber with too complicated course of the force-velocity characteristic. The requirement for the relatively small number of points of the characteristic as the design parameters is also suitable regarding the computational time of optimization. The design parameters are arranged into vector $p = [F_1, F_2, \ldots, F_N]^T$.

The measured five-point force-velocity characteristic of the front axle hydraulic shock absorbers was parametrized in all non-zero points (see fig. 3). The measured eleven-point characteristic of the rear axle hydraulic shock absorbers (in fig. 3, a full line with circular markers) included too many points the position of which could be tuned for the optimization process. That is why the original characteristic was reduced to a seven-point one (in fig. 3, a dashed line with square markers). The point $[0, 0]$ of the characteristics was constant because it is obvious that for a zero velocity a zero force must act in the shock absorbers. The facts that both the shock absorbers of the front axle suspension have identical force-velocity characteristics and that all four shock absorbers of the rear axle suspension also have identical characteristics were respected in the optimization process.

3.2. Choice of the objective function

The specification of the objective function, which should clearly quantify the degree of the objective achievement, is a further step in solving the problem. At first it had to be decided for which operational situation the force-velocity characteristics of the APCSA would be optimized. Simulations of driving on a artificially created test track according to the ŠKODA VÝZKUM road vehicles testing methodology (see fig. 4) were chosen. The test track according to the ŠKODA VÝZKUM road vehicles testing methodology (e.g. [19]) consists of three standardized artificial obstacles (according to the Czech Standard ČSN 30 0560 Obstacle II — see fig. 5) spaced out on the smooth road surface 20 meters apart. The first obstacle is run over only with right wheels, the second one with both and the third one only with left wheels (fig. 4) at bus speed 40 km/h. I.e. the simulation of another driving situation than in [12, 13, 14, 15, 16] (or [17]), was chosen.

Vertical coordinates of the standardized artificial obstacle $z(x)$ are given by the formula

$$z(x) = \sqrt{R^2 - \left(x - \frac{d}{2}\right)^2} - (R - h), \tag{1}$$

where $R = 551$ mm is the obstacle radius, $h = 60$ mm is the obstacle height, $d = 500$ mm is the obstacle length and x is the obstacle coordinate in the vehicle driving direction.

Dynamic responses of the vehicle from the moment immediately prior to running over the obstacle with front wheels to 6 seconds of the simulation (practically decay of the responses) were compared. Time histories of relative deflections of the axles' air springs were the compared quantities. The reference time histories were the relative deflections of the air springs calculated by the simulation with the multibody model of the bus loaded to 71.5 % of the maximum load in all cases.

The approach based on the calculation of the statistical quantities that express directly the relation between two time series was chosen (like in [12, 13, 14, 15, 16] or [17]) for the design of the force-velocity characteristics of the APCSA.

Correlation coefficient $R(\boldsymbol{p})$ defined for two discrete time series $x^{(1)}$ (the relative deflections of the air springs of the bus loaded to 71.5 % of the maximum load) and $x^{(2)}(\boldsymbol{p})$ (the relative deflections of the air springs of the bus of other examined weights, function of design parameters $\boldsymbol{p}$) [18] was calculated

$$R(\boldsymbol{p}) = \frac{\sum_{i=1}^{n}\left(x_i^{(1)} - \mu_1\right) \cdot \left[x_i^{(2)}(\boldsymbol{p}) - \mu_2(\boldsymbol{p})\right]}{\sqrt{\sum_{i=1}^{n}\left(x_i^{(1)} - \mu_1\right)^2 \cdot \sum_{i=1}^{n}\left[x_i^{(2)}(\boldsymbol{p}) - \mu_2(\boldsymbol{p})\right]^2}}, \tag{2}$$

where μ_1 and $\mu_2(\boldsymbol{p})$ are mean values of the appropriate time series and n is the number of the member of the discrete time series $x^{(1)}$ and $x^{(2)}(\boldsymbol{p})$. The correlation coefficient values range between zero and one. The more compared time series are similar to each other, the more the correlation coefficient tends to one. The advantage of the correlation coefficient is that it quantifies very well the similarity of two time series by scalar value, which is obtained by a simple calculation. In order to verify the designed force-velocity characteristics of the APCSA the problem was formulated (like in [12, 13, 14, 15] or [16]) as the minimization of the objective function

$$\psi(\boldsymbol{p}) = [1 - R(\boldsymbol{p})]^2. \tag{3}$$

3.3. The optimization procedure

The whole optimization procedure is summarized in figs. 6 and 7. The methodology can be divided into two loops. The first one is shown in fig. 6 and together with tab. 1 it describes the procedure of the subsequent selection of the force-velocity characteristics and their design for the particular bus weights. The initial designs of the force-velocity characteristics and the constraints defining bounds in the optimization process are given in tab. 1. The second inner loop is shown in fig. 7. It illustrates the design procedure for the given force-velocity characteristic of the APCSA.

In order to guarantee the applicability of the optimized force-velocity characteristics within the whole range of the required operational velocities (approx. between -0.5 m/s and 0.5 m/s)

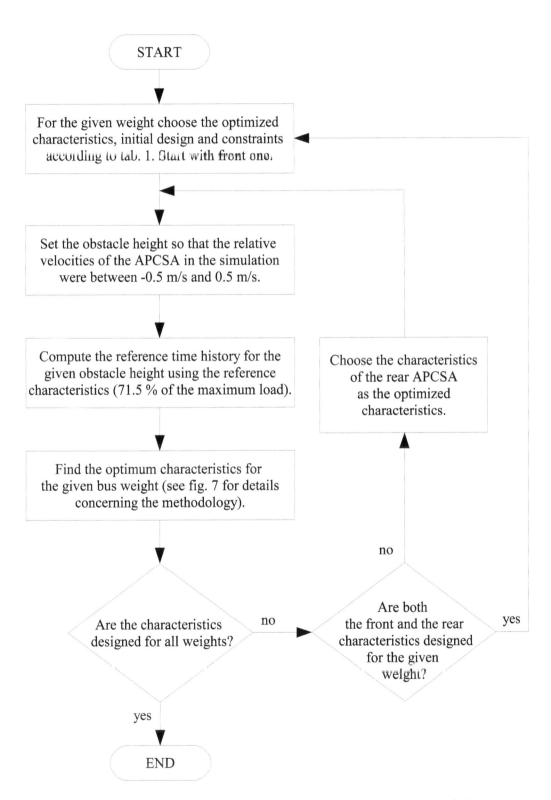

Fig. 6. The methodology of the design of the APCSA optimum characteristics

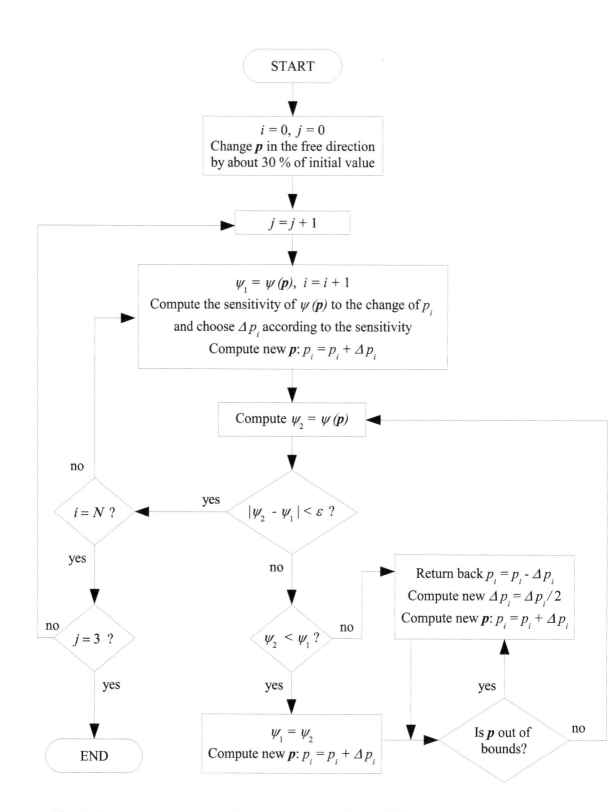

Fig. 7. The optimization methodology for the design of the APCSA characteristics for the given bus weight

Table 1. The initial designs and the constraints defining bounds in the optimization process of the force-velocity characteristics of the APCSA

Step	Optimized force-velocity characteristics for the bus weight	Initial design of the force-velocity characteristics	Constraints
1st	Fully loaded bus	71.5 % of the maximum load	71.5 % of the maximum load (lower bound for $v > 0$, upper bound for $v < 0$)
2nd	50 % of the maximum load	71.5 % of the maximum load	71.5 % of the maximum load (upper bound for $v > 0$, lower bound for $v < 0$)
3rd	20 % of the maximum load	Optimum design for 50 % of the maximum load	Optimum design for 50 % of the maximum load (upper bound for $v > 0$, lower bound for $v < 0$)
4th	Empty bus	Optimum design for 20 % of the maximum load	Optimum design for 20 % of the maximum load (upper bound for $v > 0$, lower bound for $v < 0$)

Table 2. Summary of the used obstacle heights in tuning the force-velocity characteristics of the shock absorbers

Bus weight	Obstacle height in tuning	
	Force-velocity characteristics of the front axle shock absorbers	Force-velocity characteristics of the rear axle shock absorbers
Empty bus	0.016 0 m	0.012 0 m
20 % of the maximum load	0.024 5 m	0.013 0 m
50 % of the maximum load	0.025 0 m	0.013 5 m
Fully loaded bus	0.025 0 m	0.013 5 m

the height of the artificial obstacle during the particular cycles (see fig. 6) was changed in such a way that the extremes of the time histories of the shock absorbers velocities might get closer to the required limits. Operational velocities of the shock absorbers were given on the basis of the producer's demands. Limit velocities, for which the producer is able to guarantee their damping properties on the basis of the customers' requirements, are concerned. The specific obstacle heights used in the optimization of the force-velocity characteristics of the shock absorbers for the various bus weights are summarized in tab. 2.

In order to automatically calculate the correlation coefficient and compare two numerical time series of the same length, the *Data Comparer* in-house software [12] was programmed in the MATLAB system.

4. Force-velocity characteristics of the air-pressure-controlled shock absorbers of the SOR C 12 bus

The optimum force-velocity characteristics of the APCSA of the SOR C 12 bus axles' suspension for various vehicle weights were designed during the simulations with the bus multibody models using the described methodology (figs. 8 and 9 show the example of the time histories of the relative deflections of the air springs before and after optimizing the force-velocity characteristics of the shock absorbers).

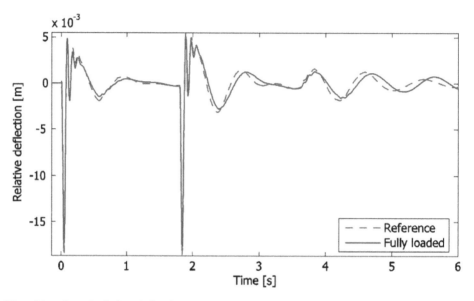

Fig. 8. Time histories of relative deflections of the right front air spring of the fully loaded bus and of the bus of the reference load (comparison of the reference case with the original force-velocity characteristics)

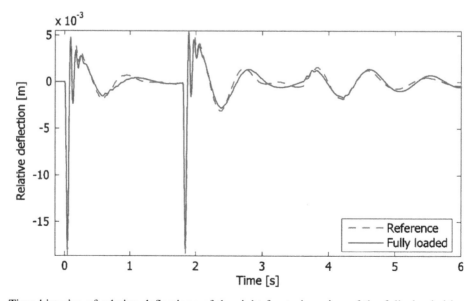

Fig. 9. Time histories of relative deflections of the right front air spring of the fully loaded bus and of the bus of the reference load (comparison of the reference case with the optimally tuned force-velocity characteristics)

From comparing the originally designed [12, 14] and the verified force-velocity character-istics of the APCSA of the front and rear axles of the SOR C 12 intercity bus in figs. 11 and 12 (the characteristics are linearly interpolated between the points in which the characteristics were tuned) it is evident that the verified force-velocity characteristics have less variance of points for all the considered vehicle weights, i.e. the range of magnitudes of forces is narrower than the originally designed force-velocity characteristics.

In fig. 10 there are differences of the right front air spring relative deflections of the fully loaded bus and of the bus of the reference load (comparison of the original and optimally tuned force-velocity characteristics). From the courses of relative deflections differences improve-ment in coincidence is not evident at first sight. The courses are given by the chosen approach based on the calculation of the scalar value of the correlation coefficient for the design of the force-velocity characteristics of the APCSA. It is necessary to note that the value of the correla-tion coefficient (equation (2)) changes (in the case of tuning the force-velocity characteristics of the APCSA of the front axle of the fully loaded bus) from the original value 0.985 5 to the value 0.988 0 at optimally tuned force-velocity characteristics (the value of correlation coefficient at total coincidence of two discrete series is 1). In order to prove the efficiency of the optimization process another quantity can be used for the difference evaluation. The norm of both curves in fig. 10 was evaluated according to

$$\|\varepsilon\| = \int_0^T |\varepsilon(t)| \, \mathrm{d}t, \tag{4}$$

where $\varepsilon(t)$ is the difference of two time histories. The value of this norm is 0.002 07 for the difference between the original and the reference time histories of the relative air spring de-flections. The value of the norm for the difference between the optimized and the reference time histories is 0.001 67. It is obvious that the second value means a better coincidence of the optimally tuned and the reference dynamic response in comparison with the original dynamic response and the reference dynamic response.

The characters of designed force-velocity characteristics of the APCSA, when comparing time histories of the relative deflections of the axles' air springs determined during the simula-tions of running over the obstacle (symmetric excitation of wheels) and determined during the simulations of driving on the artificially created test track (general excitation of wheels), are similar. Both in the originally designed and the verified force-velocity characteristic of the rear axle shock absorbers of the fully loaded bus at speed 0.264 m/s a certain singularity occurs — see fig. 12. The singularity follows from the used methodology of optimization (on the basis of the scalar value of the correlation coefficient) and from the nonlinear character of numerical simulations [12, 14].

5. Conclusion

The modified methodology for the design of the force-velocity characteristics of the semi-active air-pressure-controlled shock absorber (APCSA) described in [12, 14] is used for the verifica-tion of the originally designed force-velocity characteristics of the APCSA of the axles' air suspension of the SOR C 12 intercity bus.

As a criterion for both the design and the verifying of the design of the optimum force-velocity characteristics of the semi-active APCSA the maximum similarity of time histories of the relative deflections of the air springs of the SOR C 12 bus multibody models for various vehicle weights to the time histories of the relative deflections of the air springs of the multibody

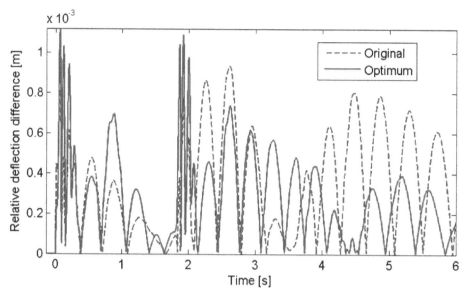

Fig. 10. Differences of time histories of relative deflections of the right front air spring of the fully loaded bus and of the bus of the reference load (comparison of the original and the optimally tuned force-velocity characteristics)

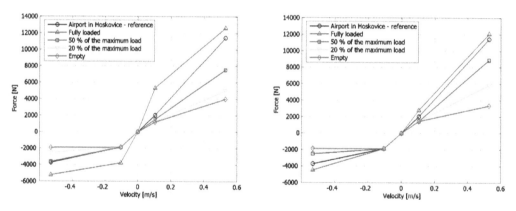

Fig. 11. The originally designed [12, 14] and the verified force-velocity characteristics of the APCSA of the front axle of the SOR C 12 intercity bus

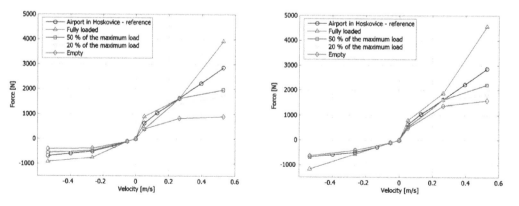

Fig. 12. The originally designed [12, 14] and the verified force-velocity characteristics of the APCSA of the rear axle of the SOR C 12 intercity bus

model of the bus of the reference vehicle weight was chosen. Simulations of running over an obstacle with all the wheels were originally (i.e. for the design of the APCSA) chosen (symmetric kinematic excitation of wheels). Verification of the suitability of the designed force-velocity characteristics of the APCSA is performed on the basis of the simulations of general kinematic excitation of wheels at driving on the artificially created test track according to the ŠKODA VÝZKUM road vehicles testing methodology (e.g. [19]). The test track consists of three standardized artificial obstacles spaced out on the smooth road surface 20 meters apart. The first obstacle of the artificially created test track is run over only with right wheels, the second one with both and the third one only with left wheels at bus speed 10 km/h.

The values of the damping forces in the selected points of the force-velocity characteristics of the non-controlled shock absorbers were the design parameters of the optimization problem. The correlation coefficient between the dynamic responses of the vehicle under the reference load (the bus loaded to 71.5 % of the maximum load) and the vehicle under the other loads was used as a suitable criterion for the evaluation of the responses similarity.

The designed force-velocity characteristics of the APCSA, when comparing the time histories of the relative deflections of the axles' air springs determined during the simulations of running over the obstacle (symmetric excitation of wheels) and determined during the simulations of driving on artificially created test track (general excitation of wheels), are similar. Though it seems to be evident that the approach to the design of force-velocity characteristics of the APCSA at the general kinematic excitation of wheels is the most correct, "higher-quality" (from the point of view of the real APCSA function) characteristics at acting only the symmetric kinematic excitation of wheels were determined. The range of the force-velocity characteristics determined at acting only the symmetric kinematic excitation of wheels is larger (except for rebound field of rear APCSA of the loaded bus at the rear shock absorber relative velocity 0.5 m/s) and thus it offers more possibilities at shock absorbers adjustment for the given operational conditions. This fact follows from the verification of force-velocity characteristics determined at acting only the asymmetric kinematic excitation of wheels, during which the force-velocity characteristics in a smaller range of magnitudes of forces [17] were obtained. At acting general kinematic excitation of wheels the influence of the symmetric excitation is "suppressed" by the asymmetric excitation and consequently the determined characteristics have a narrower range of magnitudes of forces. Evaluation of results at the general kinematic excitation of wheels is also more demanding and time consuming at these simulations. From these points of view the originally used characteristics' determination only at the symmetric excitation of the wheels seems to be more suitable.

Acknowledgements

The article has originated in the framework of solving the Research Plan of the Ministry of Education, Youth and Sports of the Czech Republic MSM4771868401.

References

[1] Danesin, D., Vercellone, P., Mastronardi, F., Fenoglio, M., Fornero, A., Velardocchia, M., Vehicle dynamics with real time damper systems, 16th European ADAMS User Conference 2001, Berchtesgaden, 2001.

[2] Eberhard, P., Piram, U., Bestle, D., Optimization of damping characteristics in vehicle dynamics, Engineering Optimization 31(4) (1999), 435–455.

[3] Eberhard, P., Schiehlen, W., Sierts, J., Sensitivity Analysis of Inertia Parameters in Multibody Dynamics Simulations, Proceedings of the 12th World Congress in Mechanism and Machine Science, Besançon, French IFToMM Committee, 2007, Vol. 4, pp. 101–106.

[4] Etman, L. F. P., Optimization of multibody systems using approximation concepts, Ph.D. thesis, Eindhoven University of Technology, Eindhoven, 1997.

[5] Holdmann, P., Holle, M., Possibilities to improve the ride and handling performance of delivery trucks by modern mechatronic systems, Journal of Society of Automotive Engineers of Japan 20(4) (1999), 505–510.

[6] Ieluzzi, M., Turco, P., Montiglio, M., Development of a heavy truck semi-active suspension control, Control Engineering Practice 14(3) (2006), 305–312.

[7] Maißer, P., Wolf, C.-D., Keil, A., Hendel, K., Jungnickel, U., Hermsdorf, H., Tuan, P. A., Kielau, G., Enge, O., Parsche, U., Härtel, T., Freudenberg, H., alaska, User manual, Version 2.3, Institute of Mechatronics, Chemnitz, 1998.

[8] Mastník, Z., Test Report No. 5-21-1004/Mz, BRANO, a. s., Jablonec nad Nisou, 2004. (in Czech)

[9] Naudé, A. F., Snyman, J. A., Optimisation of road vehicle passive suspension systems. Part 1. Optimisation algorithm and vehicle model, Applied Mathematical Modelling 27(4) (2003), 249–261.

[10] Naudé, A. F., Snyman, J. A., Optimisation of road vehicle passive suspension systems. Part 2. Qualification and case study, Applied Mathematical Modelling 27(4) (2003), 263–274.

[11] Polach, P., Hajžman, M., Approaches to the creation of the intercity SOR bus multibody models, Proceedings of the 21st conference with international participation Computational Mechanics 2005, Hrad Nečtiny, FAS UWB in Pilsen, 2005, Vol. II, pp. 477–484. (in Czech)

[12] Polach, P., Hajžman, M., Design of Characteristics of Air Pressure Controlled Hydraulic Shock Absorbers in an Intercity Bus, Proceedings of III European Conference on Computational Mechanics: Solids, Structures and Coupled Problems in Engineering, Lisbon, LNEC, 2006, CD-ROM.

[13] Polach, P., Hajžman, M., Design of the hydraulic shock absorbers characteristics using the acceleration of the sprung mass, Applied and Computational Mechanics 1(1) (2007), 233–242.

[14] Polach, P., Hajžman, M., Design of Characteristics of Air-Pressure-Controlled Hydraulic Shock Absorbers in an Intercity Bus, Multibody System Dynamics 19(1–2) (2008), 73–90.

[15] Polach, P., Hajžman, M., Design of Characteristics of Air Pressure Controlled Hydraulic Shock Absorbers Using Engine Vertical Similarity Criterion, Proceedings of The Fourth Asian Conference on Multibody Dynamics ACMD2008, Jeju, KSME, 2008, CD-ROM.

[16] Polach, P., Hajžman, M., Design of the Hydraulic Shock Absorbers Characteristics Using Tire Nominal Forces, Proceedings of ECCOMAS Thematic Conference Multibody Dynamics 2009, Warsaw, Warsaw University of Technology, 2009, CD-ROM.

[17] Polach, P., Hajžman, M., Design of the Hydraulic Shock Absorbers Characteristics Using Relative Springs Deflections at Asymmetric Excitation of the Bus Wheels, Proceedings of The 1st Joint International Conference on Multibody System Dynamics, Lappeenranta, Lappeenranta University of Technology, 2010, CD-ROM.

[18] Rektorys, K., et al., Survey of applicable mathematics, Vol. II, Kluwer Academic Publishers, Dordrecht, 1994.

[19] Řehoř, P., Kepka, M., Kotas, M., Václavík, J., Frémund, J., Operating test of the ŠKODA 14Tr San Francisco Trolleybus on a Test Track, Research Report ŠKODA VÝZKUM s.r.o., VYZ 0204/98, Plzeň, 1998.

[20] Valášek, M., Kortüm, W., Šika, Z., Magdolen, L., Vaculín, O., Development of semi-active road-friendly truck suspensions, Control Engineering Practice 6(6) (1998), 735–744.

13

Airflow visualization in a model of human glottis near the self-oscillating vocal folds model

J. Horáček[a,*], V. Uruba[a], V. Radolf[a], J. Veselý[a], V. Bula[a]

[a]Institute of Thermomechanics, Academy of Sciences of the Czech Republic

Abstract

The contribution describes PIV (Particle Image Velocimetry) measurement of airflow in the glottal region of complex physical models of the voice production that consist of 1 : 1 scaled models of the trachea, the self-oscillating vocal folds and the human vocal tract with acoustical spaces that correspond to the vowels /a:/, /u:/ and /i:/. The time-resolved PIV method was used for visualization of the airflow simultaneously with measurements of subglottal pressure, radiated acoustic pressure and vocal fold vibrations. The measurements were performed within a physiologically real range of mean airflow rate and fundamental phonation frequency. The images of the vibrating vocal folds during one oscillation period were recorded by the high-speed camera at the same time instants as the velocity fields measured by the PIV method.

In the region above the models of the ventricular folds and of the epilaryngeal tube it is possible to detect large vortices with dimensions comparable with the channel cross-section and moving relatively slowly downstream. The vortices disappear in the narrower pharyngeal part of the vocal tract model where the flow is getting more uniform. The basic features of the coherent structures identified in the laryngeal cavity models in the interval of the measured airflow rates were found qualitatively similar for all three vowels investigated.

Keywords: biomechanics of human voice, voice production modelling, PIV measurement of streamline patterns

1. Introduction

Physical theoretical background of the human voice production is the so-called source-filter theory [6]. The airflow coming from the lungs induces the vocal-folds self-oscillations generating a primary laryngeal acoustic signal. The acoustic resonances in the human vocal tract modify the spectrum of the primary laryngeal tone according to the vocal tract cavity shape typical for each vowel or voiced consonant. However, an exact physical mechanism changing the airflow energy into the acoustic energy in the glottis is not yet properly known. Because the investigation of the airflow pattern in the glottis region in vivo is problematic, the measurements of the flow characteristics and regimes are provided on various physical models.

Sophisticated experiments were recently performed by Neubauer et. al [3] studying the coherent structures in a free air jet near self-oscillating vocal folds. Influence of a vocal folds asymmetry on skewing of the glottal free jet was studied by Pickup & Thomson [4] using self-oscillating vocal folds made of two-layer silicon rubber modelling the vocal fold body and cover. Becker et. al [1] modelled a full fluid-structure-acoustic interaction in a test rig using self-oscillating polyurethane model of the vocal folds and taking into account influence of a simplified vocal tract model on the air jet focusing on Coanda effect.

*Corresponding author. e-mail: jaromirh@it.cas.cz.

The present contribution describes a complex physical models of the voice production that consist of simplified 1 : 1 scaled models of the trachea, the self-oscillating vocal folds and the vocal tract with acoustical spaces that correspond to the vowels /a:/, /u:/ and /i:/. The time-resolved PIV (Particle Image Velocimetry) method was used for visualization of the airflow inside the vocal tract models simultaneously with measurements of subglottal pressure, radiated acoustic pressure and vocal fold vibrations.

2. Measurement set-up

The schema of the measurement set-up is shown in Fig. 1. Prior to the measurement, the storage tank was filled by the tracing particles using the cigarette smoke. The airflow was coming from a big pressure vessel and the mean airflow rate was controlled by the digital flow controller AALBORG DFC4600 and measured by the float flowmeter.

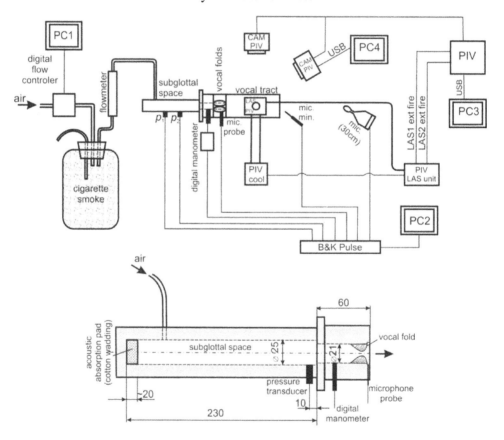

Fig. 1. Schematic simplified measurement set-up and a detail of the subglottal and glottal part

The subglottal pressure in the trachea, modeled by a Plexiglas tube, was measured by the dynamic semiconductor pressure transducers IT AS CR and the mean value by the digital manometer Greisinger Electronic GDH07AN. The vocal folds model, joined to the model of the subglottal spaces, was fabricated from a latex thin cover filled by a very soft polyurethane rubber prepared from VytaFlex 10 (parts A and B and softener So-Flex mixed in the ratio: 1 : 1 : 3). The Plexiglas "2D" vocal tract models developed from acoustically equivalent 3D FE models [7] are shown in Fig. 2. The double laser light sheet generated by the PIV system DAN-TEC was focused on a part of the vocal tract model observed by the PIV high-speed camera.

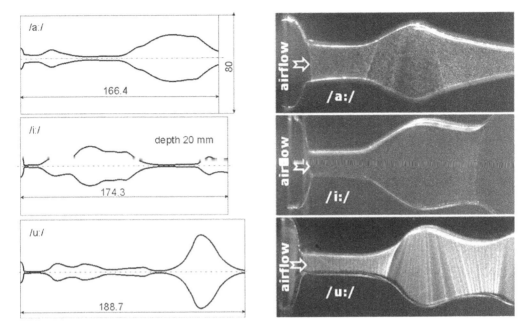

Fig. 2. Models of the human vocal tract for vowels /a:/, /i:/ and /u:/ (left) and field of view of the glottal region with flowing particles in the PIV laser light (right)

The self-oscillating vocal folds were synchronously recorded by the second high-speed camera NANOSENSE Mk III, Nikon at the same time instants as the velocity fields measured by the PIV method. The generated acoustic signal was monitored by the miniature 1/8" pressure field microphone B&K 4138 at the mouth and by the sound level meter B&K 2239 in the distance 30 cm from the outlet of the vocal tract model. The time signals from the pressure transducers and microphones were measured by the B&K system PULSE 10 with the Controller Module MPE 7537A and controlled by a personal computer. Another computer was used for recording the vocal folds vibrations by the high-speed camera at the same instants as the velocity fields measured by the PIV method. PIV laser frequency was 1 kHz and 2 000 snapshots were recorded.

The measurements were performed within a physiologically real range of input parameters for the mean airflow rate ($Q_{mean} = 0.2 - 0.6$ l/s), the mean subglottal pressure ($P_{sub} = 0.9 - 2.1$ kPa) and the fundamental frequency ($F0 = 140 - 192$ Hz) — see tab 1.

Table 1. Basic measurement data and settings

vowel	mean flow rate	subglottal pressure			microphone signal (at the "lips")	fundamental frequency	PIV laser double pulse delay
	Q	P_{sub}	RMS	SPL	SPL	F_0	Δt
	[l/s]	[Pa]	[Pa]	[dB]	[dB]	[Hz]	[μs]
/a:/	0.23	990	989	133	98.1	180	40
/i:/	0.21	940	974	138	95.4	148	30
/u:/	0.21	930	888	131	107	192	30

3. Results

The glottal gap width evaluated from the series of the images of the vibrating vocal folds in the cross-section plane, where the flow visualization by PIV was performed, are in Fig. 3 and the measured subglottal pressure and spectra of the microphone signals are shown in Fig. 4.

The signals are not perfectly periodic, because the vocal fold vibrations were not exactly repeatable in each oscillation cycle and the sampling frequency of the high-speed camera was not sufficient due to the limits of the frequency range of the PIV system. The fundamental frequency F_0 (see Table 1) dominates in all signals. The acoustic signals contain essential higher harmonics in the lower frequency region and clearly visible resonant frequencies in higher frequency

Table 2. Calculated formant frequencies of the "2D" vocal tracts for vowels /a:/, /u:/ and /i:/ (input parameters: speed of sound 343 m/s, air density 1.2 kg/m^3, with radiation losses and boundary conditions: a) C–O ... closed at the vocal folds – open at the mouth, b) O–O ... open at the vocal folds – open at the mouth)

vowel		F_1 [Hz]	F_2 [Hz]	F_3 [Hz]	F_4 [Hz]	F_5 [Hz]
/a:/	C–O	572	987	2863	3557	4321
	O–O	897	1805	2985	3920	5254
/i:/	C–O	246	2182	2620	3266	4205
	O–O	516	2475	2728	3958	4629
/u:/	C–O	386	739	2044	2618	4035
	O–O	561	864	2224	3926	4982

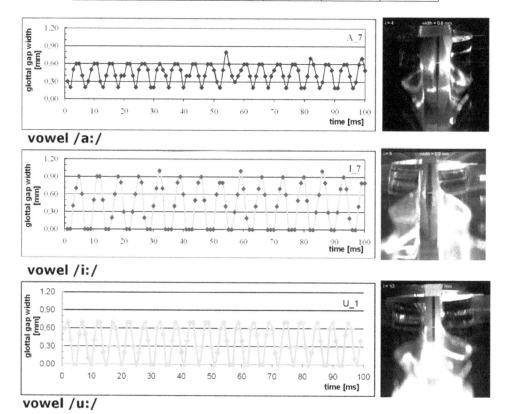

Fig. 3. Measured glottal gap in time domain (left) evaluated for all vowels at each time instant from the images of the self-oscillating vocal folds (right)

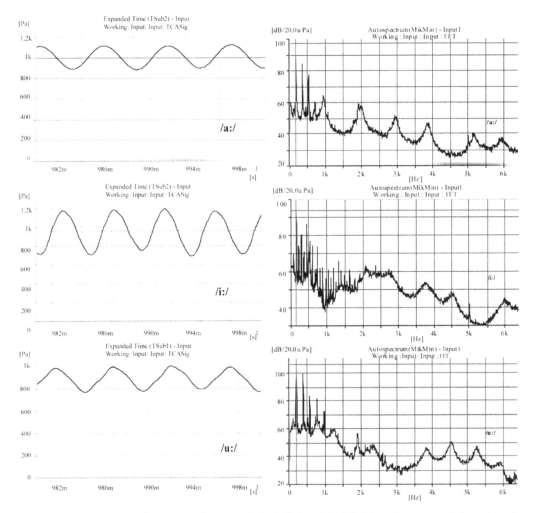

Fig. 4. Measured subglottal pressure for vowels /a:/, /i:/ and /u:/ (left) and spectra of the microphone signal at the mouth models (right)

region (see Fig. 4). The formant frequencies, e.g. for the vowel /a:/ at about $F_1 \cong 900$ Hz, $F_2 \cong 1.9$ kHz, $F_3 \cong 3$ kHz and $F_4 \cong 3.9$ kHz detected in the microphone spectrum approximately agree with the computed formant frequencies for open-open boundary conditions in Table 1, similar correspondence between calculated and measured formants is detected for the vowel /i:/, however some other parasitic resonant frequencies of an unknown origin can be seen in the spectrum for vowel /u:/, e.g. near 1.2 kHz.

The airflow streamline patterns evaluated from the PIV measurement in the laryngeal and epiglottis part of the vocal tract model for vowels /a:/, /u:/ and /i:/ are shown in Figs. 5–7. The denoted images ($i = 1, 2, \ldots, 10$) and the time instants exactly correspond to the sampling frequency of the glottal gap width as shown in Fig. 3. The images $i = 1 - 10$ of the vibrating vocal folds recorded at the same time instants are added to the left hand side of each streamline pattern. A small circle on each image denotes the position of a point with the maximum value of the airflow velocity evaluated at each time instant. The maximum airflow velocities up to about 10 m/s were observed in the epilaryngeal tube of the model. The flow is asymmetric; the jet is skewed and attached to the upper or lower wall of the channel resembling the Coanda effect. Large eddies with dimensions comparable with the channel cross-section can be identified in a

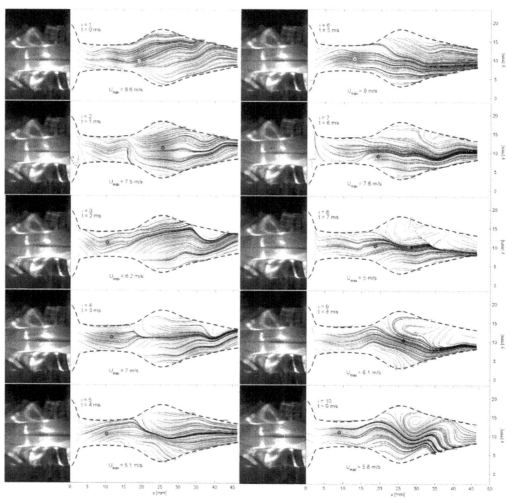

Fig. 5. Airflow streamlines measured in the model of the glottal region for vowel /a:/ and the snapshots of the self-oscillating vocal folds (left part of the panels) registered at the time instants corresponding to the time steps $i = 1$ 10 in Fig. 3. The air flows from left to right. ($Q_{\mathrm{mean}} = 0.21$ l/s, $P_{\mathrm{sub}} = 940$ Pa, $F_0 = 180$ Hz)

wider region above the laryngeal vestibule (ventricular folds and epilaryngeal tube) model. The vortices disappear in the narrower pharyngeal part of the vocal tract model where the flow is getting more uniform. The basic features of the coherent structures identified in the laryngeal cavity models in the interval of the measured airflow rates were found qualitatively similar for all three vowels investigated.

4. Conclusions

The results show the following tendencies:

- the airflow streamline patterns measured in the models of the vocal tract for vowels /a:/, /u:/ and /i:/ showed large eddies with dimensions comparable with the channel cross-section detected in a wider region above the ventricular folds in the laryngeal cavity,

- the vortices generated by the pulsating jet behind the self-oscillating vocal folds, nearly periodically closing the channel, disappear in the narrower pharyngeal part of the vocal tract model where the flow accelerates and is getting more uniform,

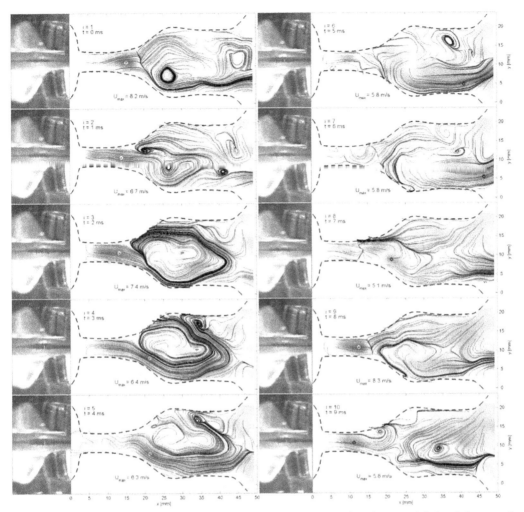

Fig. 6. Airflow streamlines measured in the model of the glottal region for vowel /i:/ and the snapshots of the self-oscillating vocal folds (left part of the panels) registered at the time instants corresponding to the time steps $i = 1 - 10$ in Fig. 3. The air flows from left to right. ($Q_{mean} = 0.24$ l/s, $P_{sub} = 910$ Pa, $F_0 = 148$ Hz)

- the basic features of the coherent structures identified in the laryngeal cavity models in the interval of the measured airflow rates were qualitatively similar for all three vowels investigated,
- substantial 3D effects were observed in the PIV experiments, see e.g. some nodes (cf. [2]) in the flow topology for $t = 0$ and 8 ms in Fig. 6 at the end of the epilaryngeal tube model.

The experimental results are important for checking the simultaneously developed numerical models of phonation, where similar coherent structures in the glottis are numerically simulated [5].

Acknowledgements

The research is supported by the project GACR 101/08/1155.

References

[1] Becker, S., Kniesburges, S., Müller, S., Delgado, A., Link, G., Kaltenbacher, M., Döllinger, M., Flow-structure-acoustic interaction in human voice model, Journal of Acoustical Society of America, 125 (2009) 1 351–1 361.

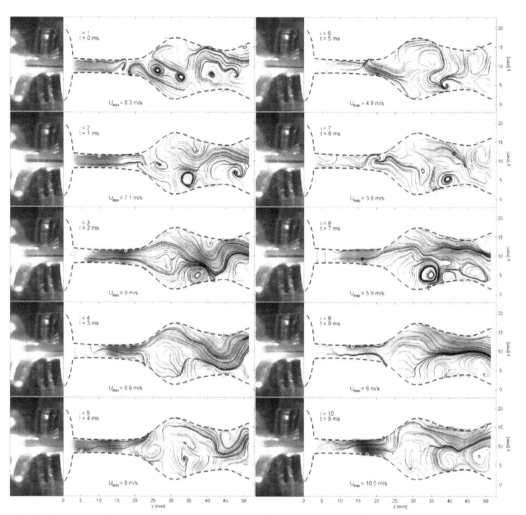

Fig. 7. Airflow streamlines measured in the model of the glottal region for vowel /u:/ and the snapshots of the self-oscillating vocal folds (left part of the panels) registered at the time instants corresponding to the time steps $i = 1 - 10$ in Fig. 3. The air flows from left to right. ($Q_{\mathrm{mean}} = 0.21$ l/s, $P_{\mathrm{sub}} = 930$ Pa and $F_0 = 192$ Hz)

[2] Jacobs, G. B., Surana, A., Peacock, T., Haller, G., Identification of flow separation in three and four dimensions, 45th AIAA Aerospace Sciences Meeting and Exhibit, 8–11 Jan. 2007, Reno, NV, American Institute of Aeronautics and Astronautics, Paper AIAA-2006-401, 20 p.

[3] Neubauer, J., Zhang, Z., Miraghaie, R., Berry, D. A., Coherent structures of the near field flow in a self-oscillating physical model of the vocal folds, Journal of Acoustical Society of America, 121 (2007), 1 102–1 118.

[4] Pickup, B. A., Thomson, S. L., Influence of asymmetric stiffness on the structural and aerodynamic response of synthetic vocal fold models. Journal of Biomechanics 42 (2009) 2 219–2 225.

[5] Punčochářová-Pořízková, P., Furst, J., Horáček, J., Kozel, K., Numerical solutions of unsteady flows with low inlet Mach numbers, Mathematics and Computers in Simulation, 80 (2010) 1 795–1 805.

[6] Titze, I. R., Principles of voice production, Iowa City, IA: National Center for Voice and Speech 2000.

[7] Vampola, T., Horáček, J., Švec, J., FE modeling of human vocal tract acoustics. Part I: Production of Czech vowels, Acta Acustica united with Acustica 94 (2008) 433–447.

14

Glass fibre reinforced cement based composite: fatigue and fracture parameters

S. Seitl[a,*], Z. Keršner[b], V. Bílek[c], Z. Knésl[a]

[a] *Institute of Physics of Materials, Academy of Sciences of the Czech Republic, v.v.i., Žižkova 22, 616 62 Brno, Czech Republic*
[b] *Institute of Structural Mechanics, Civil Engineering Faculty, Brno University of Technology, Veveří 331/95, 602 00 Brno, Czech Republic*
[c] *ZPSV, a.s., Testing laboratory Brno, Křižíkova 68, 660 90 Brno, Czech Republic*

Abstract

This paper introduces the basic fracture mechanics parameters of advanced building material – glass fibres reinforced cement based composite and its fracture and fatigue behaviour is investigated. To this aim three-point bend (3PB) specimens with starting notch were prepared and tested under static (l–d diagram) and cyclic loading (Paris law and Wöhler curve). To evaluate the results, the finite element method was used for estimation of the corresponding values of stress intensity factor for the 3PB specimen used. The results obtained are compared with literature data.

Keywords: cement based composite, glass fibre, effective fracture toughness, Paris law, S–N curve

1. Introduction

In recent years, interest has risen concerning the behaviour of high-strength/high-performance concrete subjected to fatigue loading can be observed because of its frequent use in structures such as long-span bridges, offshore structures and reinforced concrete pavements.

Fatigue is a process of progressive and permanent internal damage in materials subjected to repeated loading. This is attributed to the propagation of internal micro-cracks that may result in the propagation of macro-cracks and unpredictable failure. Fatigue phenomena related to metallic structures have been analyzed since the 19th century (for instance, see book by Suresh [20] for review), whereas the behaviour of reinforced/concrete (RC) structures under cyclic loading has been studied for only a few decades (see article by Lee and Barr [9], for review). Concrete is a highly heterogeneous material and the processes operating in its structure and leading to its degradation under cyclic loading are more complicated in comparison with these in metals. The fatigue mechanism may be attributed to progressive bond degradation between coarse aggregates and the cement paste or by development of cracks existing in the cement paste. Similarly to metals, the process leading to fatigue failure caused by macro-crack propagation consists of three phases. The first one is connected with crack initiation and typically takes place in the vicinity of stress concentrators in the weaker phase(s) of the microstructure. The second phase is characterized by the stable growth of the initiated crack up to its critical length. The final part is associated with unstable growth of the macro-crack and leads to the final fracture (usually of brittle type) of the structure. With regard to the service life

---

*Corresponding author. e-mail: seitl@ipm.cz.

Table 1. Classes of fatigue load, initiate (by Lee and Barr [9])

Low-cycle fatigue			High-cycle fatigue				Super-high-cycle fatigue		
1	10^1	10^2	10^3	10^4	10^5	10^6	10^7	10^8	10^9
Structures subjected to earthquakes			Airport pavements and bridges		Highway and railway bridges, highway pavements		Mass rapid transit structure		Sea structures

of the structure, the most important is the second part which represents up to 80 % of the total life cycle. Quantification of the crack behaviour in this phase is of paramount importance.

Fatigue loading is usually divided into three categories, i.e. low-cycle, high-cycle loading and super-high-cycle fatigue. Table 1 summarizes the different classes of fatigue loading that Lee and Barr published in their overview article [9]. It is supposed that the studied material is intended for using in high cycle fatigue region.

Based on linear elastic fracture mechanics concepts, various fatigue crack propagation laws have been proposed. In the 1980s, Baluch et al. [3] and Perdikaris and Calomino [12] reported that Paris' law [11] is a useful method for characterizing the stable fatigue crack growth behaviour of concrete. A more sophisticated propagation law, including loading history and specimen size, has been suggested by e.g. Slowik et al. [19]. Experimental fatigue crack growth data for normal (Bazant and Xu in [5]) and high strength (Bazant and Shell in [4]) concrete show that, for a given value of the stress intensity factor range, crack growth rate decreases by increasing the structural size.

The aim of the paper is to present selected fatigue and fracture mechanics parameters of advanced building materials marked here as BS 080405. The experimental measurements were made at two levels. The first one was a static measurement and its results are represented by values of effective fracture toughness of the material. The second level is connected with stable fatigue crack propagation under cyclic loading. For this purpose, fatigue crack propagation rate was determined on a three-point bend specimen and correlated with the applied stress intensity factor range (da/dN–ΔK curve) corresponding to simple Paris law. To complete basic fatigue parameters of the materials a Wöhler curve was determined. Note that the paper is connected with and expands the paper of co-authors Seitl et al. [14] that was published on the 8th HSC–HPC SYMPOSIUM.

2. Material and Methods of Measurement

In this section the material and methodology used in this paper are introduced.

2.1. Material BS 080405

The specimens tested were prepared as high performance concrete/mortar developed by ZPSV, a.s., company for production of thin-walled panels/elements. The dosage of cement CEM I 42.5R Mokra was 1 000 kg per m^3 of fresh mixture, water to cement ratio was 0.28, superplasticizer Spolostan; sand aggregates of 4 mm maximum size were used. Alkali-resistant glass fibres (glass with high content of zirconium oxide) are applied with a dosage of 5 kg per m^3 of fresh mixture (0.2 %). Properties of fibres were as follows: tensile strength 3 500 MPa, modulus of elasticity 73 GPa, diameter 14 μm, length 12 mm. The feature of the investigated specimens fracture surface is presented for illustration in fig. 1.

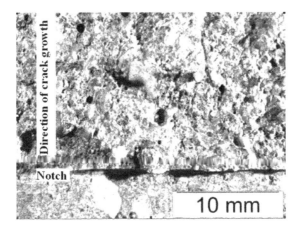

Fig. 1. The feature of the fracture surface of investigated material concrete BS 080405

2.2. Testing Procedures

The experimental data are carried out from the three-point bending (3PB) tests. Fig. 2. shows the geometry of the 3PB specimens. The 3PB specimen dimensions (in mm) were $L = 160$, $S = 120$, $W = 40$ and $t = 40$ for the first variant and $L = 400$, $S = 300$, $W = 100$ and $t = 100$ for the second one. The initial notch was made by a diamond saw that fabricated the 2–2.5 mm wide notches with controlled notch profiles and orientation. In this way 3PB, specimens with notch to width a_n/W ratios of about i) 0.33 were produced for subsequent static tests and ii) 0.10 were produced for subsequent fatigue crack growth testing.

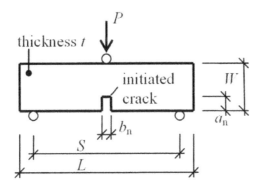

Fig. 2. The scheme of three-point bend (3PB) specimen geometry

The temperature and relative humidity were not controlled precisely. Nevertheless, both static and fatigue tests were carried out in laboratories where temperature and relative humidity values did not undergo significant fluctuations. The controlled values for temperature and relative humidity were $22 \pm 2°C$ and 50 %, respectively.

2.3. Numerical modelling

For the correct evaluation of parameters obtained from experimental data a numerical study of the crack initiation and propagation in used 3PB specimens was carried out.

The influence of the initiation notch was investigated in Seitl et al. [15], Vesely et al. [22] and Seitl et al. [17] by means of a comparison of numerically simulated fracture process in the

Fig. 3. Magnified view of the double V-notch created using a diamond disc saw. The crack is initiated at one corner of the starting notch and propagates throughout the specimen

cracked specimen and the specimens with the double V-notch of several widths. Typically, the crack initiated from the one of the rectangular notches, see fig. 3.

The numerical simulations of the fracture according to standard linear elastic fracture mechanics (LEFM) for cracks and generalized LEFM of general singular stress concentrators for notches were performed by finite element method (FEM) programs using ANSYS [1] and FRANC2D [7]. The FEM simulations were performed under plane strain conditions. All stresses were assumed to remain in the elastic range and the assumptions of LEFM were taken into account. Details are mentioned in e.g. Seitl et al. [16].

The explanation of the reasons for the application of LEFM (LEFM of general singular stress concentrators) within these analyses consists in the fact that the techniques of determination of fracture-mechanical properties of quasi-brittle materials (based on classical non-linear fracture models mentioned above) employ the approach of equivalent elastic crack, which essentially is the concept of LEFM supplemented with additional assumptions. The computational framework of LEFM is used both within the determination of effective crack models parameters (effective crack length or its extension, effective fracture toughness or effective toughness, i.e. fracture energy) and cohesive crack models (specific fracture energy, current – local – specific fracture energy). As these techniques work with the presumption that a crack (equivalent elastic, i.e. effective, but definitely no notch) is propagating in the loaded body, it is important to know how much the conditions (stresses, displacements) in the body differ in the cases where the initial stress concentrator is a crack or a notch. Since the length of the imaginary effective crack (or the crack extension) propagating from the concentrator tip is then calculated without regard to its shape (possibly together with the other fracture parameters appropriate to the models used, for which the effective crack length serves as an input) the values of such parameters can be substantially affected by this simplification, see details in Seitl et al. [15] and Veselý et al. [22].

The stress intensity factor range of the 3PB specimen for the propagation cracks is calculated as follows e.g. (Murakami et al. [10]):

$$\Delta K = \frac{3S\Delta P}{2tW^2} \sqrt{\pi a} f\left(\frac{a}{W}\right),\tag{1}$$

where S, t and W are characteristic sizes of the specimens/testing geometry, see fig. 2, ΔP is the amplitude of the cyclic load, a is crack length and f is a dimensionless function of a/W that depends on the finite size of the specimen.

In the literature, e.g. (Tada at al. [21]), it is possible to find functions $f(a/W)$ for 3PB configuration for ratio $S/W = 4$ or 8. For specimen used here the ratio $S/W = 3$ and the dimensionless function $f(a/W)$ has to be calculated. The calculation was performed by finite element software ANSYS using the standard procedure KCALC. For $0.1 \leq a/W \leq 0.8$ the results obtained were expressed in the following approximation:

$$f\left(\frac{a}{W}\right) = 51.738 \left(\frac{a}{W}\right)^4 - 47.98 \left(\frac{a}{W}\right)^3 + 19.440 \left(\frac{a}{W}\right)^2 - 2.3873 \left(\frac{a}{W}\right) + 1.041. \quad (2)$$

Consequently, the values of the stress intensity factor range for used 3PB specimen were calculated from equation (2) in the following.

2.4. Static Tests

The static tests were carried out in a testing machine made by the Zwick/Roell Company. The deflection control was used; the loading rate was 0.05 mm/min. During tests a load-deflection diagram was recorded, see fig. 5. Effective fracture toughness was measured using the Effective Crack Model (see, [8, 18]). This model combines linear elastic fracture mechanics and the crack length approach. A three-point bending test of a specimen with a central edge notch is used in this approach [13]. Two nominal sizes of the beams are used $40 \times 40 \times 160$ mm and $100 \times 100 \times 400$ mm, the depth of the central edge notch is about 1/3 of the depth of the specimen (40 mm, 100 mm) and the loaded span are equal to 120 mm and 300 mm, respectively, see fig. 2.

2.5. Fatigue Tests

The fatigue crack growth experiments were carried out in a computer-controlled servo hydraulic testing machine (INOVA-U2). Fatigue testing was conducted under load control. Stress ratio $\sigma_{min}/\sigma_{max} = 0.1$ and 10 Hz frequency rate were adjusted in all monitored cases. Crack length was monitored on both sides using an optical microscope with resolution of 0.01 mm. Because the maximum size of aggregates was 4 mm, see subsection 2.1, the crack increment da was larger than 4 mm. The 3PB fatigue test configuration is shown in the fig. 4, see ASTM [2] for details about measurement of fatigue crack growth rates.

As an important parameter to describe the fatigue rupture resisting ability of structures, fatigue crack propagation (FCP) rate da/dN is used to estimate the residual fatigue life. It can be seen that the FCP rate da/dN and the stress intensity range ΔK are related to each other. Many experimental results have shown that (da/dN)–ΔK log-log curve can be for stable crack propagation (stage II) expressed in simple form [20]. Paris and Erdogan [11] first described the crack propagation phase. They found, by analyzing experimental data using regression analysis, for repetitive loading conditions that the crack propagation rate da/dN is:

$$\frac{da}{dN} = C\Delta K^m \quad (3)$$

where C and m are experimentally determined parameters, $\Delta K = (K_{max} - K_{min})$ is the range of the stress intensity factor, a is the crack length, and N is a load excursion cycle. The law is mostly valid at stage II (stable crack propagation) and makes it possible to estimate the number of loading cycles to final fracture.

Another widely accepted approach for engineering practice is based on empirically derived S–N diagrams, also known as Wöhler curves. The S–N approach is still a useful tool to assess

Fig. 4. The three-point bending fatigue test configuration

fatigue failure of many modern structures that are subjected to repeated loading, where the applied stress is under the elastic limit of the material and the number of cycles to failure is large, see e.g. Farahmand et al in [6]. Fatigue test data can be provided to the analyst in tabular form or in the form of an $S\text{-}N$ diagram. Along with data points, the two typical analytical expressions for the curves in the following form were obtained through linear regression:

$$\sigma_f = cN^d \tag{4}$$

or in the form

$$S_n = a \log N + b, \tag{5}$$

where σ_f / S_n is stress amplitude expression, N is cycle and c, d or a, b are the material parameters.

3. Results and Discussion

3.1. Results from Static Tests

Experimental static load-deflection curves ($l\text{-}d$ diagrams) were used and for specimen size $100 \times 100 \times 400$ mm are displayed in fig. 5. Every curve was assessed separately, and the variability of the effective fracture toughness is described by the estimation of the first two statistical moments (mean value and standard deviation) – see table 2.

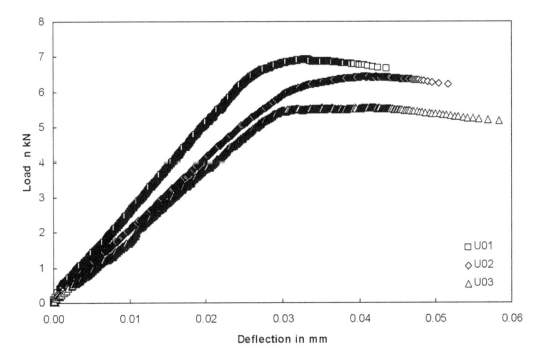

Fig. 5. Load-deflection diagram of BS 080405 under three-point-bending static test

Table 2. Results of static tests: parameter value, mean value, standard deviation and coefficient of variation

Specimen	Value [MPa · m$^{1/2}$]	Mean Value [MPa · m$^{1/2}$]	Standard Deviation [MPa · m$^{1/2}$] (COV [%])
BS080405_U01	1.190		
BS080405_U02	1.229	1.161	0.086 (7.4)
BS080405_U03	1.064		

3.2. Results from Fatigue Tests

The result of the fatigue crack growth tests performed at stress ratio $\sigma_{min}/\sigma_{max} = 0.1$ using the 3PB specimen geometries for material BS 080405 are presented in figs. 6–8 and in table 3. Note that the fatigue test data of material BS 080405 show considerable scatter because of the random orientation of fibres.

3.2.1. Fatigue Crack Growth Rate – da/dN–ΔK

The fig. 6 shows the dependence of the fatigue crack propagation rate da/dN on the stress intensity factor range ΔK in the region of the Paris law (equation (3)) validity. From the Paris equation, the relationship of $\log(da/dN)$ and $\log \Delta K$ can be obtained,

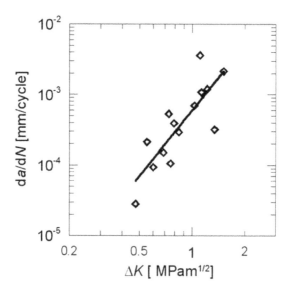

Fig. 6. Fatigue crack growth rate data obtained for concrete BS 080405

$$\log\left(\frac{\mathrm{d}a}{\mathrm{d}N}\right) = \log C + m \log \Delta K \qquad (6)$$

In log-log grid, it is expressed as a straight line with the intercept $\log C$ and slope m. At stage II (stable crack propagation), a line segment was used for linear fitting. Linear fit parameters of experimental data at crack steady growth stage gives values $C = 6 \cdot 10^{-4}$ and $m = 3.100\,6$, respectively index of dispersion is $R^2 = 0.66$.

3.2.2. Wöhler Curve

The results of the fatigue tests under varying maximum bending stress level are summarized in fig. 7. where maximum bending stress in the fatigue experiment is plotted against the logarithm of number of cycles to failure. Along with data points, the analytical expressions for the curves (in the form $\sigma_f = cN^d$) were obtained through linear regression. The regression equation and the regression coefficient for the present tested material are $\sigma_f = 5.84N^{-0.033\,3}$ and $R^2 = 0.74$ (index of dispersion).

As it was mentioned in table 1, the tested material is considered in the range of high cycle fatigue, therefore an upper limit on the number of cycles to be applied was selected as 2 million cycles. The test was terminated when the failure of the specimen occurred or the upper limit of loading cycles was reached, whichever occurred first.

Finally, let's compare the linear regression lines for the present and the literature found results for 3PB tests. The literature results were taken from [9], where authors (Lee and Barr) provide an overview of recent developments in study of the fatigue behaviour of plain and fibre reinforced concrete. They consider three kinds of concrete plain and reinforced by steel fibre with 0.5 % and 1 % fibre content.

The results of these tests are recorded in a Wöhler diagram, see fig. 7. where on one axis the normalized stresses ($S_n = \sigma_f/\sigma_s$; σ_f – the values of fatigue loading stress and σ_s – values of static maximal stress) is given and on the other axis the numbers of cycles until failure on log scale are presented. The Wöhler curves coefficients for analytical expression in the form

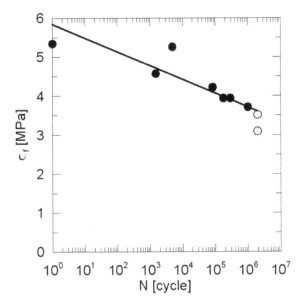

Fig. 7. Wöhler diagram (σ_f–N curve) obtained from measurement of concrete BS 080405

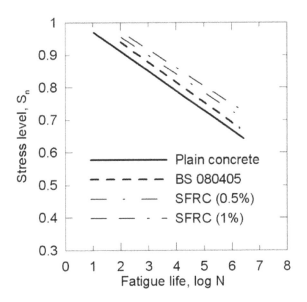

Fig. 8. Comparison between S_n–N curves for plain concrete, SFRC (0.5 % and 1.0 % fibre content) from [9] and presented results for BS 080405

$S_n = a \log N + b$ equation (5) are presented in table 3. The indexes of dispersion R^2 are in the last column.

The fatigue life increases with a decrease in the amplitude of the loading cycle. Moreover, it can be seen that for small values of N, the S_n–N curves tend to converge to σ_f values that are greater than the static value $N = 1$. This is mainly because the compressive strength used as a reference was obtained from static tests in which the loading rate is much lower than that of the fatigue tests.

Table 3. Coefficients of S_n–N curves and indexes of dispersion

Material	a and b in the fatigue equation		R^2
	a	b	
Plain concrete	$-0.060\,6$	$1.032\,7$	$0.724\,3$
BS 080405	$-0.061\,7$	$1.063\,2$	$0.744\,4$
SFRC (0.5 %)	$-0.057\,5$	$1.072\,7$	$0.606\,2$
SFRC (1 %)	$-0.055\,9$	$1.085\,4$	$0.730\,9$

There appears to be significant benefit derived from the addition of fibres. It can be seen the improvement of fatigue life due to fibre content increase from 0 % to 0.2 % and is comparable with improvement due to increase of fibre content from 0.5 % to 1 %.

4. Conclusions

The basic fracture mechanics parameters of advanced building material BS 080405 – glass fibres reinforced cement based composite – were measured. To this aim three-point bend specimens with starting double V-notch were prepared and tested under static and cyclic loading. To evaluate the results the finite element method was used for the estimation of the corresponding values of stress intensity factor for the 3PB specimen used.

From experimental tests on 3PB specimens made from concrete BS 080405, the following conclusions can be drawn:

1. Effective fracture toughness values about 1.2 MPa $\cdot$ m$^{1/2}$ from static fracture tests are slightly higher compared with typical values of this type of composite without fibres (0.8–1.0 MPa $\cdot$ m$^{1/2}$).

2. The fatigue behaviour characterized by da/dN versus ΔK values was obtained in the region of fatigue stable crack propagation and represented by Paris equation (3) with parameters ($C = 6 \cdot 10^{-4}$, $m = 3.100\,6$).

3. The S–N curve for the material studied has been presented in terms of linear relations between the maximum stress level σ_f and N in the form $\sigma_f = 5.84 N^{-0.033\,3}$, where N is the fatigue life in cycles.

4. The results obtained should contribute to a more reliable estimation of service life of structures/elements.

5. Authors suppose further directions of the research: i) Finding of correlation fatigue and fracture characteristics with the technological influences; ii) Numerical simulation/prediction of the cracking of material due to variable–amplitude loading.

Acknowledgements

The work has been supported by the grant project GA CR 103/08/0963 from the Czech Science Foundation and research project AV OZ 20410507.

References

[1] ANSYS, Users Manual Version 10.0, Swanson Analysis System, Inc., Houston, Pennsylvania (2005).

[2] ASTM, Standard E 647–99: Standard Test Method for Measurement of Fatigue Crack Growth Rates, 2000 Annual Book of ASTM Standards, Vol. 03.01, (2000) 591–630.

[3] Baluch, M. H, Qureshy, A. B., Azad, A. K., Fatigue crack propagation in plain concrete, SEM/RILEM International Conference on Fracture of Concrete and Rock, Houston, 1987.

[4] Bazant, Z. P., Shell, W. F., Fatigue fracture of high-strength concrete and size effect, ACI Materials Journal, 90 (5), (1993) 472–478.

[5] Bazant, Z. P., Xu, K., Size effect in fatigue fracture of concrete, ACI Materials Journal, 88 (4), (1991) 390–399.

[6] Farahmand, B., Bockrath, G., Glassco, J., Fatigue and fracture mechanics of high risk parts, Chapman & Hall, 1997.

[7] FRANC2D A Crack Propagation Simulator for Plane Layered Structures, http://www.cfg.cornell.edu.

[8] Karihaloo, B. L., Fracture mechanics of concrete, New York: Longman Scientific & Technical 1995.

[9] Lee, M. K., Barr, B. I. G., An overview of the fatigue behaviour of plain and fibre reinforced concrete, Cement & Concrete Composites, 26, (2004) 299–305.

[10] Murakami, Y., et al., Stress Intensity Factor Handbook I, II, III, Pergamon Press, Oxford, 1987.

[11] Paris, P., Erdogan, F., A critical analysis of crack propagation laws, Journal of Basic Engineering, Transactions of the American Society of Mechanical Engineers, 85, (1963) 528–534.

[12] Perdikaris, P. C., Calomino, A. M., Kinetics of crack growth in plain concrete, SEM/RILEM International Conference on Fracture of Concrete and Rock, Houston, 1987.

[13] RILEM, Committee FMC 50 (Recommendation), Determination of the fracture energy of mortar and concrete by means of three-point bend test on notched beams, Materials and Structures, 18, (1985) 285–290.

[14] Seitl, S., Kersner, Z., Routil, L., Knesl, Z., Selected Fatigue and Fracture parameters of glass fiber cement based composite, 8th International Symposium on Utilization of High-Strength and High-Performance Concrete, 27–29 October 2008 Tokyo Japan, (2008a) (On CD).

[15] Seitl, S. Klusák, J., Keršner, Z., "Influence of notch width and length on crack initiation in 3PB specimens", Engineering mechanics 2008, (2008b) 807–811.

[16] Seitl, S., Klusák, J., Keršner, Z., The influence of a notch width on a crack growth for various configurations of three-point bending specimens, Materials Engineering, 14 (3), (2007) 213–219 (in Czech).

[17] Seitl, S., Řoutil, L., Klusák, J., Veselý, V., The influence of the shape of a saw-cut notch in quasi-brittle 3PB specimens on the critical applied force, Applied and Computational Mechanics, 2 (1), 2008 123–132.

[18] Shah, S. P., High Performance Concrete: Strength vs. Ductility and Durability, In: Proceedings of the Symposium on Non-Traditional Cement and Concrete, Bílek, V. and Keršner, Z. (eds.), Brno, (2002) 347–358.

[19] Slowik, V., Plizzari, G., Saouma, V., Fracture of concrete under variable amplitude loading, ACI Materials Journal, 93 (3), (1996) 272–283.

[20] Suresh, S., Fatigue of Materials, Cambridge University Press, Cambridge, 1998.

[21] Tada, H., Paris, P. C., Irwin, R. G., The Stress Analysis of Cracks Handbook (Hardcover), ASM International; 3rd edition, 2000.

[22] Veselý, V., Keršner, Z., Seitl, S. Klusák, J., Influence of notch width on fracture response of bended concrete specimens, Engineering mechanics 2008, (2008) 1 113–1 120.

15

Three-body segment musculoskeletal model of the upper limb

L. Valdmanová[a,*], H. Čechová[b]

[a]*Department of Mechanics, Faculty of Applied Sciences, University of West Bohemia, Univerzitní 8, 306 14 Plzeň, Czech Republic*
[b]*New Technologies — Research Centre, University of West Bohemia, Univerzitní 8, 306 14 Plzeň, Czech Republic*

Abstract

The main aim is to create a computational three-body segment model of an upper limb of a human body for determination of muscle forces generated to keep a given loaded upper limb position. The model consists of three segments representing arm, forearm, hand and of all major muscles connected to the segments. Muscle origins and insertions determination corresponds to a real anatomy. Muscle behaviour is defined according to the Hill-type muscle model consisting of contractile and viscoelastic element. The upper limb is presented by a system of three rigid bars connected by rotational joints. The whole limb is fixed to the frame in the shoulder joint. A static balance problem is solved by principle of virtual work. The system of equation describing the musculoskeletal system is overdetermined because more muscles than necessary contribute to get the concrete upper limb position. Hence the mathematical problem is solved by an optimization method searching the least energetically-consuming solution. The upper limb computational model is verified by electromyography of the biceps brachii muscle.

Keywords: upper limb musculoskeletal model, muscle modeling, Hill-type muscle model, EMG measurement

1. Introduction

Human body modeling becomes a powerful tool for safety studies in automobile industry, helps to propose working environments or operations tools, helps to improve endoprothesis or therapies. Proposed study is motivated by comfort problems.

The main aim of this study is to develop a computational model of an upper limb for determining muscle forces generated to keep a given loaded position.

The upper arm model consists of three segments (arm, forearm, hand) and of all major muscles. The segments are represented by rigid bodies and connected by rotational joints. Muscles are represented by string elements. Their origins and insertions are fixed to the segments according to a real anatomy. Muscle behaviour is defined by the Hill-type muscle model consisting of a contractile element and a viscoelastic element. The segments and the muscles are positioned in a 3D space, nevertheless an limb movement is performed only in a 2D space. The whole upper limb is fixed in the shoulder due to neglecting of pectoral muscles

A principle of virtual work is used to solve a static balance problem. Defined musculoskeletal system is overdetermined. It means that more muscles cooperate to get the given loaded position than it is necessary. Therefore this problem is solved using an optimization method searching the least energetically-consuming solution. Since it is a complicated control system, three different objective functions are used and obtained results are compared.

The upper limb model is verified by previously measured data using a standard clinical method called electromyography. The measurement is performed with the biceps brachii muscle, the biggest muscle of the upper limb.

---

*Corresponding author. e-mail: lvaldman@kme.zcu.cz.

2. Segmental model of an upper limb

Proposed study is focused on a computational model of an upper limb. Morphological proportions of this model correspond to values of a mid-sized man [6].

2.1. Structure of the segmental model

The upper limb model consists of three segments representing arm, forearm and hand. All segments are modeled by rigid bodies connected by rotational joints. These connections represent shoulder, elbow and wrist. The rigid bodies are defined by centers of gravity and by masses. All segments are positioned in a 3D space. Joint movements are restricted in a planar rotation around joint midpoints. The whole upper limb is fixed in the shoulder.

Presented model includes muscles modeled by string elements. The muscles are fixed to the segments according to their real anatomical location [8]. Only main flexors and extensors of the upper limb are considered.

2.2. Coordinate systems

A global coordinate system is defined by a right-handed cartesian coordinate system. A center of the global coordinate system is located in so called H-point [8]. The H-point is a point which is situated in the middle of the hip joints connection (Fig. 1). X-axis is situated in a transversal plane in ventral direction. Y-axis is in a same plane in mediolateral direction. Z-axis is lying in the middle axis of a human body in cranial direction.

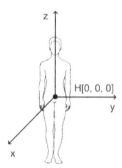

Fig. 1. Global coordinate system of the human body complex, H-point, [6]

Each segment includes own local coordinate system. The center of each local system is situated in the middle of joints connection (i.e. arm – shoulder, forearm – elbow, hand – wrist). The initial position is defined so as the upper limb hangs free along the human body, the palm is rotated forward. In the initial position, the axis of the local systems are oriented in parallel with the global system (Fig. 2). The local systems are fixed to the segments during the segment motions.

2.3. Muscle modeling

Implemented muscles enable to keep a given static position of the upper limb. They are modeled by string elements. Muscle origin and insertion are fixed to the relevant segments. Muscles cross one or more joints. To avoid them some method for muscle wrapping must be implemented, such as described in [9, 12]. To simplify the muscle model special points prescribing the muscle course around the joint are defined (Fig. 3).

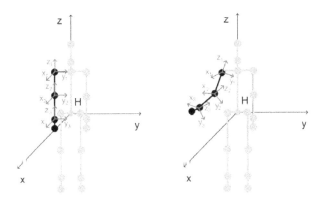

Fig. 2. Local coordinate systems created by segments; initial position (left), rotated general position (right)

Fig. 3. Prescribing of the muscle course around the joint; muscle without prescribed course (left), muscle with prescribed course (right)

Determination of the special point localizations are described using the simplified example including two segments and one muscle string. The special point is defined in the initial position of the model (Fig. 4). The plane, Ω, is oriented in parallel with the plane xy. The joint connection of segments is in Ω plane. Intersection point of the muscle string and the Ω plane is the special point prescribing the muscle course. This point belongs to the local coordinate system of the second segment. Thus, movement of the point depends on the movement of the segment. The point prescribing the muscle course is on the midline of angle formed by segments, see Fig. 4.

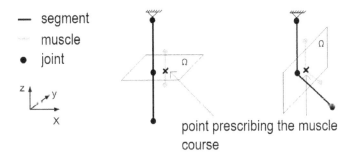

point prescribing the muscle course

Fig. 4. Localization of the point prescribing the muscle course; initial position of the model (left), general position of the model (right)

Muscle properties correspond to real anatomical and physiological data [8]. Parameters characterizing of each muscle are: the maximal force [4], an optimal muscle length, a physiology cross section ares (PCSA), their origin and insertion location kind of muscle, i.e. if the muscle belongs to a group od flexors or extensors.

Muscles including more muscle heads, such as biceps brachii, or having large physiological cross-sectional areas are modeled by several number of independent strings.

2.4. Static balance problem

The mechanical system representing the upper limb model consists of three rigid bodies depicted in Fig. 5. The rigid bodies are defined by given lengths, l_i, and masses, m_i, where $i = 1, 2, 3$. Center of gravity of each rigid body is placed in the middle of appropriate joint connection. The system is fixed to a stationary frame. Rigid bodies are connected by rotational joints. Joint movements are restricted in 2D space. The system is influenced by the gravitational field, by muscle forces and external loads.

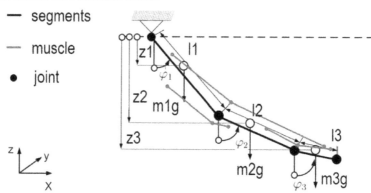

Fig. 5. Mechanical system representing the upper limb; segment parameters: l_i – length, m_i – mass, φ_i – rotation angle

The solution of balance problem comes out of the principle of virtual work [7]:

$$Q_i = -\frac{\partial E_p}{\partial q_i}, \tag{1}$$

where Q_i represents generalized force (joint torque), q_i is generalized coordinate (joint angles) and E_p is potential energy. E_p is given by the following relation:

$$E_p = \sum_{i=1}^{M} m_i \cdot g \cdot h_i, \tag{2}$$

where m_i is rigid body mass, g is gravitational constant ($g = 9.81$ ms^{-2}), h_i is the distance between instantaneous rigid body position and a surface of zero potential energy. M denotes the number of rigid bodies (segments).

The generalized force, Q_i, is given by the sum of unknown muscle forces, F_k, and external loads, $\bar{F}_l$:

$$Q_i = \sum_{k=1}^{K} F_k \cdot r_{ik} + \sum_{l=1}^{L} \bar{F}_l \cdot \bar{r}_{il}, \tag{3}$$

where K is the total number of all muscles and L is the number of external loads. Further r_{ik} and $\bar{r}_{il}$ denotes corresponding moment arm with respect to the ith joint center as depicted in Fig. 6.

Merging Eqs (1) and (3), the energy balance is obtained as:

$$\sum_{k=1}^{K} F_k \cdot r_{ik} + \sum_{l=1}^{L} \bar{F}_l \cdot \bar{r}_{il} = -\frac{\partial E_p}{\partial q_i}. \tag{4}$$

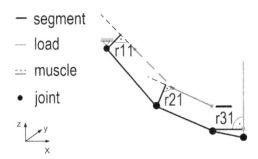

Fig. 6. Arms of forces generated by muscles and external loads

Finally Eq (4) can be written in a matrix notation:

$$\mathbf{AF} + \bar{\mathbf{A}}\bar{\mathbf{F}} = \mathbf{b}. \tag{5}$$

Used matrices and vectors in (5) can be itemized as:

$$\mathbf{A} = \begin{bmatrix} r_{11} & r_{12} & \cdots & r_{1K} \\ r_{21} & r_{22} & \cdots & r_{2K} \\ & & \ddots & \\ r_{M1} & r_{M2} & \cdots & r_{MK} \end{bmatrix}, \quad \bar{\mathbf{A}} = \begin{bmatrix} \bar{r}_{11} & \bar{r}_{12} & \cdots & \bar{r}_{1L} \\ \bar{r}_{21} & \bar{r}_{22} & \cdots & \bar{r}_{2L} \\ & & \ddots & \\ \bar{r}_{M1} & \bar{r}_{M2} & \cdots & \bar{r}_{ML} \end{bmatrix}, \tag{6}$$

$$\mathbf{F} = \begin{bmatrix} F_1 \\ F_2 \\ \vdots \\ F_K \end{bmatrix}, \quad \bar{\mathbf{F}} = \begin{bmatrix} \bar{F}_1 \\ \bar{F}_2 \\ \vdots \\ \bar{F}_L \end{bmatrix}, \quad \mathbf{b} = \begin{bmatrix} -\partial E_p/\partial q_1 \\ -\partial E_p/\partial q_2 \\ \vdots \\ -\partial E_p/\partial q_M \end{bmatrix}, \tag{7}$$

where $\mathbf{F}$ represents the vector of unknown muscle forces, $\bar{\mathbf{F}}$ are known external loads, M is the number of segments, K represents the total number of muscle forces and L is the total number of external loads.

The number of muscle forces is higher than the number of rigid bodies ($M \ll K$). Thus, this system of algebraic equations is overdetermined.

2.5. *Optimization*

Demanded static position of the upper limb is the result of the complex muscles cooperation. Each muscle contributes with another muscle activation rate. This rate is established by a central nervous system.

The upper limb model is represented by the overdetermined system of Eqs (5). Many combinations of muscle activations exist to keep each given position. The number of unknown muscle forces is much more higher than the number of equations. Thus, the optimization method searching the least energetically-consuming solution is used [9]. The optimization problem is defined as:

the unknown muscle forces: $\mathbf{F} = \{F_k\}, k = 1, 2, \ldots, K,$

objective function: $F_0(\mathbf{F}),$

equality constraint function: $f_m(\mathbf{F}) = 0, m = 1, 2, \ldots, M,$

inequality constraint function: $F_i^{lower} \le F_i \le F_i^{upper}, i = 1, 2, \ldots, K.$

A feasible region is then defined by equality and inequality constraint functions. The equality constraints are given by system of Eqs (5). The inequality constraints respect on the real muscle behaviour:

- $F_i^{lower} = 0$, i.e., muscles can not push,

- $F_i^{upper} = F_i^{max}$, i.e., muscles can not generate force greater than their maximal.

Each human task is controlled by the central nervous system using a particular criterion or a set of criteria such as pain, physical endurance of an individual, time of activity, fatigue, etc. Thus, so many cost functions are described in the literature. The cost function should be able to reflect the inherent physical activity or pathology as well as it should be able to include relevant physiological characteristics and functional properties such as maximum force or activity [10]. Some of the most commonly used non-linear cost function presented in [9] are used and then compared:

- sum of the square of the individual muscle forces: $F_0 = \sum_{k=1}^{K} \left(F^k\right)^2$,

- sum of the cube of the individual average muscle stresses: $F_0 = \sum_{k=1}^{K} \left(\sigma^k\right)^3$,

- sum of the square of the individual normalized muscle forces: $F_0 = \sum_{k=1}^{K} \left(\frac{F^k}{F_{max}^k}\right)^2$.

The optimization problem is solved by Python optimize package providing several commonly used optimization algorithms. Namely Sequential Least Squares Programming (SLSQP) algorithm is used. The SLSQP optimizer uses a slightly modified version of Lawson and Henson's nonlinear least-squares solver [3].

3. Results and discussion

3.1. Comparison of the objective functions

The optimization method is used to solve an overdetermined problem of the upper limb muscular balance. Three objective functions are used. Their convergence and number of iteration are compared. One model case is presented — the arm hangs vertically along the body, the upper arm and the forearm form the right angle, the palm is turned to the body. The external load is situated vertically down to the palm and its size is 30 N. The results are summarized in Table 1, muscle forces are shown for the biceps brachii muscle.

Table 1. Comparison of used objective functions

Objective function	Number of iterations	Force of the biceps brachii muscle [N]
$F_{01} = \sum_{k=1}^{K} \left(F^k\right)^2$	4	138.708 108
$F_{02} = \sum_{k=1}^{K} \left(\sigma^k\right)^3$	2	138.707 543
$F_{03} = \sum_{k=1}^{K} \left(\frac{F^k}{F_{max}^k}\right)^2$	20	135.844 856

The first and the second objective functions have the comparable resulting values. The second one has in addition the low number of iterations. Therefore this function is used for the following computation.

3.2. Muscle forces in various positions of the upper limb

Tested positions of the upper limb model are described in Table 2 and shown in Figs. 7–10. The model is located in the global cartesian coordinate system. The all modeled segments (represented by black lines), the considered major muscles (represented by gray lines), the all joints (represented by black dots) and all muscle origins and insertions (represented by gray dots) are shown. The gray square represents the H-point located in the center of the global coordinate system.

Table 2. Tested position of the upper limb model

Position number	Arm rotation [rad]	Forearm rotation [rad]	Hand rotation [rad]
1	0	0	0
2	0	$3/4\,\pi$	$\pi/2$
3	0	$\pi/2$	$\pi/2$
4	$\pi/2$	$\pi/2$	$\pi/2$

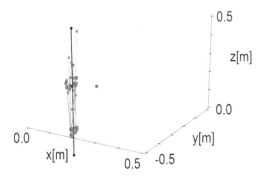

Fig. 7. Position number 1

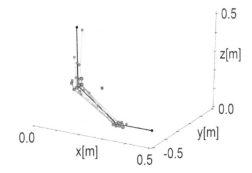

Fig. 8. Position number 2

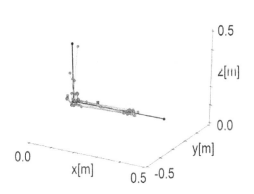

Fig. 9. Position number 3

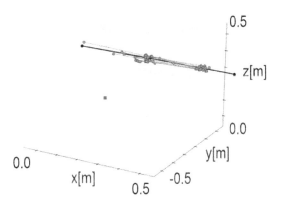

Fig. 10. Position number 4

Discussed positions differ in segments positions defined by arm rotation, forearm rotation and hand rotation.

The upper limb is loaded by the weight of 30 N. The load is applied to the end of the hand. Its orientation is vertically down for each discussed case. Table 3 summarizes a comparison of resulting forces generated by the biceps brachii muscle to keep the four discussed static positions.

Table 3. Resulting forces generated by the biceps brachii muscle for different static position of the upper limb model

ID	Muscle name	Muscle force [N]			
		Position 1	Position 2	Position 3	Position 4
1	biceps brachii (LH)	0.0	125.981	138.706	139.191
2	brachioradialis	0.0	169.028	215.142	215.892
3	triceps brachii	0.0	0.0	0.0	0.0
4	triceps brachii	0.0	0.0	0.0	0.0
5	brachialis	0.0	59.334	74.492	75.500
6	anconeus	0.0	0.0	0.0	0.0
7	pronator teres	0.0	273.811	351.334	354.255
8	extensor carpi radialis longus	0.0	0.0	0.0	0.0
9	extensor carpi radialis brevis	0.0	0.0	0.0	0.0
10	extensor dig. com.	0.0	0.0	0.0	0.0
11	extensor car. ul.	0.0	0.0	0.0	0.0
12	flexor car. ul.	0.0	55.929	73.162	74.357
13	flexor carpi radialis	0.0	42.636	57.842	58.786
14	flexor pollicis longus	0.0	68.861	93.420	94.945
15	flexor dig. sub.	0.0	14.896	20.209	23.200

Obviously, the muscles don't generate any activation to keep the first static position (Table 3). The comparison shows that the muscle activation grows up for the next static positions. Several muscles such as triceps brachii muscle generate the zero activation all the time. These muscles are antagonists for discussed positions.

4. Model verification using biceps brachii muscle

4.1. Experiment set up

Presented upper limb model is verified by previously measured data using a clinical method called electromyography (EMG) [11]. EMG is a standard measuring method based on an analysis of electrical signals closely associated with muscle activations [5].

The test is performed by measuring the EMG activity on the biceps brachii muscle when carrying a given increasing load. The EMG signal is measured using surface electrodes.

The volunteer holds his right upper limb flexed in the elbow so that the arm and the forearm form the right angle. The palm is turned to the body. The weight is hung on the hand so that

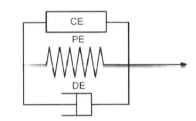

Fig. 11. Measurement of biceps brachii EMG signal   Fig. 12. Hill-type muscle model

the load is applied on the supposed center of gravity of the hand. The electrodes are stuck on the skin. The experiment set up is shown in Fig. 11. The weight is subsequently increased from 0.5 kg to 5 kg with the step 0.5 kg. For each load the EMG signal of biceps brachii muscle is monitored.

As EMG output the EMG activity-time relation is obtained. The raw signal is then filtered, rectified and normalized as is published in detail in [11].

4.2. Hill-type muscle model implementation

EMG measurement is useful for verification of muscular forces determination. Up to now the particular total muscle force of the upper limb model were determined. Obviously the normalized EMG signal is compared to the active part of the total muscle force. Hence the Hill-type muscle model respecting the active and passive muscle properties [12] is implemented.

The Hill-type muscle model consists in general of three elements as depicted in Fig. 12. The contractile element (CE) represents an active muscle part, the parallel elastic element (PE) represents a passive part and the parallel dumping element (DE) substitutes viscous muscle properties. The parallel elements represent a collagen and elastin network of muscle. The resulting muscle force is than calculated with the following equations:

$$F_{muscle}(t, l, v) = N_a(t)F_{CE}(l, v) + F_{PE}(l) + F_{DE}(v), \qquad (8)$$
$$F_{CE}(l, v) = F_l(l)F_v(v), \qquad (9)$$

where the total muscle force, F_{muscle}, is obtained from the presented upper limb model, $N_a(t)$ is a function determining the muscle active state, $F_{CE}(l, v)$ is a force generated by contractile element, $F_{PE}(l)$ is given by parallel elastic element, $F_{DE}(v)$ is the force in viscous element, $F_l(l)$ represents an active force-length characteristic, $F_v(v)$ is an active force-velocity characteristic.

Mathematical expressions of mentioned characteristics, F_l, F_v, F_{PE}, and their parameters are described by equations in [12]. The active muscle force-length relation, $F_l(l)$, is given by the following formula:

$$F_l(l) = F_{max}\exp\left(-\left(\frac{\frac{l}{l_{opt}} - 1}{C_{sh}}\right)^2\right), \qquad (10)$$

where F_{max} substitutes the maximal muscle force, l is the instantaneous muscle length, l_{opt} is the optimal muscle length when the muscle can generate the maximal force and C_{sh} is the shape parameter determining concavity of muscle force-length characteristic.

The force-velocity characteristic, $F_v(v)$, is defined as the relation between the maximum muscle force and instantaneous rate of the muscle length change when a muscle is fully activated, described in [12]. In considered loaded static position of the upper arm, the muscles generate forces without changing their length. In this case of isometric contraction, the force-velocity characteristic is constant of value one ($F_v(v) = 1$).

The parallel elastic element, F_{PE}, is calculated as:

$$F_{PE} = \frac{F_{max}}{\exp(C_{PE}) - 1} \left\{ \exp\left[\frac{C_{PE}}{PE_{max}} \left(\frac{l}{l_{opt}} - 1 \right) \right] - 1 \right\}, \tag{11}$$

where C_{PE} and PE_{max} are the shape parameters of defined dependencies. According to [12] they are set as follows:

$$C_{sh} = 0.4, \qquad C_{PE} = 5.0, \qquad PE_{max} = 0.6.$$

The force in the parallel damper element, F_{DE}, is given by the formula:

$$F_{DE} = k_{DE} v, \tag{12}$$

where k_{DE} is the damping coefficient, v is the muscle contraction velocity. Due to presented case of isometric contraction, the force of dumper element is zero ($F_{DE} = 0$).

Substituting (9)–(12) into (8) the relation for the muscle activation, N_a, is obtained:

$$N_a(t) = \frac{F_{muscle} - F_{PE}(l)}{F_{CE}(l)}. \tag{13}$$

The external loading of the upper arm model is constant for each mentioned position. Thus, the generated muscle force is constant too and the muscle activity is than constant in time.

4.3. Comparison of muscle activation using biceps brachii muscle

For the upper limb model verification it is necessary to normalize obtained muscle activations. The activations are normalized by the maximal activations that can be generated by the muscle [1, 2]. However, determination of the maximal muscle activation is usually not flawless in practice. Thus, instead of the maximal activation the activation generated with 5 kg of load (N_{amax}) is considered to normalize the results:

$$N_{anorm} = \frac{N_{ai}}{N_{amax}}. \tag{14}$$

Table 4 shows the comparison of the measured and the computed muscle activations of biceps brachii muscle using three presented objective function. These values are computed and measured, for ten different loads. Obtained values determine muscle activities that are exerted by the biceps brachii muscle to keep the limb position loaded from 0.5 kg to 5 kg. All cases are normalized by the case with 5 kg of load.

Fig. 13 shows the positioned upper limb model.

The values of normalized muscle activations, as well as differences, are the same using the first and the second objective function. The third function has much different resulting values. Moreover, the second one has the low number of iterations. Thus, this function is considered to be the most suitable of all discussed functions.

The values of measured muscle activation of biceps brachii muscle are comparable to the computed values. The upper limb is verified.

Table 4. The comparison of the measured and computed activation of the biceps brachii muscle normalized by case with 5 kg of load, where F_{01}, F_{02}, F_{03} are the used objective function

Loading [kg]	Normalized muscle activations [–]				Difference [%]		
	Model	Experiment					
		F_{01}	F_{02}	F_{03}	F_{01}	F_{02}	F_{03}
0.5	0.180	0.209	0.209	0.203	13.06	13.6	16.1
1.0	0.271	0.297	0.297	0.294	12.6	12.6	13.5
1.5	0.362	0.385	0.385	0.383	8.6	8.6	9.1
2.0	0.454	0.473	0.473	0.411	10.1	10.1	21.9
2.5	0.545	0.561	0.561	0.488	2.9	2.9	15.6
3.0	0.636	0.648	0.648	0.564	9.6	9.6	4.5
3.5	0.727	0.736	0.736	0.735	11.3	11.3	11.2
4.0	0.818	0.824	0.824	0.823	3.3	3.3	3.1
4.5	0.909	0.912	0.912	0.912	13.3	13.3	13.3
5.0	1.000	1.000	1.000	1.000	0.00	0.0	0.0

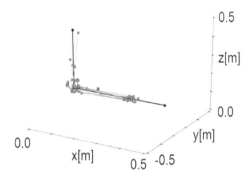

Fig. 13. Resulting model of the upper limb

5. Conclusion

The main aim of proposed study is to compose a computational upper limb model of a human body. The model computes muscle forces generated to keep a given loaded static upper limb position. The upper limb model is implemented in a programming language called Python.

Model consists of three rigid segments representing the arm, the forearm and the hand. These segments are connected by rotational joints. Joint movements are restricted to a planar. The whole upper limb model is fixed to a frame in the shoulder joint. Muscles are modeled by strings fixed to the segments according to the real anatomy.

A static balance problem is solved by a principle of virtual work. The musculoskeletal system is overdetermined. It means that more muscles contribute to keep a given static position than it is necessary. Thus, this problem is solved by an optimization method searching the least energetically-consuming solution. Three objective functions are used and then compared. The normalized muscle activations, as well as differences, are the same using the first and the second function. The third function has different resulting values. The second function has in addition the lower number of iterations. Thus, the second objective function is considered to be the most suitable.

The model is verified by EMG measurement. The normalized measured and computed muscle activations of the biceps brachii muscle are compared. The analysis shows that the values are comparable.

Acknowledgements

This work is supported by the internal grant project SGS-2010-007 and by New Technologies-Research centre.

References

[1] Craik, R. L., Oatis, C. A., Gait analysis, Mosby, 1994.

[2] Pathobiomechanics and pathokinesiology – Electromyography, Kompendium, (2013), (in Czech) http://biomech.ftvs.cuni.cz/pbpk/kompendium/biomechanika/experiment_metody_emg.php.

[3] Kraft, D., A software package for sequential quadratic programming, Technical Report DFVLR-FB 88–28, DLR German Aerospace Center — Institute for Dynamics of Flight Systems, Germany, 1988.

[4] Křen, J., Janíček, P., Rosenberg, J., Biomechanics, University of West Bohemia, Pilsen, 2001. (in Czech)

[5] Merletti, R., Parke, P. A., Electromyography — Physiology, engineering and noninvasive applications, John Wiley & Sons, 2004.

[6] Robbins, D. H., Anthropometric specifications for mid-sized male dummy, Technical report, University of Michigan, December 1983.

[7] Rosenberg, J., Theoretical mechanics, University of West Bohemia, Pilsen, 2003. (in Czech)

[8] Seiger, A., Arvikar, R., Biomechanical analysis of the musculoskeletal structure for medicine and sports, Hemisphere Publishing Corporation, 1989.

[9] Tavares da Silva, M. P., Human motion analysis using multibody dynamics and optimization tools, Ph.D. thesis, Universidade Técnica de Lisboa, Instituto Superior Técnico, 2003.

[10] Tsirakos, D., Baltzopoulos, V., Bartlett, R., Inverse optimization: Functional and physiological considerations related to the force-sharing problem, Critical Reviews in Biomedical Engineering 4–5 (25) (1997) 371–407.

[11] Valdmanová, L., Čechová, H., Usage of electromyography measurement in human body modeling, Applied and Computational Mechanics 5 (1) (2010) 67–76.

[12] Wittek, A., Mathematical modeling of the muscle effects on the human body responses under transient loads, Ph.D. thesis, Chalmers University of Technology, 2000.

16

Vibration analysis of tapered rotating composite beams using the hierarchical finite element

R. Ghayour[a], M. Ghayour[a,*], S. Ziaei-Rad[a]

[a]*Department of Mechanical Engineering, Isfahan University of Technology, Isfahan 84156-83111, Iran*

Abstract

A hierarchical finite element model is presented for the flapwise bending vibration analysis of a tapered rotating multi-layered composite beam. The shear and rotary inertia effects are considered based on the higher shear deformation theory to derive the stiffness and mass matrices of a tapered-twisted rotating and composite beam element. Certain non-composite beams for which comparative results are available in the literature are used to illustrate the application of the proposed technique. Dimensionless parameters are identified from the equations of motion and the combined effects of the dimensionless parameters on the modal characteristics of the rotating composite beams are investigated through numerical studies. The results indicate that, compared with the conventional finite element method, the hierarchical finite element has the advantage of using fewer elements to obtain a better accuracy in the calculation of the vibration characteristics of rotating beams such as natural frequencies and mode shapes.

Keywords: vibration, tapered, composite beam, hierarchical FEM, rotating

1. Introduction

Rotating, tapered, laminated composite beams are basic structural components with applications in a variety of engineering structures such as airplane wings, helicopter blades, and turbine blades. The great possibilities provided by composite materials can be used to alter favorably the response characteristics of these structures. Due to their outstanding engineering properties, such as high stiffness-to-weight ratio, composite beam structures play a significant role in designing structures in which weight and strength are of primary importance. The behavior of composite beam structures can also be effectively and efficiently tailored by changing the lay-up parameters. It need be mentioned that it is far more difficult to analyze composite beams than it is to analyze their metallic counterparts.

An important element in the dynamic analysis of composite beams is the computation of their natural frequencies and mode shapes. This is important because composite beam structures often operate in complex environmental conditions and are frequently exposed to a variety of dynamic excitations. The characteristics of rotating flexible structures differ significantly from those of non-rotating ones. Centrifugal inertia force due to rotational motion causes variation in bending stiffness, which naturally results in variations in natural frequencies and mode shapes. Moreover, the stiffness property of composite structures can be easily modulated through changing their fiber orientation angles and number of layers.

The finite element method (FEM) is one of the most powerful numerical procedures for solving mathematical problems in engineering and physics. Nowadays, advanced formulations

---
*Corresponding author. e-mail: ghayour@cc.iut.ac.ir.

of the method such as the hierarchical FEM (HFEM) have been introduced. In conventional FEM, a beam element is modeled using two nodes at the end. Therefore, a large number of elements are needed to achieve an acceptable accuracy. In HFEM, however, a number of polynomial or trigonometric terms is introduced into the displacement and rotation function that yield higher degrees of freedom. Thus, the same accuracy can be achieved by using a much smaller number of elements. This results in rapid convergence.

Over the past four decades, investigators have carried out intensive studies on the dynamic analysis of rotating structures to improve their efficiency and dynamic characteristics. L. Chen and H. Chen [1] used the finite element model and incorporated the effect of rotation to study the transient response of a rotating blade of generally orthotropic materials. Sabuncu and Thomas [2] studied the vibration characteristics of pre-twisted aerofoil cross-section blade packets under rotating conditions. An improved two-node Timoshenko beam finite element was derived by Friedman and Kosmatka [3].The vibration of Timoshenko beams with discontinuities in cross-section was investigated by Farghaly and Gadelab [4, 5]. Corn *et al.* [6] derived finite element models through Guyan condensation method for the transverse vibration of short beams. Gupta and Rao [7] considered the finite element analysis of tapered and twisted Timoshenko beams. Gupta and Rao [8] applied finite element method for the analysis of rotating Timoshenko beams. A modeling method for the flapwise bending vibration analysis of a rotating multi-layered composite beam is presented in [9]. According to [10], a method is developed for dynamic response analysis of spinning tapered Timoshenko beams utilizing the finite element method. In [11], the effect of centrifugal forces on the eigenvalue solution obtained from using two different nonlinear finite element formulations is examined. In [12], the free and forced vibration of a rotating, pretwisted blade modeled as a laminated composite, hollow (single celled), uniform box-beam is studied. The structural model includes transverse shear flexibility, restrained warping, and centrifugal and Coriolis effects.

Most of these analytical works on composites are limited to static analysis. At the same time, the works on dynamic analysis of composite plates or beams have concentrated on uniform laminates. Tapered laminated beams have rarely ever been investigated despite their applications in important structures. Hoa and Ganesan [13] presented a review of recent developments in the analysis of tapered laminated composite structures with an emphasis on interlaminar stress analysis and delamination analysis. EL-Maksoud [14] studied the dynamic analysis of uniform and mid-plane tapered composite beams by using conventional and higher order finite element formulations. Borneman [15] presents a new dynamic finite element formulation for the free vibration of composite wings modeled as beam assemblies. W. Liu [16] studied the instability of tapered laminates under dynamic loading conditions. In [17], a dynamic finite element method for free vibration analysis of generally laminated composite beams is introduced on the basis of first order shear deformation theory. The influences of Poisson effect, couplings among extensional, bending and torsional deformations, shear deformation and rotary inertia are incorporated into the formulation. Conventional cubic Hermitian finite element formulation requires a large number of elements to obtain reasonably accurate results in the analysis of tapered laminated beams. Since the continuity of curvature at element interfaces cannot be guaranteed with the use of conventional formulation, the stress distribution across the thickness is not continuous at element interfaces. The material and geometric discontinuities at ply drop-off locations leads to additional discontinuities in stress distributions. As a result, efficient and accurate calculation of natural frequencies becomes very difficult.

In order to overcome these limitations, HFEM has been recently developed in many papers. Zabihollah [18] presents the vibration and buckling analysis of uniform and tapered composite beams using advanced finite element methods based on the classical laminate theory and the first shear deformation theory. Barrette [19] presented the vibration analysis of stiffened plates using hierarchical finite element with a set of local trigonometric interpolation functions. The functions have shown great numerical stability. Ramtekkar [20] used a mixed finite element formulation to calculate the natural frequencies of laminated beams. Nigam [21] used the hierarchical finite element method to investigate the static and dynamic responses of uniformly laminated composite beams. He used both polynomial and trigonometric functions and compared the convergences and accuracies to find that the latter outperforms the former. L. Chen [22] compared the conventional finite element with hierarchical finite element method in calculating natural frequencies. HFEM has the advantage of achieving a higher accuracy by using fewer elements.

In this paper, a hierarchical finite element technique is applied to find the natural frequencies and mode shapes of composite beams in the bending mode of vibration by taking into account the taper and the rotation simultaneously. The element mass and stiffness matrices are derived and the effects of offset, rotation, taper ratio, and shear deformation on the beam natural frequencies are investigated.

2. Derivation of the equations of motion

The configuration of a cantilever beam attached to a rotating rigid hub with the radius r_e is shown in Figure 1. The elastic deformation of the beam is denoted by $\vec{u}$ in the Figure.

Neglecting u along the beam in flapwise vibration analysis of rotating beams, the degrees of freedom for every point of the beam are $w(x,t)$ and $\theta(x,t)$.

The strain energy of a solid body in Cartesian coordinates can be expressed as:

$$U = \frac{1}{2} \iiint (\sigma_x \varepsilon_x + \sigma_y \varepsilon_y + \sigma_z \varepsilon_z + \tau_{yz} \gamma_{yz} + \tau_{xz} \gamma_{xz} + \tau_{xy} \gamma_{xy}) \, \mathrm{d}x \, \mathrm{d}y \, \mathrm{d}z -$$
$$\frac{1}{2} \iint \left[N_x \left(\frac{\partial w}{\partial x} \right)^2 + 2 N_{xy} \frac{\partial w}{\partial x} \frac{\partial w}{\partial y} + N_y \left(\frac{\partial w}{\partial y} \right)^2 \right] \mathrm{d}x \, \mathrm{d}y. \tag{1}$$

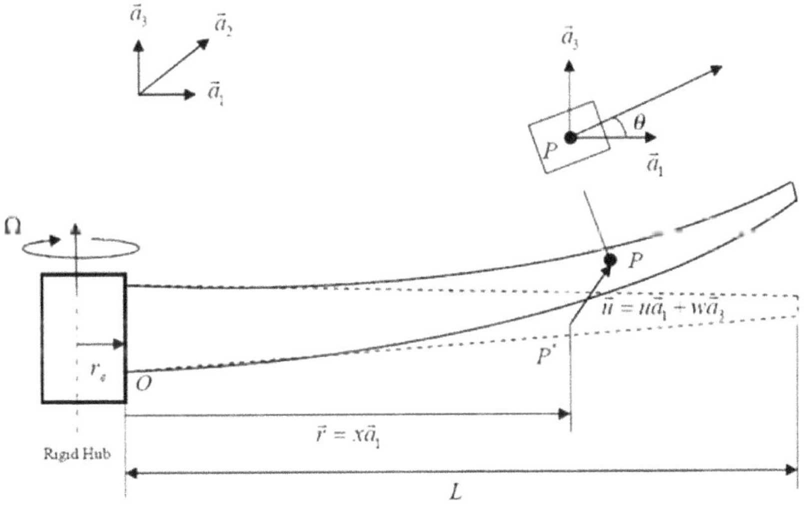

Fig. 1. Configuration of a rotating tapered cantilever beam

In rotating beam, the only load is the axial one due to the centrifugal force; thus

$$N_x = -\int_{r_e+x}^{r_e+L} \frac{\rho}{b}\Omega^2 x \, \mathrm{d}x = -\frac{\rho\Omega^2}{2b}\left((r_e+L)^2 - (r_e+x)^2\right) =$$

$$-\frac{\rho\Omega^2}{2b}\left(L^2 - x^2 + 2r_e(L-x)\right). \tag{2}$$

In the above equation, ρ is the mass per unit length of the beam and b is the width of the rotating beam. The relation between stress and strain in the layers of a tapered laminated composite beam is

$$\begin{Bmatrix} \sigma_x \\ \sigma_y \\ \sigma_z \\ \tau_{yz} \\ \tau_{xz} \\ \tau_{xy} \end{Bmatrix} = \begin{bmatrix} \bar{C}_{11} & \bar{C}_{12} & \bar{C}_{13} & \bar{C}_{14} & \bar{C}_{15} & \bar{C}_{16} \\ & \bar{C}_{22} & \bar{C}_{23} & \bar{C}_{24} & \bar{C}_{25} & \bar{C}_{26} \\ & & \bar{C}_{33} & \bar{C}_{34} & \bar{C}_{35} & \bar{C}_{36} \\ & & & \bar{C}_{44} & \bar{C}_{45} & \bar{C}_{46} \\ & & & & \bar{C}_{55} & \bar{C}_{56} \\ sym & & & & & \bar{C}_{66} \end{bmatrix} \begin{Bmatrix} \varepsilon_x \\ \varepsilon_y \\ \varepsilon_z \\ \gamma_{yz} \\ \gamma_{xz} \\ \gamma_{xy} \end{Bmatrix}. \tag{3}$$

The shear stresses are related to the strains by

$$\begin{Bmatrix} \tau_{yz} \\ \tau_{xz} \end{Bmatrix} = \begin{bmatrix} \bar{C}_{14} & \bar{C}_{24} & \bar{C}_{34} & \bar{C}_{44} & \bar{C}_{45} & \bar{C}_{46} \\ \bar{C}_{15} & \bar{C}_{25} & \bar{C}_{35} & \bar{C}_{45} & \bar{C}_{55} & \bar{C}_{56} \end{bmatrix} \begin{Bmatrix} \varepsilon_x \\ \varepsilon_y \\ \varepsilon_z \\ \gamma_{yz} \\ \gamma_{xz} \\ \gamma_{xy} \end{Bmatrix}. \tag{4}$$

Since we assume that $w(x, y, z, t) = w^\circ(x, t)$, the strain ε_z is zero. Therefore, the shear stresses are a function of five strains. If one neglects the inplane strains ε_x, ε_y and γ_{xy}, the shear stresses relate to the shear strains by

$$\begin{Bmatrix} \tau_{yz} \\ \tau_{xz} \end{Bmatrix} = k \begin{bmatrix} \bar{C}_{44} & \bar{C}_{45} \\ \bar{C}_{45} & \bar{C}_{55} \end{bmatrix} \begin{Bmatrix} \gamma_{yz} \\ \gamma_{xz} \end{Bmatrix}. \tag{5}$$

The factor k called the shear factor is equal to 5/6. Due to the first order shear theory for composite beam, the strains in the one dimension case are

$$\varepsilon_x = z\frac{\partial\theta}{\partial x}, \qquad \gamma_{xz} = \theta + \frac{\partial w}{\partial x}, \tag{6}$$

where w, θ are functions of x, t. Let us define

$$A_{55} = b\int_{-\frac{H}{2}}^{\frac{H}{2}} \bar{C}_{55} \, \mathrm{d}z, \qquad D_{11} = b\int_{-\frac{H}{2}}^{\frac{H}{2}} \bar{C}_{11} z^2 \, \mathrm{d}z. \tag{7}$$

Using the above parameters, the strain energy of the tapered composite rotating beam will be

$$
\begin{aligned}
U &= \frac{1}{2} \iiint \left(\bar{C}_{11} \varepsilon_x^2 + k\bar{C}_{55} \gamma_{xz}^2 \right) \, \mathrm{d}x \, \mathrm{d}y \, \mathrm{d}z + \\
&\quad \frac{1}{2} \int \frac{\rho\Omega^2}{2} \left(L^2 - x^2 + 2r_e(L-x) \right) \left(\frac{\partial w}{\partial x} \right)^2 \mathrm{d}x = \\
&\quad \frac{1}{2} \iiint \left(\bar{C}_{11} z^2 \left(\frac{\partial \theta}{\partial r} \right)^2 + k\bar{C}_{55} \left(\theta + \frac{\partial w}{\partial x} \right)^2 \right) \mathrm{d}x \, \mathrm{d}y \, \mathrm{d}z + \\
&\quad \frac{1}{2} \int \frac{\rho\Omega^2}{2} \left(L^2 - x^2 + 2r_e(L-x) \right) \left(\frac{\partial w}{\partial x} \right)^2 \mathrm{d}x = \\
&\quad \frac{1}{2} \iint b \left(\bar{C}_{11} z^2 \left(\frac{\partial \theta}{\partial x} \right)^2 + k\bar{C}_{55} \left(\theta + \frac{\partial w}{\partial x} \right)^2 \right) \mathrm{d}x \, \mathrm{d}z + \\
&\quad \frac{1}{2} \int \frac{\rho\Omega^2}{2} \left(L^2 - x^2 + 2r_e(L-x) \right) \left(\frac{\partial w}{\partial x} \right)^2 \mathrm{d}x = \\
&\quad \frac{1}{2} \int_0^L \left(D_{11} \left(\frac{\partial \theta}{\partial x} \right)^2 + kA_{55} \left(\theta + \frac{\partial w}{\partial x} \right)^2 \right) \mathrm{d}x + \\
&\quad \frac{1}{2} \int_0^L \frac{\rho\Omega^2}{2} \left(L^2 - x^2 + 2r_e(L-x) \right) \left(\frac{\partial w}{\partial x} \right)^2 \mathrm{d}x .
\end{aligned} \tag{8}
$$

The strain energy in its final form will be

$$
\begin{aligned}
U &= \frac{1}{2} \int_0^L kA_{55} \left(\frac{\partial w}{\partial x} \right)^2 \mathrm{d}x + \frac{1}{2} \int_0^L kA_{55} \left(\frac{\partial w}{\partial x} \right) \theta \, \mathrm{d}x + \\
&\quad \frac{1}{2} \Omega^2 r_e \rho \int_0^L (L-x) \left(\frac{\partial w}{\partial x} \right)^2 \mathrm{d}x + \frac{1}{4} \Omega^2 \rho \int_0^L (L^2 - x^2) \left(\frac{\partial w}{\partial x} \right)^2 \mathrm{d}x + \\
&\quad \frac{1}{2} \int_0^L kA_{55} \theta \left(\frac{\partial w}{\partial x} \right) \mathrm{d}x + \frac{1}{2} \int_0^L D_{11} \left(\frac{\partial \theta}{\partial x} \right)^2 \mathrm{d}x + \frac{1}{2} \int_0^L kA_{55} \theta^2 \, \mathrm{d}x .
\end{aligned} \tag{9}
$$

The kinetic energy of the tapered composite rotating beam can be written as

$$
\begin{aligned}
T &= \frac{1}{2} \iiint \rho' \left[\left(\frac{\partial u}{\partial t} \right)^2 + \left(\frac{\partial v}{\partial t} \right)^2 + \left(\frac{\partial w}{\partial t} \right)^2 \right] \mathrm{d}x \, \mathrm{d}y \, \mathrm{d}z = \\
&\quad \frac{1}{2} \int_0^L \rho \left(\frac{\partial w}{\partial t} \right)^2 \mathrm{d}x + \frac{1}{2} \int_0^L \rho \frac{I_z}{A} \left(\frac{\partial \theta}{\partial t} \right)^2 \mathrm{d}x ,
\end{aligned} \tag{10}
$$

where L denotes the length of the beam; k, the shear correction factor; θ, the cross-section rotation angle; ρ, the mass per unit length of the beam; b, the width of the beam; I_2, the area moment of inertia in $\hat{a}_2$ axis; and A is the cross-section area of the beam. Also A_{ij}, B_{ij} and D_{ij} can be obtained by integrating the properties of the tapered composite beam layers (see [22]).

3. Hierarchical Finite element formulation

The finite element configuration of a rotating tapered cantilever beam is shown in Figure 2.

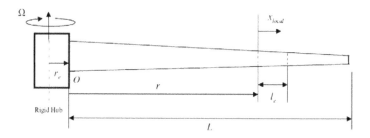

Fig. 2. Finite element configuration of a rotating tapered cantilever beam

For nodal analysis by HFEM, displacement and rotation functions are assumed to be as below:

$$w(x) = \left(1 - \frac{x}{l_e}\right) w_1 + \frac{x}{l_e} w_2 + \sum_{n=1}^{N} A_n \sin \frac{n\pi x}{l_e} = \tag{11}$$

$$\left[\begin{array}{ccccc} 1 - \frac{x}{l_e} & \frac{x}{l_e} & \sin \frac{\pi x}{l_e} & \cdots & \sin \frac{N\pi x}{l_e} \end{array}\right] \left\{\begin{array}{c} w_1 \\ w_2 \\ A_1 \\ \vdots \\ A_N \end{array}\right\},$$

$$\theta(x) = \left(1 - \frac{x}{l_e}\right) \theta_1 + \frac{x}{l_e} \theta_2 + \sum_{n=1}^{N} B_n \sin \frac{n\pi x}{l_e} =$$

$$\left[\begin{array}{ccccc} 1 - \frac{x}{l_e} & \frac{x}{l_e} & \sin \frac{\pi x}{l_e} & \cdots & \sin \frac{N\pi x}{l_e} \end{array}\right] \left\{\begin{array}{c} \theta_1 \\ \theta_2 \\ B_1 \\ \vdots \\ B_N \end{array}\right\},$$

where N is the number of hierarchical terms. In compact form

$$w(x) = [N^w] \{W\}, \qquad \theta(x) = [N^\theta] \{\Theta\}, \tag{12}$$

where $\{W\}$, $\{\Theta\}$ are the nodal displacements and rotations, respectively.

The expanded interpolation functions are:

$$[N^w] = [N^\theta] = \left[\begin{array}{c} 1 - \frac{x}{l_e} \\ \frac{x}{l_e} \\ \sin \frac{\pi x}{l_e} \\ \vdots \\ \sin \frac{n\pi x}{l_e} \end{array}\right]_{(2+n)\times 1}. \tag{13}$$

The following two notations are used:

$$[N^{dw}] = \frac{d[N^w]}{dx}, \tag{14}$$

$$[N^{d\theta}] = \frac{d[N^\theta]}{dx}. \tag{15}$$

The strain energy and kinetic energy of the system are:

$$U = \frac{1}{2} u^T [K] u, \qquad T = \frac{1}{2} \dot{u}^T [M] \dot{u}. \tag{16}$$

The components of the mass matrix are:

$$M_{11} = \int_0^{l_e} \rho [N^w]^T [N^w] \, dx, \tag{17}$$

$$M_{22} = \int_0^{l_e} \rho \frac{I_2}{A} [N^\theta]^T [N^\theta] \, dx. \tag{18}$$

For the stiffness matrix, the components are:

$$K_{11} = \int_0^{l_e} k A_{55} [N^{dw}]^T [N^{dw}] \, dx +$$
$$\Omega^2 \left\{ r_e \rho \left(\int_0^{l_e} (L - (x + r)) [N^{dw}]^T [N^{dw}] \, dx \right) + \right.$$
$$\left. \frac{1}{2} \rho \left(\int_0^{l_e} (L^2 - (x + r)^2) [N^{dw}]^T [N^{dw}] \, dx \right) \right\} \tag{19}$$

$$K_{12} = \int_0^{l_e} k A_{55} [N^{dw}]^T [N^\theta] \, dx \tag{20}$$

$$K_{21} = \int_0^{l_e} k A_{55} [N^{d\theta}]^T [N^w] \, dx \tag{21}$$

$$K_{22} = \int_0^{l_e} D_{11} [N^{d\theta}]^T [N^{d\theta}] \, dx + \int_0^{l_e} k A_{55} [N^\theta]^T [N^\theta] \, dx. \tag{22}$$

By solving the following equation, the natural frequencies and the mode shapes of the composite rotating beam are obtained as:

$$\left| [K] - \omega^2 [M] \right| = 0, \tag{23}$$

where

$$[M] = \begin{bmatrix} M_{11} & 0 \\ 0 & M_{22} \end{bmatrix}, \tag{24}$$

$$[K] = \begin{bmatrix} K_{11} & K_{12} \\ K_{21} & K_{22} \end{bmatrix}. \tag{25}$$

4. Numerical results

Based on the above formulation, a finite element code was developed for the rotating composite beams. In what follows, the code will be verified using the data available in the literature.

4.1. Free vibration of a non-rotating simply-supported composite beam

In order to validate the present dynamic stiffness formulation, a symmetric cross-ply $[90°/0°/0°/90°]$ laminated beam with the simply-supported boundary condition is considered. This example is selected due to the comparative results already available in [23]. The properties of the laminated beam are presented in Table 1.

Table 1. Material properties of the laminated beam

E_1 (GPa)	E_2 (GPa)	G_{12} (GPa)	G_{13} (GPa)	G_{23} (GPa)	ν_{12}	ρ (Kg/m^3)	L (m)	b (m)	h (m)
241.5	18.98	5.18	5.18	3.45	0.24	2015	6.35	0.2794	0.2794

The first six natural frequencies of the simply-supported laminated beam for the first six modes are calculated using the HFEM presented in Table 2. The number of hierarchical elements used in the calculation is 100. Table 2 also shows a comparison of the results with those of [23] and the Abaqus solutions in [24]. It can be observed that the present results are in good agreement with those presented in [23, 24].

Table 2. Natural frequencies (in Hz) of simply-supported laminated beam

Mode	ω Ref [23]	ω Abaqus [24]	ω Present Study
1	14.9	14.95	15.00
2	58.1	57.6	58.1
3	124.5	122.8	124.7
4	208.6	204.2	208.8
5	304.8	296.6	305.0
6	408.9	396.2	409.2

4.2. Vibration of a rotating fixed-free composite beam using HFEM

In this example, a tapered composite beam is considered and the results are presented for both stationary and rotating cases. To obtain the numerical results, the composite beams consisting of 4 skew symmetric fiber orientation layers $[0°/90°/-90°/0°]$ are considered in this example. All the layers have identical thicknesses and the composite beams are made of graphite-epoxy. The beam aspect ratio is assumed to be $L/h = 10$, where L is the length of the beam and h denotes beam width and thickness. The material properties of the graphite-epoxy are given in Table 3.

Table 3. Material properties of the graphite- epoxy used for the composite beams

E_1 (GPa)	E_2 (GPa)	E_3 (GPa)	G_{12} (GPa)	G_{13} (GPa)	G_{23} (GPa)	ν_{13}	k
145	9.6	9.6	4.1	4.1	3.4	0.3	5/6

To check the accuracy of the modeling method proposed in this study, the numerical results obtained are compared with those presented in [9] and those obtained from the commercial program Ansys. The number of hierarchical terms is set to 100.

In Table 4, $\bar{\omega}$ denotes the dimensionless natural frequencies (i.e. natural frequencies multiplied by $T \equiv \sqrt{\frac{\rho L^4}{D}}$, where D denotes the value of D_{11} when all the layer angles are zero). For the composite beam with rotation, a constant $\gamma = T\Omega$ is defined where Ω is the angular speed of the rigid hub.

Table 4. Comparison of the first five dimensionless natural frequencies for a stationary composite beam

Mode	$\bar{\omega}$ Ref [25]	$\bar{\omega}$ Ref [9]	$\bar{\omega}$ Present Study
1	3.073	3.064	3.062
2	14.44	14.36	14.18
3	31.75	31.40	30.91
4	49.68	48.87	47.98
5	66.23	66.21	65.15

Table 5. Comparison of the first three dimensionless natural frequencies for the rotating composite beam

γ	Mode	Ref [9]	ANSYS [9]	Present Study
0	1	3.067	3.06	3.062
	2	14.359	14.172	14.183
	3	31.397	30.878	30.908
10	1	10.698	10.63	10.62
	2	28.802	28.525	28.478
	3	52.397	51.729	51.696
20	1	20.522	20.356	20.324
	2	51.492	51.05	50.97
	3	86.791	85.786	85.779

4.3. Vibration of a rotating tapered composite beam using HFEM

A tapered composite beam is made of NCT301 graphite-epoxy is shown in Figure 3. Its mechanical properties are shown in Table 6.

Table 6. Mechanical properties of NCT301 graphite-epoxy

E_1 (GPa)	E_2, E_3 (GPa)	ν_{21}, ν_{31}	ν_{23}	G_{12}, G_{13} (GPa)	G_{23} (GPa)	ρ (Kg/m^3)
144	12.14	0.017	0.458	4.48	3.2	1 660.8

Fig. 3. Free-fixed tapered composite beam

The geometric properties of the beam are: length, $L = 0.304\,8$ m; and individual ply thickness, $t = 0.000\,152\,4$ m. There are 32 plies at the left end and 30 plies at the right end. The configuration of both ends are $[(0/90)_8]_S$ and $[(0/90)_7/0]_S$, respectively.

The parameters related to the tapered properties of the composite beam are:
$$A_{55} = 18\,726\,912 - 3\,200\,000x \ (\text{N} \cdot \text{m}^{-1}),$$
$$D_{11} = 817.122 - 490.366x + 95.509\,7x^2 - 1.015\,15x^3 \ (\text{N} \cdot \text{m}),$$
$$D = -12.044x^3 + 176.19x^2 - 859.2x + 1\,396.6 \ (\text{N} \cdot \text{m}).$$

Table 7 presents the first four natural frequencies of the non-rotating tapered composite beam with simply supported boundary conditions. This sub case was selected to further validate the proposed method and the associated code developed. The results calculated by using the code are compared with those reported in [22], which have been obtained by using the Ritz method. It is noteworthy that there is no exact solution for the tapered composite beams.

Table 7. Natural frequencies of non-rotation simply supported tapered composite beam

Mode	ω (Rad/s) Using Ritz method [22]	ω (Rad/s) Present Study
1	1 031.89	1 063.99
2	4 096.45	4 219.83
3	9 101.65	9 363.77
4	15 906.20	16 337.24

The first five natural frequencies of the rotating fixed-free tapered beam are presented in Table 8. Natural frequencies are calculated for the following three different conditions: 1) non-rotating ($\gamma = 0$), and the rotating cases ($\gamma = 10$, $\gamma = 20$).

Table 8. Natural frequencies of fixed-free tapered composite beam (Rad/Sec)

γ	mode	$m = 10$ $n = 0$	$m = 10$ $n = 1$	$m = 10$ $n = 2$	$m = 10$ $n = 3$	$m = 10$ $n = 4$	$m = 10$ $n = 5$	$m = 10$ $n = 6$	$m = 10$ $n = 7$	$m = 10$ $n = 8$
	1	606.93	389.38	388.78	385.78	385.744 24	385.322 85	385.317 17	385.204 49	385.202 9
	2	3 816.74	2 427.84	2 416.83	2 398.91	2 398.178 9	2 395.667 3	2 395.527 4	2 394.855 3	2 394.812 7
0	3	10 822.77	6 745.77	6 680.89	6 635.06	6 630.660 1	6 624.252 2	6 623.393 7	6 621.676 9	6 621.410 5
	4	21 652.32	13 082.52	12 855.53	12 778.09	12 762.989	12 752.195	12 749.229	12 746.331	12 745.404
	5	36 727.51	21 368.42	20 774.29	20 671.47	20 633.429	20 619.137	20 611.658	20 607.808	20 605.465
	1	1 649.750 4	1 566.372	1 565.428 5	1 564.276 7	1 564.206 1	1 564.044 6	1 564.030 4	1 563.987 2	1 563.982 7
	2	5 288.555 7	4 381.221 8	4 373.395	4 362.888	4 362.341 1	4 360.875 7	4 360.768 8	4 360.377 3	4 360.344 1
10	3	12 428.722	9 037.720 1	8 986.745 4	8 950.758	8 947.272 8	8 942.261 3	8 941.577 9	8 940.237	8 940.024 2
	4	23 387.187	15 636.352	15 442.359	15 374.617	15 361.704	15 352.297	15 349.757	15 347.235	15 346.441
	5	38 570.16	24 105.481	23 570.153	23 475.037	23 440.807	23 427.634	23 420.904	23 417.361	23 415.252
	1	3 058.334 7	2 994.325 7	2 992.050 1	2 990.948 3	2 990.773 4	2 990.618 4	2 990.582 4	2 990.541	2 990.529 5
	2	8 221.556 3	7 621.025 2	7 612.304 4	7 604.968	7 604.328 4	7 603.309 1	7 603.180 4	7 602.908 4	7 602.867 8
20	3	16 241.623	13 605.421	13 561.763	13 533.673	13 530.646	13 526.756	13 526.156	13 525.117	13 524.93
	4	27 874.147	21 320.01	21 156.104	21 099.273	21 088.355	21 080.511	21 078.357	21 076.26	21 075.585
	5	43 573.883	30 681.784	30 217.059	30 133.062	30 103.445	30 091.893	30 086.066	30 082.969	30 081.141

Parameter D is defined t as in Table 5; however it is here defined at the root place (i.e., at $x = 0$). In this Table, m denotes the number of elements and n is the number of trigonometric terms. The table indicates that by increasing the trigonometric terms, the accuracy of the solutions is enhanced. This is more apparent for higher modes. It is noticeable that for the first natural frequency of the non-rotating beam, even with 2 000 conventional elements, the results are different from those obtained with $m = 10$ and $n = 8$. The Table also shows that the natural frequencies of the beam increase with beam rotating speed.

Figures 4 to 7 depict the first four natural frequencies of the rotating tapered composite beam versus the number of elements.

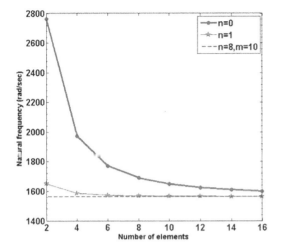

Fig. 4. The first natural frequency of rotating fixed-free tapered composite beam ($\gamma = 10$)

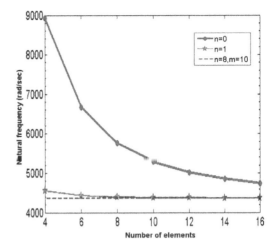

Fig. 5. The second natural frequency of rotating fixed-free tapered composite beam ($\gamma = 10$)

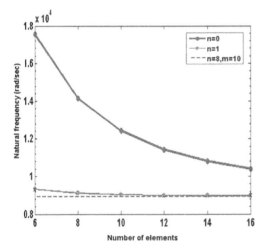

Fig. 6. The third natural frequency of rotating fixed-free tapered composite beam ($\gamma = 10$)

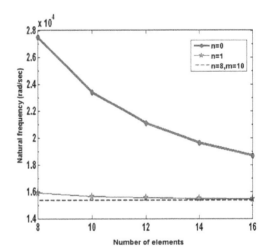

Fig. 7. The fourth natural frequency of rotating fixed-free tapered composite beam ($\gamma = 10$)

In each Figure, the results obtained from the conventional finite element code are compared with those of the HFEM with one trigonometric term (i.e. $n = 1$). The dashed line in each Figure is calculated for $m = 10$ and $n = 8$, which is assumed to be the exact solution.

The first five modes of vibrations are shown in Figures 8(a)–(e). In these Figures, the solid lines represent the mode shapes of the non-rotating beam while the dashed lines represent the same for the rotating beam. The Figures indicate that the deflection shape of a rotating beam is smaller than that of a non-rotating beam due to the centrifugal forces.

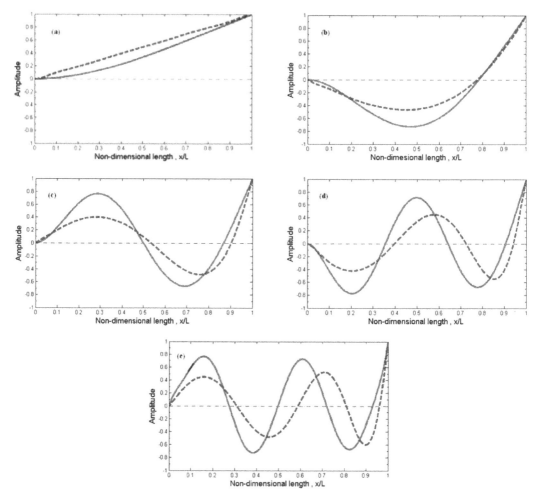

$— \gamma = 0$; ---- $\gamma = 100$ Mode number, $\omega_{\gamma=100}$: (a) 1, 14 448.63; (b) 2, 35 437.36; (c) 3, 56 618.81; (d) 4, 79 044.43; (e) 5, 102 898.88

Fig. 8. Mode shape of rotating fixed-free tapered composite beam

5. Conclusions

A hieratical finite element formulation was developed for the vibration analysis of rotating tapered composite beams. The taper angle of the composite beam changes not only its geometric properties but also the stiffness of the oblique plies. This causes the mechanical behavior of the tapered composite beam to be different from that of the uniform beam. Therefore, it is necessary to consider the effect of the laminate stiffness of the composite beam caused by the taper angle.

Based on the proposed formulation, the mass and stiffness matrices of a tapered composite rotating beam element were developed for the eigenvalue analysis of rotating, doubly tapered beams. The element was found to give reasonably accurate results. The consideration of shear deformation was found to reduce the values of the higher natural frequencies of beam vibration.

The results indicate that the hieratical finite element formulation uses fewer elements to obtain accurate results, which, in turn, leads to less costly computational processes. Comparison with available data reveals that the method is accurate and can be used for a large class of rotating beams.

References

[1] Chen, L. W., Chen, H. K., Transient responses of a pre-twisted rotating blade of general orthotropy, Finite Elements Anal. Des. (13) (1993) 285–298.

[2] Sabuncu, M., Thomas, J., Vibration characteristics of pretwisted aerofoil cross-section blade packets under rotating conditions, American Institute of Aeronautics and Astronautics Journal (30) (1992) 241–250.

[3] Friedman, Z., Kosmatka, J.B., An improved two-node Timoshenko beam finite element, Computers and Structures (47) (1993) 473–481.

[4] Farghaly, S. H., Vibration and stability analysis of Timoshenko beams with discontinuities in cross-section, Journal of Sound and vibration (174) (1994) 591–605.

[5] Farghaly, S. H., Gadelrab, R.M., Free vibration of a stepped composite Timoshenko cantilever beam, Journal of Sound and vibration (187) (1995) 886–896.

[6] Corn, S., Buhaddi, N., Piranda, J., Transverse vibrations of short beams: finite element models obtained by a condensation method, Journal of Sound and vibration (201) (1997) 353–363.

[7] Gupta, R. S., Rao, S. S., Finite element eigenvalue analysis of tapered and twisted Timoshenko beams, Journal of Sound and vibration (56) (1978) 187–200.

[8] Gupta, R. S., Rao, S. S., Finite element vibration analysis of rotating Timoshenko beams. J. Sound Vibration 242(1) (2001) 103–24.

[9] Yoo, H. H., Lee, S. H., Shin, S. H., Flapwise bending vibration analysis of rotating multi-layered composite beams, Journal of Sound and Vibration (286) (2005) 745–761.

[10] Bazoune, A., Khulief, Y.A., Stephen, N. G., Mohiuddin, M. A., Dynamic response of spinning tapered Timoshenko beams using modal reduction, Finite Elements in Analysis and Design (37) (2001) 199–219.

[11] Maqueda, L. G., Bauchau, O. A., Shabana, A. A., Effect of the centrifugal forces on the finite element eigenvalue solution of a rotating blade: a comparative study, Springer Science Multibody Syst Dyn (19) (2008) 281–302.

[12] Chandiramania, N. K., Shetea, C. D., Librescu, L. I., Vibration of higher-order-shearable pretwisted rotating composite blades, International Journal of Mechanical Sciences (45) (2003) 2 017–2 041.

[13] He, K., Hoa, S. V., Ganesan, R., The study of tapered laminated composite structures: a review, composites science and technology 60 (14) (2000) 2 643–2 657.

[14] EL-Maksoud Abd, Mohamed, A., Dynamic analysis and Buckling of variable thickness laminated composite beams using conventional and advanced finite element formulation, M.A.Sc. Thesis, Concordia University, 2000.

[15] Borneman, S. R., A New Dynamic Finite Element Formulation with Application To Composite Aircraft Wings, M.A.Sc. Thesis, Ryerson University, 2004.

[16] Liu, W., Dynamic instability analysis of tapered composite plates using Ritz and finite element methods, M.A.Sc. Thesis, Concordia University, 2005.

[17] Jun, L., Hongxing, H., Rongying, S. H., Dynamic finite element method for generally laminated composite beams, International Journal of Mechanical Sciences, (50) (2008) 466–480.

[18] Zabihollah, A., Vibration analysis of tapered composite beams using a higher-order finite element formulations, composite structures, (77) (2007) 306–318.

[19] Barrette, M., Berry, A., Vibration of stiffened plates using Hierarchical Trigonometric Functions, Journal of Sound and Vibration, 235(5) (2000) 727–747.

[20] Ramtekkar, G. S., Desai, Y. M. Natural Vibration of Laminated Composite Beams by Mixed Finite Element Modeling, Journal of Sound and Vibration, Vol. 257(4) (2002) 635–651.

[21] Nigan, Amit, Dynamic Analysis of Composite Beams using Hierarchical Finite Element Meyhod, M.A.Sc. Thesis Concordia University, 2002.

[22] Chen, L., Free Vibration Analysis of Tapered Composite Beams using Hierarchical Finite Element Method, M.A.Sc. Thesis Concordia University, 2004.

[23] Jun, L., Hongxing, H., Rongying, S., Dynamic stiffness analysis for free vibrations of axially loaded laminated composite beams, Composite Structures (84) (2008) 87–98.

[24] Karama, M., Abou Harb, B., Mistou, S., Caperaa, S., Bending, buckling and free vibration of laminated composite with a transverse shear stress continuity model, Composite (29) (1998) 223–234.

[25] Singh, M., Abdelnaser, A., Random response of symmetric cross-ply composite beams with arbitrary boundary conditions, AIAA Journal (30) (1992) 201–210.

17

Influence of delayed excitation on vibrations of turbine blades couple

L. Půst[a],*, L. Pešek[a]

[a]Institute of Thermomechanics ASCR, Dolejškova 5, 182 00 Praha 8, Czech Republic

Abstract

In the presented paper, the computational model of the turbine blade couple is investigated with the main attention to the influence two harmonic excitation forces, having the same frequency and amplitude but with moderate delay in time. Time delay between the exciting harmonic forces depends on the revolutions of bladed disk, on the number of blades on a rotating disk and on the number of stator blades. The reduction of resonance vibrations realized by means of dry friction between the shroud blade-heads increases roughly proportional to the difference of stator and rotor blade-numbers and also to the magnitude of dry friction force.

From the analysis of blade couple with direct contact it was proved that the increase of friction forces causes decrease of resonance peaks, but the influence of elastic micro-deformations in the contact surfaces (modeled e.g. by the modified Coulomb dry friction law) is rather small.

Analysis of a blade couple with a friction element shows that the lower number of stator blades has negligible influence on the amplitudes of both blades, but decreases amplitudes of the friction element oscillations. Similarly the increase of friction forces causes a decrease of resonance peaks, but an increase of friction element amplitudes.

Keywords: time delay, phase delay, blades couple, amplitude reduction, dry friction

1. Introduction

The enormous great resonance vibrations of turbine blades are very dangerous and are often the cause of serious crashes of power plants. The reduction of undesirable vibrations of turbine blades is very often realized by using the blade damping heads. A lot of theoretical, numerical and experimental studies were done in the Institute of Thermomechanics ASCR in cooperation with the University of West Bohemia on the problems of ascertaining the dynamic properties of bladed disks and of reduction of undesirable vibrations.

The main experimental set in laboratories of Institute of Thermomechanics ASCR is a model of a turbine disk, with blades connected either by direct contact or by an inserted friction element. There are many articles and books related to theoretical and experimental investigations of friction properties, e.g. [4, 13]. However, the literature sources on friction properties are mainly oriented to the study of friction properties at constant or slowly variable relative velocity in the friction contact surfaces, which is important e.g. for bearings, clutch, brakes, etc., but the friction at vibrations, where the contact velocity varies from positive to negative values in one period, has been given small attention. As an example let us mention book [2], where the friction processes are investigated on the various types of analytical models. Friction at vibrating, particularly stick-slip motion, are solved in [1, 3, 16], mainly for sphere contacts.

---

*Corresponding author. e-mail: pust@it.cas.cz.

The application of friction contact to the damping of blades systems occurs very often in praxis and also in technical literature. The friction properties in blade contact surfaces are analyzed in [5], properties of damper near the blade root are solved in [8] and [12]. The Influence of contact stiffness is considered in [15]. Numerical analysis of shroud friction blades contact by FE method is presented in [14]. No solution of phase-delayed excitation of blade couple with friction contact has been found in any accessible literature.

For detail discovering of friction processes and their influence on blades vibrations, the dynamic tests of separated blade couple connected by [11] describes the influence of various mathematical models of dry friction forces (modified Coulomb [9], spring-dry friction model [6], etc.) on the response curves of harmonically excited blade couple. In paper [7], there it is shown the additional effect of elastic stops, fixed to the friction element in order to prevent falling out of the slot during vibrations, both on reduction of amplitudes, but also on appearance of instability regions and existence of chaotic oscillations.

The dynamic systems investigated in both papers have two or three degrees of freedom, shown in Fig. 1 and were (unlike to here investigated system) excited only by one harmonic force $F_0 \cos \omega t$ acting on the first blade. The right hand subsystem was without any external excitation.

In the present paper, the same blades systems modeled by two or three degrees of freedom mathematical models are investigated with the main attention to the influence of the second excitation force, having the same frequency and amplitude but being moderately delayed in time. Parameters of these mathematical models were determined from the experimental models used in laboratory IT ASCR by means of eigenfrequency measurements and vibration amplitude decay of blade after the abrupt switching of excitation in resonance.

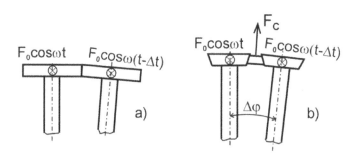

Fig. 1. Friction connection of blades

The reduction of undesirable vibrations of blades is realized by using blade damping heads, which are connected by either a direct friction contact (position a) or by inserted friction elements (position b), as seen in Fig. 1. In the first case, due to the de-twisting of both blades at rotation, the pressure in the appropriate contact surface produces friction losses and in consequence of this also the reduction of vibrations. In alternative b), the head tops of the blades are provided with the friction surfaces creating the wedge-shaped inter-head slot. The friction element is pushed in the slot by the centrifugal force under rotation or for non-rotating stationary tests by the static force F_c.

The blades vibrate in bending and torsion modes. It has been shown in [3], that blades in the real turbines have sufficiently high torsion eigenfrequencies and therefore their mutual interaction with the first bending mode is negligible. In this contribution, only the bending modes will be taken into account.

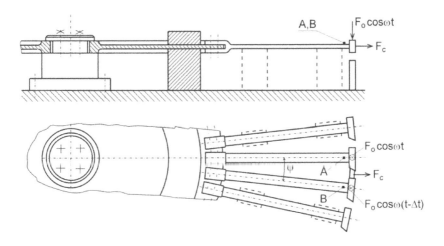

Fig. 2. Measurement of blade couple with inserted friction element

Laboratory measurements of a blade couple were realized on two selected blades, the roots of which were joined to the experimental disk, which was rigidly fastened to a steel plate basement. The other blades, except for the mentioned couple, were fastened to the steel plate as well — see Fig. 2.

2. Delay of excitation

In both cases of the blade-heads connection, the right blade is forced by a delayed harmonic force $F_0 \cos \omega(t - \Delta t)$. The time delay Δt of periodic excitation depends on the revolutions

$$n = \frac{60\omega_r}{2\pi} \tag{1}$$

of the bladed disk, on number l_r of blades on rotating disk and on number l_s of stator blades. Basic frequency f_e of excitation of an individual blade from the periodic distribution of pressure on the outflow behind the stator blade row is

$$f_e = \frac{n}{60} l_s, \qquad \omega_e = 2\pi f_e = \frac{2\pi}{60} n l_s. \tag{2}$$

The next blade is excited by the same excitation frequency f_e, but delayed on the time interval Δt proportional to the angle between l_r blades $\Delta\varphi = 2\pi/l_r$. This time interval is given by

$$\Delta t = \Delta\varphi/\omega_r = \frac{2\pi}{l_r} \bigg/ \frac{2\pi}{60} n = \frac{60}{l_r n}. \tag{3}$$

The exciting angular frequency at static experiments is $\omega - \omega_e$. Using (1) and (2) gives

$$\Delta t = \frac{60}{l_r n} = \frac{60}{l_r} \cdot \frac{1}{60\omega_e/2\pi l_s} = \frac{2\pi}{\omega} \cdot \frac{l_s}{l_r}. \tag{4}$$

The shifted excitation force acting on the second blade is

$$F_0 \cos \omega(t - \Delta t) = F_0 \cos \omega \left(t - \frac{2\pi}{\omega} \cdot \frac{l_s}{l_r} \right) = F_0 \cos \left(\omega t - 2\pi \cdot \frac{l_s}{l_r} \right), \tag{5}$$

where the delay is in the last formula expressed as phase angle shift, in the middle formula as the time shift.

3. Vibrations of a blade couple with a direct friction contact

A simplified mathematical model of such a couple is shown in Fig. 3. This model consists of two identical 1 DOF slightly damped subsystems connected by a direct friction contact. Blade's bending and damping were modeled by stiffness k and damping coefficient b, roughly corresponding to the experimentally ascertained values. As this analysis is limited to the lowest resonance frequency, the modeling by 1 DOF is eligible.

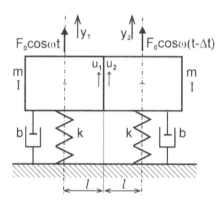

Fig. 3. Mathematical model of two blades system with direct friction contact

The analysis of up to now investigated model of blade couple with friction contact has been solved at the assumption that blades vibrate only in the bending mode. If we neglect a torsion vibration of blades, the velocities $\dot{u}_1$, $\dot{u}_2$ in the friction surfaces are

$$\dot{u}_1 = \dot{y}_1, \qquad \dot{u}_2 = \dot{y}_2. \tag{6}$$

Differential equations of motion are

$$\begin{aligned}
m\ddot{y}_1 + b\dot{y}_1 + ky_1 + F_t(\dot{u}_1 - \dot{u}_2) &= F_0 \cos \omega t, \\
m\ddot{y}_2 + b\dot{y}_2 + ky_2 - F_t(\dot{u}_1 - \dot{u}_2) &= F_0 \cos \omega (t - \Delta T),
\end{aligned} \tag{7}$$

where $\dot{u}_1 - \dot{u}_2 = \dot{y}_1 - \dot{y}_2$.

After substituting $\dot{u}_1$, $\dot{u}_2$ from (6) into (7) and using (5) we get equations with two unknown quantities y_1, y_2:

$$\begin{aligned}
m\ddot{y}_1 + b\dot{y}_1 + ky_1 + F_t(\dot{y}_1 - \dot{y}_2) &= F_0 \cos \omega t, \\
m\ddot{y}_2 + b\dot{y}_2 + ky_2 - F_t(\dot{y}_1 - \dot{y}_2) &= F_0 \cos \left(\omega t - 2\pi \frac{l_s}{l_r} \right).
\end{aligned} \tag{8}$$

Expression $F_t(\dot{y}_1 - \dot{y}_2) = F_t(\dot{u}_1 - \dot{u}_2)$ describes the dry friction forces in the heads slot.

Differential equations (7), (8) as well as (11) together with additional expressions (9), (10), (12) were solved in MATLAB R2012a version, using Runge-Kutta 4th order integrating methods. The time steps were 0.000 1 s in order to describe the sudden jumps of dry friction forces and other strong nonlinearities with sufficient accuracy. Numerical simulations give time histories of motion $y_1(t)$, $y_2(t)$, $y_3(t)$, from which the maxima of y_i i.e. amplitudes a_i were ascertained and plotted.

4. Dry friction properties

Dry friction is very complicated, strongly nonlinear process and the generally used Coulomb's model is only the first approximation of real properties. For a better description of friction process, the stick-slip (or micro slip-full slip) model is often used. The short survey of basic mathematical models giving at least approximate true pictures of real forces is in [4]. The influence of application of some dry friction model on the blade couple vibration will be presented in the next chapters.

The first improvement of the classical Coulomb friction law

$$F_t = F_{t_0} \operatorname{sgn}(v) \quad \text{for } |v| > 0,$$
$$-F_{t_0} < F_t < F_{t_0} \quad \text{for } v = 0$$

(9)

is the modified Coulomb law, where instead of the sudden jump at zero velocity at the very low velocity v, the complicated processes caused mostly by elastic micro-deformations of bodies near the friction surfaces, accompanied by partial micro-slip in several points of the contact area, are modeled by a oblique line, a linear increase of friction force, as shown in Fig. 4.

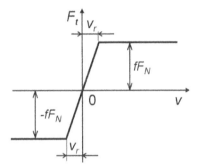

Fig. 4. Modified Coulomb friction characteristics

Micro-slips arise in the contact points, where owing to non-uniform distribution of contact pressure a part of the area is less loaded or even without contact. Processes, which happen during this motion period, are therefore always highly influenced by wear, geometry of contact bodies, precision of surfaces, etc. Their mathematical model is therefore very uncertain and the oblique line is the first approximation of the real micro-deformations and micro-slips processes.

Critical velocity v_r [m/s] is a velocity, at which the micro-slip motion changes into full relative motion, F_{t_0} is Coulomb friction force, proportional to the normal pressure $F_{t_0} = f F_N$ [N]. Mathematical description of the simply modified Coulomb law with the constant dry friction force $F_{t_0} = \pm f F_N$ in the full slip phase of motion is:

$$F_t = F_{t_0} \left[\frac{v}{v_r} H(v_r - |v|) + \operatorname{sgn}(v) H(|v| - v_r) \right],$$

(10)

where H is the Heaviside function. Normal force F_N [N] acts in the contact surface between the modelled bodies. This force is in the real turbine blading realized by the un-twisting of blades due to the centrifugal force at couples with direct contact, or by indentation of friction element into slot between blades heads, again due to the centrifugal force at rotation.

This basic dry-friction model can be completed by further functions expressing e.g. a simple linear increase or decrease of friction force at higher relative velocities. To express friction force that at great velocity v settles on a constant value, it is possible to use the functions $\operatorname{atan}(v)$ or $\exp(-v)$.

5. Example of a system with direct friction contact

Applying equations (4) for parameters roughly corresponding to the experimental set, i.e. $m = 0.2$ kg, $k = 100\,000$ N/m, $F_0 = 1$ N, $F_1(t) = F_0 \cos \omega t$, $F_2(t) = F_0 \cos \omega(t - \Delta t)$, the amplitude response curves of all three coordinates y_1, y_2, $u_1 - u_2$ can be calculated for several cases of time delay (i.e. different number l_s, l_r of stator and rotor blades), friction forces, types of friction characteristics and damping coefficients of the separate blades.

The acceleration of sweeping excitation frequency ω at simulation is sufficiently low

$$\frac{\mathrm{d}\omega}{\mathrm{d}t} = accel = 0.25 \ \mathrm{rad/s^2}$$

so that the transient response is very close to the stationary one. It can be proved by recording response curves of mathematical model with increasing and decreasing excitation frequency — as shown in Fig. 5 for the twofold passing acceleration $0.5 \ \mathrm{rad/s^2}$ and for the system with inserted friction element. Damping of both blades is modeled by small viscous damping with coefficients $b_1 = b_2 = 0.1$ Ns/m.

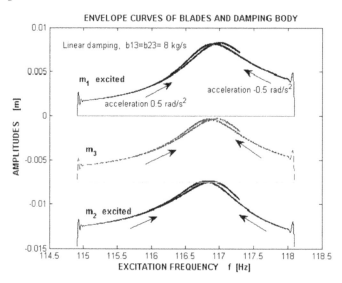

Fig. 5. Check of distortion at sweep excitation

The shifts of peaks is $df = 0.03$ Hz, which related to the resonance frequency gives error smaller than 0.03 %.

6. Phase-shift effect on a system with direct Coulomb friction contact

If there is no phase shift between fully synchronized exciting forces, no relative motion in the contact surface exists and the system is damped only by the small subsystem's damping forces $b\dot{y}_i$, $i = 1, 2$. Resonance amplitudes in such a case are very high (the frequency range in the figures is only 1.5 Hz). However due to delay of one harmonic exciting force against the other, relative motion connected with the friction energy losses in the contact surface occurs and resonance amplitudes get lower. For the equal subsystems with masses $m = 0.2$ kg and spring stiffness $k = 100\,000 \ \mathrm{kg \cdot s^{-2}}$, the amplitude response curves $a_1(f)$, $a_2(f)$ are drawn in Fig. 6 for dry friction force $F_t = 0.2$ N and for six blade-number ratios

$$l_s/l_r = 1; 0.9; 0.8; 0.7; 0.6; 0.5.$$

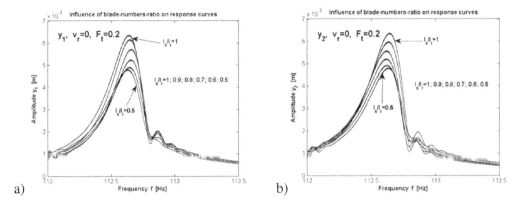

Fig. 6. Influence of excitation delay at dry friction force $F_T = 0.2$

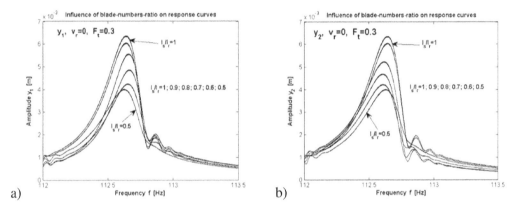

Fig. 7. Influence of excitation delay at dry friction force $F_T = 0.3$

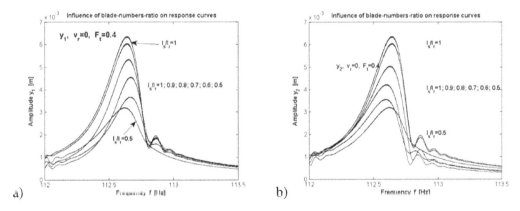

Fig. 8. Influence of excitation delay at dry friction force $F_T = 0.4$

Similar curves are plotted in Fig. 7 for the higher dry friction force $F_t = 0.3$ N and again for six blade-number ratios. Influence of the dry friction force $F_t = 0.4$ N is shown in Fig. 8. It is evident that the damping increases with higher friction force and with greater difference between the number l_s of stator blades and number l_r of rotor blades.

The elastic micro-deformations in contact surfaces (as well as small torsion deformations-in this analysis neglected) can reduce the positive dry friction damping effect. It can be shown on the case where a modified Coulomb dry friction model (see Fig. 4) is used.

7. Phase-shift effect — modified Coulomb dry friction

The influence of elastic micro-deformations in the contact surfaces can be analyzed by using various more sophisticated mathematical models. The simplest one is the modified Coulomb dry friction model containing two parameters: critical velocity v_r at which the partial micro-slip motion changes into full slip motion and vice versa and the constant friction force $F_{t_0} = \pm f F_N$ in the full slip at higher velocities.

Because the maximum amplitude is the decisive value for the reliability of blades systems, the influence of phase-shift excitation and critical velocity v_r on the high of resonance amplitude will be considered.

Response curves for four values of critical velocity $v_r = 0, 2, 4, 6$ and for ratio of the number of stator and rotor blades $l_s/l_r = 0.7$ are shown in Fig. 9. The greater is the critical velocity, the smaller is the damping ability of friction connection. Interesting phenomenon is the increase of first blade's amplitudes in the under-resonance zone and the increase of the second blade's amplitudes in the over-resonance zone.

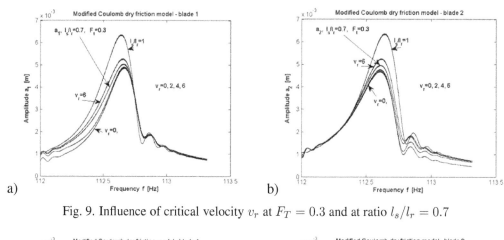

Fig. 9. Influence of critical velocity v_r at $F_T = 0.3$ and at ratio $l_s/l_r = 0.7$

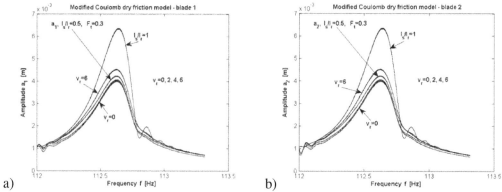

Fig. 10. Influence of critical velocity v_r at $F_T = 0.3$ and at ratio $l_s/l_r = 0.5$

In order to estimate the damping contribution caused by the phase-shift excitation, one response curve at in phase excitation $l_s/l_r = 1$ is plotted in each diagram.

For the same system parameters but for smaller ratio of the numbers of stator and rotor blades $l_s/l_r = 0.5$, the response curves again for four values of critical velocity $v_r = 0, 2, 4, 6$ are shown in Fig. 10. The quenching of amplitudes is now greater than in the previous case and the damping ability of friction connection decreases again with growing critical velocity.

Interesting phenomenon in this case is the identity of both sets of amplitude response curves $a_1(f)$ and $a_2(f)$ (the phase response curves are however different), as well as the increase of amplitudes both in the before-resonance and in the after-resonance zone with the increasing of critical velocity v_r.

8. Vibrations of a blade couple with friction element

Experimental research gives important results useful for design and development of new machines, but it is e.g. difficult to measure motion of friction element, dry friction forces and friction coefficient during operation, etc.

Therefore the additional analytical and numerical solution of simplified mathematical model with exact parameters is very useful and enables to complete knowledge of dynamic behavior of studied system with new information. Experimental system in Fig. 1 can be modeled by a simple three masses system shown in Fig. 11, where the blades are replaced by 1 DOF systems.

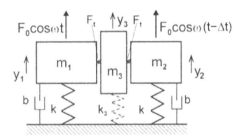

Fig. 11. Mathematical model of two blades system with friction element

Damping of both blades is in Fig. 11 modeled by small viscous damping with coefficients $b_1 = b_2 = 0.1$ Ns/m. For elimination of gravitational force, the friction element $m_3 = 0.02$ kg was supported by a very weak spring with stiffness $k_3 = 100$ N/m. Differential equations of motion are then

$$m_1\ddot{y}_1 + b_1\dot{y}_1 + k_1 y_1 + g_1(\dot{y}_1 - \dot{y}_3) = F_0 \cos \omega t,$$
$$m_2\ddot{y}_2 + b_2\dot{y}_2 + k_2 y_2 + g_2(\dot{y}_2 - \dot{y}_3) = F_0 \cos \omega(t - \Delta t), \qquad (11)$$
$$m_3\ddot{y}_3 + k_1 y_3 + g_1(\dot{y}_1 - \dot{y}_3) - g_2(\dot{y}_2 - \dot{y}_3) = 0,$$

where the excitation frequency of force $F_0 \cos \omega t$ varies near to the eigenfrequencies of main subsystems

$$\omega \approx \sqrt{k_1/m_1} \approx \sqrt{k_2/m_2}.$$

The nonlinear functions g_1, g_2 consist of nonlinear Coulomb dry friction forces:

$$g_i = F_{ti} \operatorname{sgn}(\dot{y}_i - \dot{y}_3), \qquad i = 1, 2, \qquad (12)$$

where H is the Heaviside function.

Motion of the investigated system is further solved by direct numerical solution of equations (11), (12).

9. Example of a blade couple with friction element

Only the dry frictions connect the three masses system. Amplitude response curves $a_1(f)$, $a_2(f)$, $a_3(f)$ of systems with four different delays given by blades' numbers $l_s/l_r = 1; 0.8;$ $0.6; 0.5$ are calculated and drawn in Fig. 12a–c for the equal main subsystems parameters: $m_1 = m_2 = 0.2\,\text{kg}$, $k = 100\,000\,\text{kg}\cdot\text{s}^{-2}$, $m_3 = 0.02\,\text{kg}$, dry friction damping force $F_t = 0.3\,\text{N}$ and for stiffness of supporting spring $k_3 = 100\,\text{N/m}$. Response curves $a_1(f)$ of mass m_1 are almost identical with the response curves $a_2(f)$ of mass m_2 and their forms are also unchanged for various delays $l_s/l_r = 1; 0.8; 0.6; 0.5$, as can be seen from the records in Fig. 12a,b, where the drawings of individual curves are vertically shifted for easy comparison. On the contrary, the amplitudes a_3 of the friction element m_3 are strongly influenced by the change of delays between excitation forces, as it is evident from the records in Fig. 12c for various ratios l_s/l_r. Motion a_3 of friction element m_3 contains chaotic components, which are also contained, however in a smaller rate, in motions a_1, a_2 of the much greater masses m_1 and m_2.

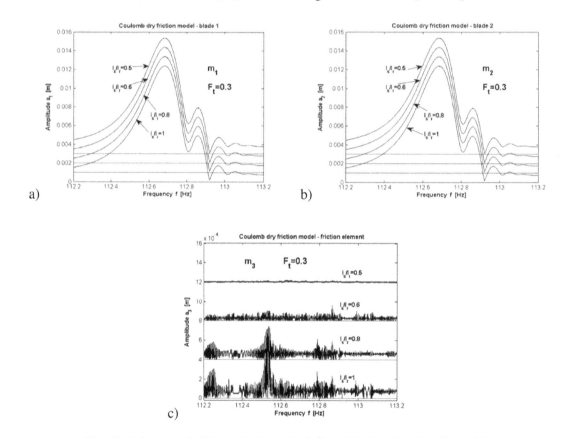

Fig. 12. Influence of different blades ratio $l_s/l_r = 0.5; 0.6; 0.8; 1$ at $F_T = 0.3$

Influence of dry friction forces F_t (Coulomb friction, equation (9)) on the response curves is represented in Fig. 13a–c. Response curves $a_1(f)$ of mass m_1 are again identical with the response curves $a_2(f)$ of mass m_2, but the increase of friction force F_t very strongly decreases the maximum resonance amplitudes, as can be seen from the records in Fig. 13a,b.

Response curves of the amplitudes a_3 of the friction element m_3 are very flat without any resonance peaks. Amplitude a_3 has — at given F_0 — constant value in the majority of frequency range. With increasing friction force F_t, the mean value of amplitude a_3 increases, as it is

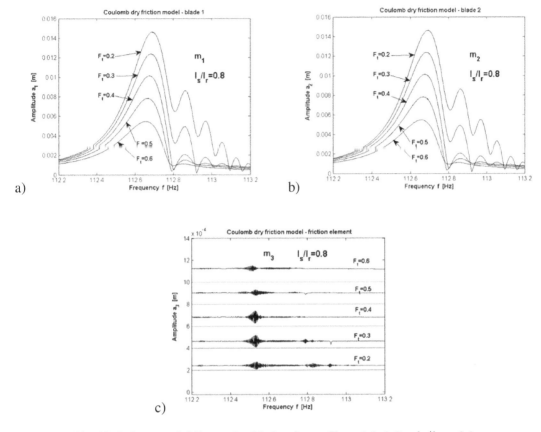

Fig. 13. Influence of different dry friction forces $F_T = 0.2$–0.6 at $l_s/l_r = 0.8$

evident from the records in Fig. 13c for various friction forces. Motion a_3 of friction element m_3 contains, except a constant value, also some oscillating components, but only in narrow frequency ranges near to the rising parts of $a_1(f)$, $a_2(f)$ response curves.

Another properties were obtained, when instead of classical Coulomb friction law (9), the modified Coulomb friction law (10) has been used. Influence of variation of critical velocity v_r on the amplitude response curves $a_1(f)$, $a_2(f)$, $a_3(f)$ of systems with five different critical velocities $v_r = 0, 0.2, 0.4, 0.6, 0.8$ m/s is presented in Fig. 14. Dry friction force $F_t = 0.8$ N is for all response curves constant, as well as the constant excitation delay characterized by the ratio blades' numbers $l_s/l_r = 0.8$. From the diagrams plotted in Fig. 14a,b it is evident that the increase of critical velocity v_r causes moderate increase of resonance peaks of both masses, but as it is shown in Fig. 14c, it causes qualitative change of friction element motion. At $v_r = 0$ (Coulomb friction), the sudden jump of friction force excites irregular, chaotic motion, but at $v_r > 0$ (modified Coulomb friction), the smooth passage between opposite friction forces makes the oscillation of friction element harmonic with smoothly variable amplitudes.

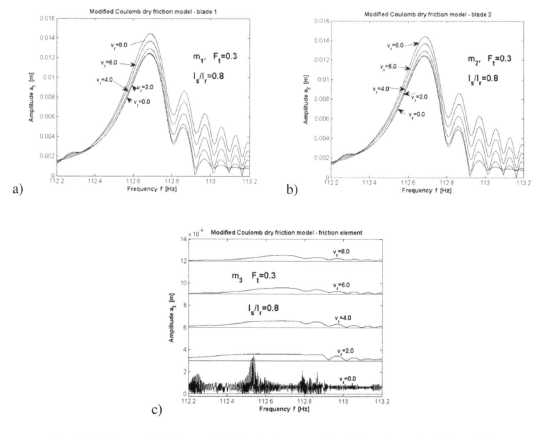

Fig. 14. Influence of different critical velocity v_r at $F_T = 0.3$ and at ratio $l_s/l_r = 0.8$

10. Conclusion

- Present paper serves as further contribution to the systematic research of dynamic properties of turbine blade couple. The introduction of excitation with delay into a mathematical model brings this model closer to a real situation in a working turbine.

- Phase shift of excitation can be expressed either by time delay or by phase (angle) delay.

- This delay is ascertained both by the revolution and by the ratio of numbers of stator and rotor blades.

Blade couple with direct contact:

- The damping ability of blade heads with direct friction contact increases with the lower number of stator blades.

- The increase of friction forces causes a decrease of resonance peaks.

- The elastic micro-deformations in contact surfaces (modelled e.g. by the modified Coulomb dry friction law) decrease the damping ability, but this influence is rather small.

Blade couple with friction element:

- The lower number of stator blades (increasing delay) has a negligible influence on the amplitudes of both blades, but decreases amplitudes of friction element oscillations.

- The increase of friction forces causes decrease of resonance peaks, but an increase of friction element amplitudes.

- Increase of critical velocity v_r causes moderate increase of resonance peaks of both masses and a qualitative change of friction element motion.

Note: This contribution is an extended text of paper [10].

Acknowledgements

This work has been elaborated in a frame of the grant project GA CR101/09/1166 "Research of dynamic behavior and optimization of complex rotating system with non-linear couplings and high damping materials" and it is also a contribution to the scientific cooperation with NAS Ukraine.

References

[1] Archard, J. F., Contact and rubbing of flat surfaces, Journal of Applied Physics 24 (8) (1953) 981-988.

[2] Awrejcewicz, J., Pyryev, Yu., Nonsmooth dynamics of contacting thermoelastic bodies, Springer, 2009.

[3] Gallego, L., Nelias, D., Modeling of fretting wear under gross slip and partial slip conditions, Journal of Tribology 129 (3) (2007) 528-536.

[4] Guran, A. (ed.), Impact and friction of solids, structures and intelligent machines, World Scientific, Singapore, Series B, Vol. 14, 2000.

[5] Koh, K.-H., Griffin, J. H., Filippi, S., Akay, A., Characterization of turbine blade friction dampers, Journal of Engineering for Gas Turbines and Power-transactions of The ASME 127 (4) (2005) 856-862.

[6] Pešek, L., Půst, L., Influence of dry friction damping on bladed disk vibration. In: Vibration Problems ICOVP 2011, Berlin, Springer, 2011, pp. 557-564.

[7] Pešek, L., Půst, L., Mathematical model of a blade couple connected by damping element, Proceedings of the 8th International Conference on Structural Dynamics, EURODYN 2011, Leuven, Katolieke Universiteit Leuven, 2011, pp. 2 006-2 011.

[8] Pfeifer, F., Hajek, M., Stick-slip motion of turbine blade dampers, Philosophical Transactions of the Royal Society A-Mathematical, Physical and Engineering Sciences 338 (1651) (1992) 503-517.

[9] Půst, L., Pešek, L., Friction in blade system, Proceedings of the conference Computational Mechanics 2011, Pilsen, Book of abstracts, CD ROM edition, 2011.

[10] Půst, L., Pešek, L., Phase delayed excitation of turbine blades couple with friction connection, Proceedings of the conference Computational Mechanics 2012, Špičák, Book of extended abstracts, CD ROM edition, 2012.

[11] Půst, L., Pešek, L., Various types of dry friction characteristics, Proceedings of the conference Dynamika strojů 2011, Prague, Institute of Thermomechanics AS CR, 2011, pp. 77-78. (in Czech)

[12] Rao, J. S., et al., Interface damping in attachment region, Proceedings of the 3rd International Conference on Rotordynamics, IFToMM, CNRS, Lyon, 1990, pp. 185-190.

[13] Sextro, W., Dynamical contact problems with friction, Springer-Verlag, Berlin Heidelberg, 2007.

[14] Szwedowicz, J., The reliable numerical analysis of shrouded bladed disk, In: International Contact Mechanics Workshop, New Orleans, 2001, pp. 1-6.

[15] Voldřich, J., Morávka, Š., Contact stiffness modeling in numerical analysis of nonlinear vibrations of bladed disk with friction contact interfaces, Proceedings of the conference Vibration Problems ICOVP 2011 — Supplement, TU Liberec, 2011, pp. 383-388.

[16] Yang, B. D., Chu, M. L., Meng, C. H., Stick-slip-separation analysis and non-linear stiffness and damping characterization of friction contacts having variable normal force, Journal of Sound and Vibration 210 (4) (1998) 461-481.

Permissions

All chapters in this book were first published in ACM, by University of West Bohemia; hereby published with permission under the Creative Commons Attribution License or equivalent. Every chapter published in this book has been scrutinized by our experts. Their significance has been extensively debated. The topics covered herein carry significant findings which will fuel the growth of the discipline. They may even be implemented as practical applications or may be referred to as a beginning point for another development.

The contributors of this book come from diverse backgrounds, making this book a truly international effort. This book will bring forth new frontiers with its revolutionizing research information and detailed analysis of the nascent developments around the world.

We would like to thank all the contributing authors for lending their expertise to make the book truly unique. They have played a crucial role in the development of this book. Without their invaluable contributions this book wouldn't have been possible. They have made vital efforts to compile up to date information on the varied aspects of this subject to make this book a valuable addition to the collection of many professionals and students.

This book was conceptualized with the vision of imparting up-to-date information and advanced data in this field. To ensure the same, a matchless editorial board was set up. Every individual on the board went through rigorous rounds of assessment to prove their worth. After which they invested a large part of their time researching and compiling the most relevant data for our readers.

The editorial board has been involved in producing this book since its inception. They have spent rigorous hours researching and exploring the diverse topics which have resulted in the successful publishing of this book. They have passed on their knowledge of decades through this book. To expedite this challenging task, the publisher supported the team at every step. A small team of assistant editors was also appointed to further simplify the editing procedure and attain best results for the readers.

Apart from the editorial board, the designing team has also invested a significant amount of their time in understanding the subject and creating the most relevant covers. They scrutinized every image to scout for the most suitable representation of the subject and create an appropriate cover for the book.

The publishing team has been an ardent support to the editorial, designing and production team. Their endless efforts to recruit the best for this project, has resulted in the accomplishment of this book. They are a veteran in the field of academics and their pool of knowledge is as vast as their experience in printing. Their expertise and guidance has proved useful at every step. Their uncompromising quality standards have made this book an exceptional effort. Their encouragement from time to time has been an inspiration for everyone.

The publisher and the editorial board hope that this book will prove to be a valuable piece of knowledge for researchers, students, practitioners and scholars across the globe.

List of Contributors

F. Fojtík and J. Fuxa
Faculty of Mechanical Engineering, V ŠB – Technical University of Ostrava, 17 listopadu 15, 708 33 Ostrava-Poruba, Czech Republic

J. Zapoměl, P. Ferfecki and J. Kozánek
Department of Dynamics and Vibrations, Institute of Thermomechanics, Department of Mechanics, Dolejškova 1402/5, 182 00 Praha 8, Czech Republic

F. Fojtík, J. Fuxa and Z. Poruba
Faculty of Mechanical Engineering, VŠB – Technical University of Ostrava, 17 listopadu 15, 708 33 Ostrava-Poruba, Czech Republic

A. Zaryankin and A. Rogalev
Department of Steam and Gas turbines, Moscow Power Engineering Institute (Technical University), Krasnokazarmennaya 14, 111250 Moscow, Russia

S. Arianov
JSC "ENTEK", Krasnokazarmennaya 17-G/3, 111116 Moscow, Russia

S. Storoguk
JSC "RAO Energy System of East", Timura Frunze 11/15, 119021 Moscow, Russia

T. Vampola
Department of Mechanics, Biomechanics and Mechatronics, Faculty of Mechanical Engineering, Czech Technical University in Prague, Karlovo nám. 13, 121 35 Prague 2, Czech Republic

A. M. Laukkanen
Department of Speech Communication and Voice Research, University of Tampere, FIN 33014 Tampere, Finland

J. Horáček
Institute of Thermomechanics, Academy of Sciences of the Czech Republic, Dolejškova 5, 182 00 Praha 8, Czech Republic

J. G. Švec
Department of Experimental Physics, Faculty of Sciences Palacký University Olomouc, 17. listopadu 12, 771 46 Olomouc, Czech Republic

J. Zapoměl and P. Ferfecki
Institute of Thermomechanics, branch Ostrava, Czech Academy of Science, 17. listopadu 15, 708 33 Ostrava, Czech Republic

M. Kotoul
Brno University of Technology, Faculty of Mechanical Engineering, Technická 2, 616 69, Brno, Czech Republic

L. Valdmanová
Department of Mechanics, Faculty of Applied Sciences, University of West Bohemia, Univerzitní 8, 306 14 Plzeň, Czech Republic

H. Čechová
New Technologies — Research Centre, University of West Bohemia, Univerzitní 8, 306 14 Plzeň, Czech Republic

M. Holeček, F.Moravec and J. Vychytil
Faculty of Applied Sciences, University of West Bohemia, Univerzitní 22, 306 14 Plzeň, Czech Republic

V. Zeman and Z. Hlaváč
Faculty of Applied Sciences, University of West Bohemia, Univerzitní 22, 306 14 Plzeň, Czech Republic

V. Pelikán, P. Hora and O. Červená
Institute of Thermomechanics of the ASCR, v.v.i., Veleslavínova 11, 301 14 Plzeň, Czech Republic

A Spielmannová and A. Machová
Institute of Thermomechanics of the ASCR, v.v.i., Dolejškova 5, 182 00 Praha, Czech Republic

P. Polach and M. Hajžman
Section of Materials and Mechanical Engineering Research, ŠKODA VÝZKUM s. r. o., Tylova 1/57, 316 00 Plzeň, Czech Republic

J. Horáček, V. Uruba, V. Radolf, J. Veselý and V. Bula
Institute of Thermomechanics, Academy of Sciences of the Czech Republic

S. Seitl and Z. Knésl
Institute of Physics of Materials, Academy of Sciences of the Czech Republic, v.v.i., Žižkova 22, 616 62 Brno, Czech Republic

Z. Keršner
Institute of Structural Mechanics, Civil Engineering Faculty, Brno University of Technology, Veveří 331/95, 602 00 Brno, Czech Republic

V. Bílek
ZPSV, a.s., Testing laboratory Brno, Křižíkova 68, 660 90 Brno, Czech Republic

L. Valdmanová
Department of Mechanics, Faculty of Applied Sciences, University of West Bohemia, Univerzitn´ı 8, 306 14 Plzeň, Czech Republic

H. Čechová
New Technologies — Research Centre, University of West Bohemia, Univerzitní 8, 306 14 Plzeň, Czech Republic

R. Ghayour, M. Ghayour and S. Ziaei-Rad
Department of Mechanical Engineering, Isfahan University of Technology, Isfahan 84156-83111, Iran

L. Půst and L. Pešek
Institute of Thermomechanics ASCR, Dolejškova 5, 182 00 Prague 8, Czech Republic

Index